Digital Book
Design and Publishing

Digital Book
Design and Publishing

Douglas Holleley

CLARELLEN

CARY GRAPHIC ARTS PRESS

This book is co-published by
Clarellen and the Cary Graphic Arts Press
2001

CLARELLEN
P.O. Box 2177
Elmira Heights, N.Y. 14903
www.clarellen.com

CARY GRAPHIC ARTS PRESS
Rochester Institute of Technology
90 Lomb Memorial Drive
Rochester, N.Y. 14623-5604
http://wally.rit.edu/cary

ISBN: 0-9707138-0-0

Printed by InterPress Limited, Hong Kong.

NOTICE TO THE READER

The material in this book is based on many years experience by the author. The principles and procedures herein therefore reflect a personal perspective only. As such the publishers do not warrant or guarantee any of the products, nor do the publishers perform
any independent analysis in connection with the products discussed herein.

The reader is also expressly warned to adopt all appropriate safety measures when
attempting the activities described in this book. By following the instructions the reader assumes all risks in connection with such instructions.

The reader is also reminded that the discussion of copyright is the opinion of the
author only and does not constitute legal advice. The reader thus assumes all responsibility with respect to the observance of copyright law. The publishers expressly disclaim any
responsibility for any consequences that may follow from the reader failing to observe
any or all laws relating to issues of copyright and/or other intellectual or property laws.

The publishers shall not be liable for any special, consequential or exemplary damages
resulting in whole or part, from the reader's use of, or reliance on, this material.

For Judy Haas

On the occasion of
the bookmaking workshop
at Anderson Ranch.

I was a great pleasure
to both meet you and
work with you.

Your book is gorgeous

With warmest wishes

Douglas Howlins

June 29 2007.

Acknowledgements

I WOULD like to express my thanks to the many individuals who have helped directly and indirectly in the writing and production of this book. My most special thanks are extended to Joan and Nathan Lyons of the Visual Studies Workshop in Rochester, N.Y. At a professional level, their appointing me Artist in Residence at the Workshop in 1997/1998 gave me a base from which I was able to re-assess and refine my personal and artistic direction. At a more personal level, their friendship, support and encouragement is gratefully appreciated and acknowledged.

I also wish to acknowledge those friends who shared with me their love of books, and their personal collections, so I might illustrate this work with a wide variety of examples of excellence in the gentle but demanding art of book-making. Dr. Peter Stanbury, Mike Hudson, Jadwiga Jarvis, Philip Zimmermann, and Joan Lyons all allowed me to photograph the wonderful books in their personal collections.

With respect to public collections, I would like to thank David Pankow, Curator of the Melbert B. Cary, Jr. Graphic Arts Collection, Wallace Library, Rochester Institute of Technology, Rochester, N.Y., and Mark Woodhouse, College Archivist, Elmira College Archives, Gannett-Tripp Library, Elmira College, Elmira, N.Y., for sharing their treasures.

Thanks are also extended to all the individual book artists who gave me permission to use photographs of their remarkable books and encouraged me while I wrote the text.

Additionally I would like to thank all the teachers who have influenced me over the course of my formal (and out-of-classroom) education. Special thanks to my Ph.D. adviser, Professor James Conner of Sydney University, for teaching me the value of organization, structure and persistence. Thanks also to my third grade teacher, Mrs. Ogden, my high school art teacher, Martin James, my high school French teacher, Robert Goode, my psychology professor at Macquarie

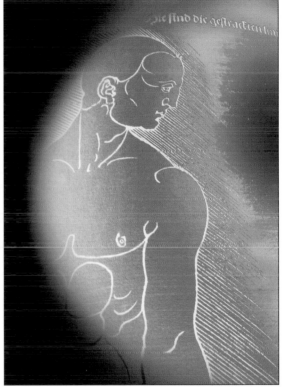

He Searched for His Muse, Douglas Holleley, 2000. Photographed from Albrecht Dürer's *Hierin sind begriffen vier Bucher von menschlicher Proportion.* Nurenberg, 1528.

University, Professor Ian K. Waterhouse, my first photographic mentor, Robert Taylor, my M.F.A. thesis advisers, Paul Diamond and Leroy Searle, and my former colleague at the Canberra School of Art, Petr Herel. Finally, thanks to Martin Sharp, Wendy Carnegie, and Eelco Wolf for sharing with me, their special view of the world.

I would also like to express my gratitude for the assistance I have received from the Australia Council over the years.

Special thanks also to my daughter Clare (after whom the imprint is named) for simply being who she is, and doing it really well.

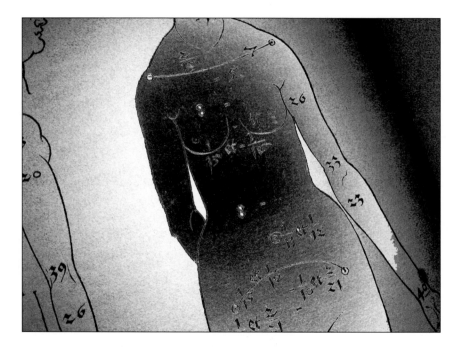

The Body Map, Douglas Holleley, 2000. Photographed from Albrecht Dürer's *Hierin sind begriffen vier Bucher von menschlicher Proportion.* Nurenberg, 1528.

Although we have never met I would like also to acknowledge the influence and example of Professor Edward Tufte. His remarkable self-published books exemplify the highest level of design and production quality and have greatly influenced my work.

Finally, I would like to thank Professor Jan Kather of Elmira College and Amelia Hugill-Fontanel of RIT, for proofreading the manuscript many times, providing much-needed feedback, Professor Frank Cost of RIT for his help and advice on digital printing, Professor Archie Provan (also of RIT) for his feedback on the typography chapter, Fred Jordan, book conservationist and master binder, for his comments and help with the chapter on bookbinding, and Laura Jaffe of InterPress, the printers of this book.

Douglas Holleley

Using this Book

Establishing a Layout Style
Chapter 2: *The Process of Design*
Chapter 3: *Typography*

Preparing Images for Reproduction
Chapter 6: *Scanning*
Chapter 7: *Correcting Images*

Assembling the Document Digitally
Chapter 4: *Setting Up*
Chapter 5: *The Page Layout Program*

Printing the Document
Chapter 9: *Printing the Book*
Chapter 10: *Printing Substrates and Materials*

Bookbinding
Chapter 11: *Binding the Book*

Where to find advice

There are many aspects to bookmaking, and the process though logical, is often not linear. You may choose to either read the book from cover to cover, or access the contents in a non-linear way, acquiring specific skills as needed. If you wish to start immediately, this table represents a typical work path, and where in the book you can find information relevant to your needs.

Angel of Hope, Douglas Holleley, 1995. Published in the author's
Love Song, Rockcorry, Woodford, New South Wales, 1995.

PREFACE

WHEN, in the mid-fifteenth century, Johannes Gutenberg rallied a number of existing technologies, including paper-making, metal-smithing, punch and die-making and the screw press, to develop a workable system of casting and printing from moveable metal type, the culture of literacy in the Western world was forever transformed. In the last forty years of that century the new craft spread throughout Europe, where more than forty thousand editions—millions of books—were printed, with an estimated 150–268 printers working in Venice alone.

Developments in book production for the next 500 years were incremental. Type continued to be printed almost exclusively from metal forms until the 1950s. The reproduction of images was advanced by new techniques in engraving, the invention of lithography by Alois Senefelder at the end of the eighteenth century, and the advent of photogravure and halftone processes in the nineteenth century. In the twentieth century ever more complex technologies necessitated a battalion of specialists to produce a book while the economics of production favored large publishers of mass editions.

Computers are leveling the playing field. Contrary to futurists' predictions that computer culture would mark the demise of the book, electronic technologies, by changing the way books are produced and distributed, are creating a renaissance in book culture. At least as significant to print publishing as Gutenberg's moveable type in its time, electronic, or desktop, publishing has brought the tools of book production to anyone who owns or has access to a personal computer. Add a scanner and printer, page layout and image processing programs and you have, at your desktop, a means to work with typography, images and page design undreamed of fifteen years ago.

This book covers all the essentials of digital bookmaking for photographers, artists, designers and writers who want to move beyond the manuscript to the page. Based on his years of work as a photographer, bookmaker and teacher, Douglas Holleley has developed a clear and considered approach to "digital book design and publishing." You will find a progression through the process of bookmaking, from a consideration of maquette and materials through printing and bookbinding, as well as a step-by-step guide to page layout and image processing software. A rich and varied selection of reproductions from historical and contemporary illustrated books and artists' books places digitally produced books in a historical continuum.

Joan Lyons
Visual Studies Workshop Press

Table of Contents

Introduction

Chapter 1: The Nature of the Book

Chapter One discusses those qualities which distinguish the book from other forms of presentation. The discussion, by implication and suggestion, will enhance your appreciation of the expressive and communicative possibilities of the medium.

Chapter 2: The Process of Design

The next three chapters address issues of page layout and design. In Chapter Two there is a discussion of how to create a "dummy" or maquette to organize your thoughts and plan your book. In Chapters Three and Four, you will find further practical advice on typography and digital document set-up.

CHAPTER 3: TYPOGRAPHY

CHAPTER 4: SETTING UP

CHAPTER 5: THE PAGE LAYOUT PROGRAM

Chapter Five is a guide to using a page layout program to enable you
to assemble your book. The discussion is based on the program Quark–
XPress but the principles are equally applicable to all such programs.

CHAPTER 5: THE PAGE LAYOUT PROGRAM, *Continued*

CHAPTER 6: SCANNING

The next three chapters address the issues involved in preparing images for publication. Chapters Six and Seven show you how to use Adobe Photoshop to scan and correct your images so they will print with the highest possible quality. Chapter Eight addresses the nature of digital imaging and suggests alternative strategies for creating images for the book which do not rely on conventional photographic means.

CHAPTER 7: CORRECTING IMAGES

CHAPTER 8:
ALTERNATIVE METHODS OF ACQUIRING IMAGES

CHAPTER 9: PRINTING THE BOOK

The following three chapters discuss the final stages of book production. Chapters Nine and Ten will help you gain optimum results from your printer by explaining ways to combine the controls of the printer with a sensitive selection of printing materials. Chapter Ten also addresses the publication of your book on CD ROM. Chapter Eleven explains various methods of bookbinding.

CHAPTER 10:
PRINTING SUBSTRATES AND MATERIALS

CHAPTER 11:
BINDING THE BOOK

CHAPTER 12:
COMPUTERS, COPYRIGHT AND THE LAW

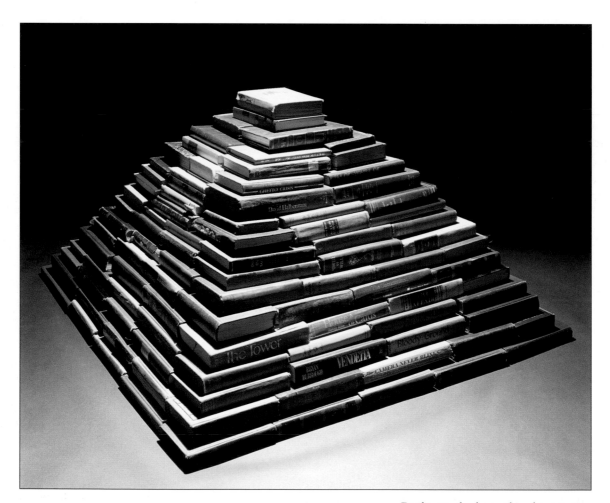

Books can also be used as elements to create works of art in other mediums. This sculpture is comprised of a solid mass of some 500 books.
The Monument to Ephemeral Facts. Sculpture and color photograph, Douglas Holleley, 1998.

INTRODUCTION

THIS book will assist the reader who wishes to construct a book utilizing contemporary digital technology. Although it is primarily aimed at photographers it will also be of use to artists, authors, historians, and others who have a collection of related material and would like to see it integrated into a single document. The emphasis is on expressive and creative work. However, the principles and procedures described throughout the book are equally applicable to introspective and arcane publications or to the production of brochures and booklets for more prosaic needs.

The primary means of assembling the book will be through the practical application of two pieces of software, Adobe Photoshop™ and QuarkXPress ™. No prior knowledge of either computer program is assumed nor does it exclude those who may be fluent in either or both. As the primary aim of this publication is to produce a book, the direct expression of an abstract idea in tangible form will always remain more important than mere technical skills. However, elementary computer competency will be assumed. You should be able to start your computer, open a program and save the results. This is sufficient to be able to follow the instructions.

The most important aspect of bookmaking is having something to say. The first thing required is having a reasonably clear idea right from the start of what the finished product will be. This is a theme that we will return to again and again during the course of this book.

To have this clear idea makes the process easier for a variety of reasons. If you are new to the programs discussed in this book, you will find it quite easy to acquire the skills necessary because they are not presented as tasks in their own right but are instead logical steps that facilitate getting the job accomplished. To learn a computer program without a goal is one of the more difficult tasks that one can attempt. Modern software programs are very complex, so much so, that one writer was prompted to make the following observation:

> The stuff we call software is not like anything that human society is used to thinking about. Software is something like a machine, and something like mathematics, and something like language, and

As the title suggests, much has been forgotten about the venerable art of bookmaking. The computer, although opening up new possibilities, cannot substitute for an understanding of these rich traditions. Progress is best when it builds upon these "lost trails" rather than simply supplanting them. It is essential to research the history of bookmaking to be aware of the richness and beauty of the medium. E. S. Ellis, *The Lost Trail,* Cassell & Co., London, New York, Toronto, and Melbourne, no date. (Inscription inside dated 1927.)

something like thought, and art, and information … but software is not in fact any of those other things. The protean quality of software is one of the great sources of its fascination. It also makes software very powerful, very subtle, very unpredictable, and very risky.[1]

1. Bruce Sterling, *The Hacker Crackdown,* Bantam Books, N.Y., 1992, *p. 34.*

This remark was made in a different context but it graphically illustrates the complex, almost intangible nature of software. It is not within the scope of this book to either understand the nature of software, or to gain competence in every subtle intricacy and function of the programs involved. Instead the approach will be to remain focussed on the production of a tangible object and employ the software to this end, rather than learning the program for its own sake. In this way we create a path through a complex and convoluted web of possibilities, so many possibilities, in fact, that choice can become a burden rather than an opportunity. The making of a book will be our Ariadne's thread as we steer a course through this complex but tantalizing maze.

However, learning and applying these computer programs is but one part of the process. To make a book one adopts a series of roles, that in the not too distant past, were whole fields of specialized study. Consider for a moment the steps involved and the level of skill required at each stage.

When one makes images for the book, one is a photographer. When one writes the words that accompany the images, one is an author. When one places these words into an appropriate format, making decisions about type styles and typefaces, one is a typographer. When one commences to assemble all this material into a coherent package, one is both editor and graphic designer. One then proceeds in turn to be the equivalent of a reprographic camera operator, a platemaker, a printer, a bookbinder, a publisher and ultimately a book distributor or bookseller.

This is a tall order. The fact that we can even do it at all, for the most part as a function of digital technology, is remarkable in itself. It is a sobering thought to realize how the very nature of what used to be such specific, individualized and highly skilled trades and crafts, is now within the reach of many of us. Part of the process of constructing a book as described here, is to gain an appreciation of the history of bookmaking and to understand that many different skills are involved. For example, Garamond and Baskerville are not just fonts, but are the names of real people. With pen and ink they drew these typefaces, a slightly different style for each type size, on real pieces of paper, to be

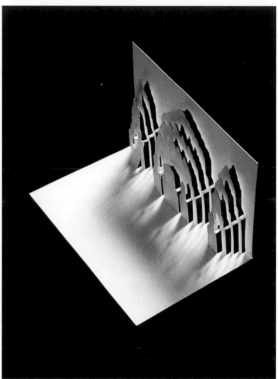

Appreciating the qualities of your materials is an essential aspect of bookmaking. Although this is a Christmas card made by a dear friend and not a book as such, the principle of utilizing the nature of paper, by exploring its qualities of translucency and its ability to create a three dimensional construction, is made clear in this illustration.
Christmas card made by Dr. Peter Stanbury.

cast in lead in foundries big and small, and assembled by typographers and compositors for hundreds of years.

Now we select fonts from a list on our computer screen and within an instant our document changes character and emphasis. This simple action should be treated as a responsibility, one that demands an appreciation of the hundreds of years of human history and effort that lies behind the simple phrase, "desktop publishing." It is quite astonishing that this range of activities, from the conception of the work, to a finished bound volume, can be performed at one's desk.

These remarks are included both as a caution to the beginner and as a homage to those who in the past kept the tradition of the book alive as it grew and evolved to the point where it is today. As you sit at your desk and work through this volume, think of the medieval monks patiently illuminating their manuscripts, the Chinese calligraphers writing their scrolls, the Victorian typesetters composing a page one lead character at a time, and all the other figures in the history of bookmaking, a medium whose fundamental purpose is to ensure that knowledge will persist through time.

The author's first "word processor." It was given to me by my parents when I was young. As such I am reluctant to disclose the date. However, this *Mettoy Elegant* tinplate, toy typewriter was made during the 1950s in Great Britain.

Not all combinations of type and image need to be made on computer. This postcard was originally published by the Rotary Photographic Series, England, c. 1900.

CHAPTER 1

THE NATURE OF THE BOOK

ONE of the more difficult tasks in life is to simply state the obvious. In this chapter we will examine those qualities that differentiate the book from other forms of creative expression. Much of this is self-evident. However, while reading this chapter, keep in mind the comments made by the early twentieth century physicist Niels Bohr who prefaced his lectures with the words… "Every sentence that I utter should be regarded by you not as an assertion but as a question."[1]

THE BOOK PROVIDES THE OPPORTUNITY TO MAKE AN EXTENDED STATEMENT

One of the book's greatest attributes is the ability to make an extended and coherent statement. The contents of a book are finite. There is a beginning and an end. The length, the content, the amount of text, the number of images, and the visual/spatial relationship between the text and images, are controlled by the bookmaker. Similarly, the time taken to make a book is also up to the maker.

Such choice permits the construction of an extended statement where the imperatives of expression are permitted to unfold in a logical, even poetic, space. There need be no rush or hurry, or feelings of disappointment that come from unexpressed ideas. A book can permit the artist/author to fully explore his or her subject, providing the opportunity for a depth of expression that is difficult to achieve in other ways. Compared with the constraints of space and time in the art gallery (most shows lasting for a month or less) the book offers a permanent and thoughtful sanctuary where the work can be accessed at any time.

Books also manifest the quality of time. The experience of the content is linear, sequential and unfolding. Again, compare this with viewing work in an art gallery. In the gallery usually all of the work can be viewed in a single scan as one enters the room. Following this initial impression, the viewer can then look at individual pieces of work, in most cases in random order depending on how she or he walks around the three-dimensional space.

L. T. Meade, *A Girl from America*, W. and R. Chambers Ltd., Edinburgh, c. 1905.

1. Bohr quoted in J. Bronowski's, *The Ascent of Man,* Little, Brown and Company, Boston, 1973.

Consider for a moment how different this is to looking at images in book form where the following qualities are in effect.

- There is a progressive unfolding of the content.
- The work is read in a pre-determined sequence.
- A range of visual concerns may co-exist in the same space.

To each in turn...

In a book one looks at images and words sequentially. Thus the author has the power to control the nature of the experience by altering the order of the pages so that the reader can be led through the work in a pre-determined path.

Photographers such as Minor White[2] and Nathan Lyons[3] have demonstrated through their art-practice and teaching, that the thoughtful sequencing of images is an almost indispensible tool of visual authorship. Keith Smith[4] in *The Structure of the Visual Book*, has codified many of Lyons' thoughts on this matter and the reader of this book is encouraged to refer to Smith's volume. Both White and Lyons see the sequence as a strategy independent of the forum in which the images are viewed, seeing it as equally valid for exhibitions, portfolios or books. However, of these choices, the book presents the greatest opportunity to realize the full power of this approach.

The reason for this lies in the fact that as each page is turned, the experience of looking at one image is replaced by that of another *within the same space.* Thus the images (and words), and the impression they create, accumulate in the mind of the reader as he or she proceeds.

One of the consequences is that work of great variety can be included in a sequence within a book. Again it is useful to think of the kinds of dynamics that are in place in other forums to help appreciate this. In an exhibition, because it is (usually) possible to see all the images at once, there is pressure to edit the work so that it presents a unified visual impression. This can sometimes result in a situation where formal concerns override issues of content, especially if the content is complex.

In contrast, the images contained within a book's enveloping structure are simultaneously connected but separated from each other. Thus images can be included that, if seen in immediate juxtaposition, might seem strange, inappropriate or even discordant. It is impossible to stand back and view the contents of a book as a whole. One must engage with the work one page at a time. Direct comparisons and simplified overall views are impossible to attain.

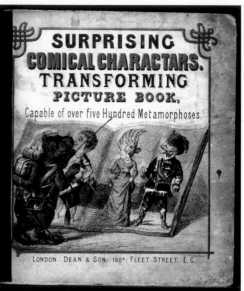

Surprising Comical Characters Transforming Picture Book, Dean and Sons, London, c. 1890.

2. For a poetic introduction to White's views on the creative possibilities offered by the sequencing of imagery see, Minor White, *Mirrors, Messages, Manifestations,* an Aperture Monograph, New York, 1969.
3. Keith Smith, *Structure of the Visual Book,* keith smith BOOKS, Rochester, N.Y., 1995.
4. *ibid.*

This gradual and progressive unfolding of the experience is a liberating quality, greatly freeing up the creative process. It enables complex, even conflicting ideas to be expressed in their own space in their own way, yet can, on reflection, be incorporated into a more enriching and vibrant tapestry of resonance and, ultimately, meaning.

THE OPPORTUNITY TO USE BOTH WORDS AND IMAGES TO REFINE A STATEMENT

A book also permits the artist/author to explore and refine nuances of meaning by experimenting with image/text relationships. The synergies that can be achieved by juxtaposing words and images cannot be over-emphasized.

It is a quality of much visual imagery, but particularly photography, that the data it represents exists entirely in the realm of disconnected fact. In his book *Looking at Photographs*, Szarkowski[5] compares an early twentieth-century photograph of a chaotic and unstructured battle field with classical paintings of "war." He observes that such photographs, in contrast to the ordered composition and coded symbolism of the paintings, have the ability to describe everything but explain nothing. Certainly this observation helps us to understand why many critics struggle with photography's slippery relationship with reality and the subsequent consequences for attributing meaning.

5. John Szarkowski, *Looking at Photographs,* Museum of Modern Art, New York, 1973.

The book illustrated below uses images to create an "exquisite corpse" effect. Contemporary bookmakers also have experimented with this method of image sequencing.
Surprising Comical Characters Transforming Picture Book, Dean and Sons, London, c. 1890.

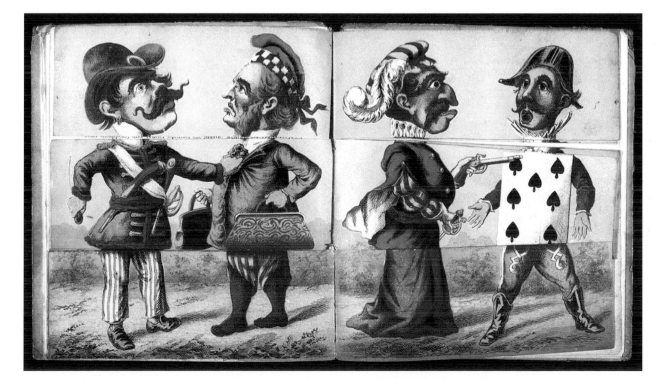

Such observations suggest that photographs are only partial data and that some sort of contextual device is necessary to give them meaning. As con-text literally means "with words," it is frequently text that serves this function. But what is the nature of this image/text relationship? Some insight is offered by the language we use when image/text relationships are discussed. The two most common terms are "the caption" and "the illustration."

The word "caption" suggests that the image is the prime carrier of the communicated content. But it also implies that the image needs clarification and that some explanatory text is necessary for it to be "correctly" interpreted. Similarly the word "illustration" carries hierarchical resonances, but in this case it suggests that the image fills in the gaps, or makes more clear, a pre-existing idea that already has been expressed in words. It implies, at worst, a kind of redundancy and at best, a process of decorative embellishment.

The fact is there is no word in the English language that describes the equal, mutual and complementary juxtaposition of image and text. This suggests there may be a hierarchy or even an innate conflict between the way content and meaning is communicated in words and how it is communicated in images. One of the reasons for this may lie in the formative experiences of early childhood.

Probably the first experience you had with image/text relationships was as a child. You were given a book with an illustration on one page, and on the facing page there was most likely a single word. This word would usually be set in large, legible type. The function of this book was to teach you, the young child, how to read.

The illustration functioned as a device to teach you to decode the collection of letters on the page. There was no reward for appreciating the image, but parental cooing and praise followed every instance when it seemed you were able to read the word. In fact the sooner you could read it without reference to the picture, the more you were encouraged. That strange little collection of signs had a meaning that transcended the particular image that was being observed. A picture of a curled-up sleeping hound, a poodle dressed in circus regalia jumping through a hoop, a collie, a retriever, a working sheep dog, all could be subsumed under the label "dog." Past a certain point your skill improved to the point where the image need only be barely looked at. A glance was sufficient, once you learned the rules of the game. You were learning to read.

However, other things were also being learned. You were not just learning to read words; you were learning to read images. You learned

The Archer Alphabet, T. Goode Publisher, London, c. 1890.

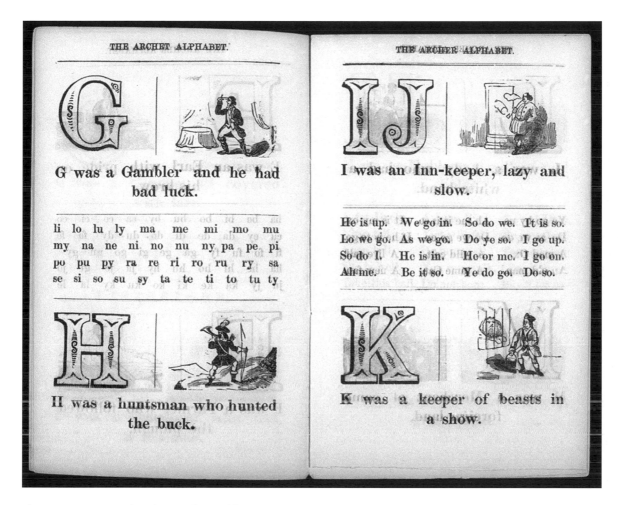

The Archer Alphabet, T. Goode Publisher, London, c. 1890.

that images are to be digested quickly and that to understand an image it was sufficient to identify the objects it pictured. You also learned that visual specifics and structure were less important than categorical thinking and abstract signs. You learned that images served the word.

In saying this I am not suggesting a position of quiet resignation. Instead these issues have been addressed to provoke the reader into a consideration of other possible ways that images and text may co-exist. The point is this: more than any other forum for viewing images and text, modern computer bookmaking offers a possibility for devising structures and creating solutions that circumvent the traditional strictures of word/image relationships. The computer's ability to acquire and then recombine many different forms of information employing a single digital code has opened up the creative process to whole new vistas and ideas which could not exist with past technology.

The reality is that the book does not care what is printed on its pages. It accepts, with indifference, images, text, drawings, diagrams or indeed any impression that the author may deem appropriate to make.

Thus carefully consider the informational and creative possibilities offered by the book to contextualize visual information. In saying this, and in keeping with the spirit of this description of the book's innate characteristics, reflect on what the nature of this process is, both in terms of conventional usage and language, and also what it might be in terms of its future potential.

The Intimacy of the Book

There are many forums for the viewing of visual images. The exhibition has been discussed already. However, images can also be presented on film, television, or computer screens. They can be viewed individually as prints, combined in portfolios or sent through the mail as postcards. In comparison with all these methods, the book has a particular quality of intimacy. Unlike the public space of the exhibition and the movies (and TV when the experience is shared with others present in the room), the book is a quiet, solitary and, indeed, intimate experience. It can be held in one's hands. This direct, tactile connection, so different from the signs in the gallery that admonish one to not touch the work, creates a different environment for appreciating content and message. The experience of holding a book in one's hands has the potential to suggest an almost direct link between the author and the reader. The space created is intimate and implies trust and connection. The gentle, quiet act of turning the pages is a subtle yet powerful signifier of intimacy and participation.

A loaf of bread, a glass of wine, and a book. How better to spend a Sunday afternoon? This book features samples of cloth, colored with aniline dyes, actually tipped into the pages. Léon Lefèvre, *Matières Colorantes*, Paris, 1896.

The book is the fundamental precursor of that most post-modern notion, interactivity. Despite earlier claims about the author having the ability to control the sequencing of the work, the reality is that the book can be read from the back, from the middle, skimmed, cut up and its pictures transferred to a scrapbook or even sliced with a bandsaw and photographed for its beauty as an object transformed.

Perhaps the ultimate expression of interactivity is to take a book and cut it with a bandsaw. This seemingly disrespectful act can produce an object with its own particular qualities of poetic logic.
The Index, Douglas Holleley. Digitally modified photograph, 1999.

THE PORTABILITY OF THE BOOK

The book accommodates to the reader, not the reader to the book. One does not have to read a book at a particular time, in a particular place. It can be read in public on the train or bus or it can be taken to bed where it has the potential to serve the function of a dream that can be entered or left at will.

Related to this quality, the book has the very simple but useful property of being a self-contained forum for the presentation of one's images. In an age where gadgetry and electronic forms of delivery are almost worshiped, the book steadfastly remains accessible to all with no need for sophisticated equipment. Although there is a paradox here in the sense that this book addresses bookmaking from the perspective of using a computer (there is even a section on transferring the book to CD ROM, see Chapter 10, *Printing Your Book Electronically, pp. 216–217*) the fact remains that at the end of the day, when the power lines are down, the batteries exhausted and the software corrupted, one can go to the shelves, select a volume, sit down and read.

Let me emphasize the simplicity of books by way of the following anecdote:

I was walking down an aisle at a computer trade fair looking at (expensive) devices that promised power, speed and control and was accosted by an earnest, youngish gentleman who felt obliged to share the wonders of his product with me and my companion. I can't remember what he was trying to sell, probably some sort of laptop computer. He was extolling its virtues with such enthusiasm and such one-sided rhetoric that I found myself gripped by an urge. With difficulty I interrupted his sales pitch to tell him that only that very morning I had been looking at a form of information storage and retrieval that had some quite remarkable qualities. I went on to tell him how I had seen a device that reproduced images and text with remarkable fidelity. How color and black and white photographs, line illustrations and other graphics were presented with equal precision. This device was also able to allow random access to the contents, enabling them to be viewed in any order. Saving the most remarkable feature for the last, I topped off the description with the announcement that it did not even require any batteries.

By this stage the salesman was totally convinced that the miracle of the twentieth century had been invented without his knowledge and he implored me to tell him the name of the product.

"It was a book," I replied.

There are no problems either finding or retrieving data when it is stored in book form on the library shelf.

THE ARCHIVAL STABILITY OF THE BOOK

It is remarkable just how permanent paper can be. Perhaps more than any other material, it has the ability to persist through time. It is true of course that there is paper and there is paper. Certainly newsprint and other wood pulp papers have relatively short lives. But often this is a function of the ephemeral nature of their content as much as the impermanency of the material itself. Even wood-pulp based paper, when stored correctly, can last many years.

There is a discussion of paper types later in this book (see *pp. 205–215*). However, for the moment let us consider other contributing factors to archival permanence. What happens, for example, when the salesman's product described previously breaks? What happens when computers change the way they store data and it becomes irretrievable?

This is no small issue. The wire recorder, the reel-to-reel tape recorder, the eight-track tape player and the vinyl record are examples of what can occur when a technological advance changes the way stored data is accessed. At present the CD ROM is the preferred form of archival data storage. However, even these require "backing up" every ten years or so to ensure that the data has not become corrupted. Even if one was sufficiently organized and conscientious enough to engage in such a program of data protection, there is no guarantee that in ten or twenty years time that there will be a working CD ROM drive left in the world to read the fragile, laser-burned surface.

The book has remained in use for centuries because of its simple nature and use of traditional materials. A book printed on good quality paper may last virtually indefinitely. It is not dependent on any technology. One only has to take it from the shelf, open it, and read.

The book also offers built in protection to the contents. When it is closed, the pages are protected from light by the covers which form a protective cocoon around the contents. It is easy to store and access and is an object that encourages protection by virtue of its beauty, and manageable scale.

In the early twentieth century, publishers often went to great lengths to make their books attractive. The covers and spines were often decorated with gold stamping, embossing and elaborate typefaces, providing the reader with a visual and tactile treat.

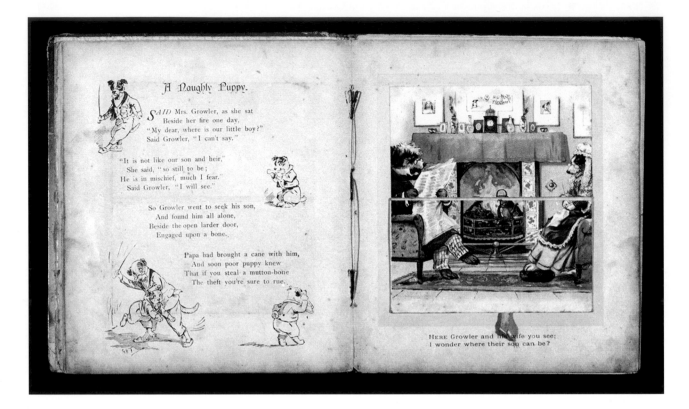

CONTROL OVER THE CONTENTS OF THE BOOK

Finally, it will become apparent as you work through these pages, that the self-made book offers a great amount of control over the presentation and subsequent viewing of the work. When the author is also the creator and publisher there is no intrusion by editors, designers, marketing experts or others who may have an interest in how a work should look to suit their own perspectives. Commercial publishers almost invariably require a mass audience and will not print a book that might sell only a score, a hundred, or even a few thousand copies. They thus exercise considerable editorial and design power.

Modern technology makes it possible for an individual to directly engage in the process of bookmaking and publishing. One may not get rich. However, one retains the satisfaction of retaining control over how the book looks, how it feels, what it says, how it is said, and how and to whom it is made available.

Publishing your own book allows you to create unusual, even idiosyncratic effects with your images. Although this, and the facing page, is from a nineteenth century commercial publication, such solutions can be adapted to more contemporary works. The small cloth tab enables the reader to interact with the image by moving it up or down to conceal or reveal the second image underneath.
Picture Pastimes for Small Folk. Published by Ernest Nister, London and E.P. Dutton & Co., New York, c. 1890.

CONCLUSION

The purpose of this chapter has been to describe the qualities of the book. They include the unfolding of the experience, the temporal nature of the experience, the portability of the book and its qualities of intimacy and scale. However, with only a slight shift in perspective, it is helpful to pose some "what if" questions.

What effect would be generated if a book were constructed that was not small and intimate, but huge, unwieldy and gigantic in scale? What if the book were the size of a book of matches? What would happen to the experience if the pages were bound in a way that thwarted the linear experience? What if the book was not bound at all?

Think about these issues, not only from the perspective of questioning the book itself, but also how it can affect the meaning of your work. Although this book addresses the issues involved in relatively straightforward production, any discussion of one way of proceeding, by implication, suggests that other solutions and other forms which break with convention may offer effective and innovative alternatives.

The bottom line in bookmaking is having something to say. The more honest and direct you are, the greater the chance of devising structures and solutions that not only respect the qualities of the traditional book, but also challenge and subvert convention, not simply for the sake of innovation, but as a specific response to your expressive and communicative concerns.

Picture Pastimes for Small Folk. Published by Ernest Nister, London and E.P. Dutton & Co., New York, c. 1890.

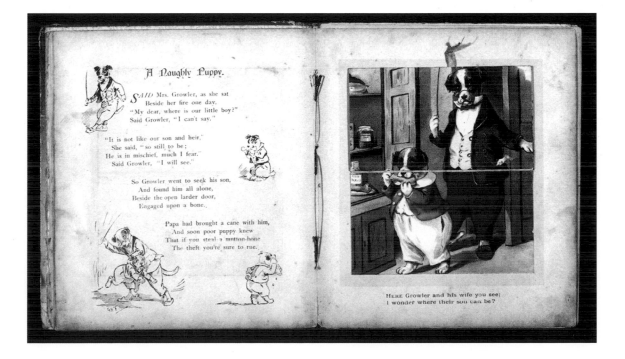

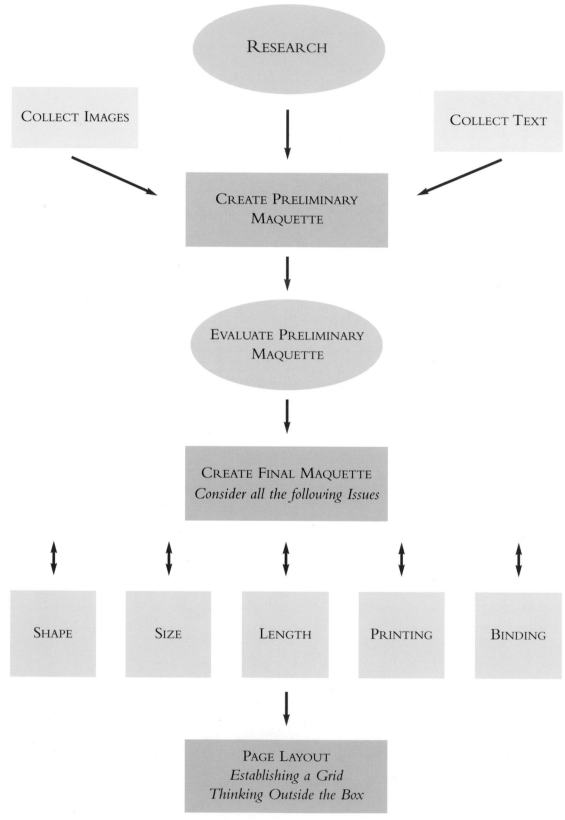

CHAPTER 2

THE PROCESS OF DESIGN

RESEARCH

To make a book is to enter a world with a long and distinguished history. As such it is essential to see, read and touch as many books as possible, critically evaluating their materials, print quality and design. Visit libraries and second-hand bookstores and inform the staff of your interest. You will most likely be shown rare and beautiful treasures if judged sincere. Most bibliophiles are happy to share their knowledge, and show you their personal favorites. Take note of any special techniques such as embossing, paper cutting, unusual shapes, unusual typeface choices, or other devices. Imagine how they would look if adapted to, not grafted on, your work. Make notes and sketches as ideas present themselves.

As you engage in this research you will notice how graphic design reflects the Zeitgeist, or spirit of the times, in a very specific manner. Cultural movements, be they Art Nouveau, punk music or Victorian times, have graphic devices and type styles so particular to them, that it becomes difficult to separate one from the other. Perhaps the greatest emblem of the 'Sixties was not the Beatles or the Vietnam War, not even the mini skirt, but the word *Love* styled by the American artist Robert Indiana.

Realize you are not a blank slate. You are constantly being influenced. Typographic and layout styles are so much a part of the everyday cultural landscape, that they are absorbed almost by osmosis. They seem to burrow into our psyche, and it is only with the greatest effort that this can be recognized, let alone ignored. Be aware of this. Consciously analyze some of the more daring examples of contemporary graphic design in magazines and on television. Start a notebook of examples that interest you and build up a personal "bank" of resources to draw upon.

To compare the design process with a spider's web is perhaps an exaggeration. It may be as complex, but it is not as dangerous. However, the metaphor reinforces the notion that design addresses the total structure of the book, and like a web, this structure is the sum of many smaller parts. A·L·O·E (an anagram for "A Lady of England"), *In the Spider's Web,* Gall and Inglis, London and Edinburgh, c. 1905.

The point of these remarks is to emphasize the need to proceed in an informed manner. Do not simply go to the computer and start. The result will be disappointing. You will most likely impose a pre-determined solution on your work. Your book will be much richer if it reflects a thoughtful process of research and reflection.

Finally, consider the function of your book. Is it a personal expressive work, or do you wish to use it for commercial purposes? Each will have different requirements. This can mean eschewing fancy type and pictures and just keeping it simple. I remember once receiving a memo from a colleague who had just attended a computer design course. The memo looked so slick, and so much like a commercial brochure, that I did not even realize it was an inter-office communication, and I threw it in the trash without even reading it. Fortunately I was not the only one to make this error. I remember myself, and other colleagues, scrambling to find the "junk" mail before the re-cyclers came through the offices in the evening.

You may consider the option of leaving some pages blank so that handwritten comments can be inserted after the book is complete. Such a solution can moderate the often overly mechanical appearance of a computer generated book.
Edmund Evans, *The Illuminated Scripture Text Book for Every Day, with Interleaved Diary for Every Day and a Colored Illustration for Every Day*, Frederick Warne and Co., New York, 1875.

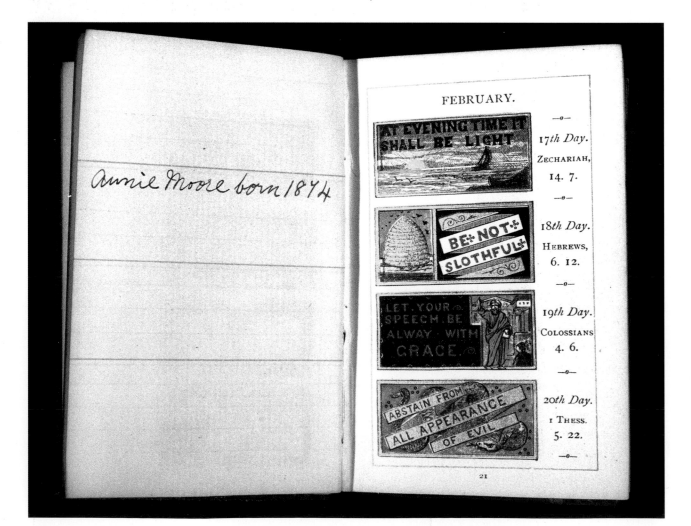

GETTING STARTED: ASSEMBLING YOUR MATERIAL

In the first instance you must collect and/or prepare the materials you need.

IMAGES

Do you have all the images? Are they of sufficient quality? Are you going to work from negatives or slides? If so, do you have the means to scan them or will they need to be sent out to be scanned? Is the material either your own or in clear title and free of copyright encumbrances? If you are using the material of others, do you have permission to use it?

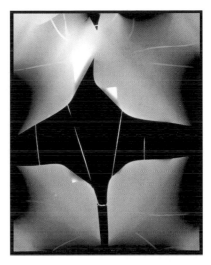

The issue of quality for a book is best decided by the simple criteria of appropriateness to the intended use. Any image should look "good," or, more correctly, look how you would like it to look if it is the same size that it will appear in your book. This applies particularly when working with prints, which for the most part can only be scanned on relatively low resolution flatbed reflective scanners. For example, if the only copy you have of an image is say 3″x 2″, then your chances of being able to scan the image and successfully reproduce it bigger than 3″x 2″ are not great. Sometimes one has little choice and it is true that some enlargement is possible. However, best results will be obtained if you ensure your images are the same size they will appear in the book, or a little larger.

Scale is less of an issue with either negatives or transparencies because they can be scanned with a film scanner if you have access to one. Otherwise slides and negatives will have to be sent out to be scanned. (See Chapter 6, *Photo CD and Custom Scanning, pp. 138–141.*)

When assembling the preliminary maquette simple black and white photocopies of your images will suffice. Proof prints of color images may be useful but in most cases it is not necessary to go to this expense. The primary consideration at this stage is size and positioning.
Untitled Photogram, Douglas Holleley, 1991.

TEXT

The way in which you prepare the text depends on how much you have. If there is only a small amount (for example, captions with your images), then it is acceptable practice to type directly into the page layout program. However, if there is a large amount this is not advisable. Page layout programs work best when you use them to manipulate both your images and your text as shapes on the page, concentrating on them as simple design elements. Although they can be used to type text, they are clumsy and inefficient compared with a dedicated word processing program.

Use a word processing program to prepare and print the text. Have it read by another person, ideally a critical and patient friend. Make the changes and spell check the document one last time. Usually it is acceptable to simply save your document in the native format of the word processing program you are using. The page layout program has "filters" which read the word processing formatting in order to translate this to your document. However, sometimes things can go wrong and the text does not open as it should. If this is the case, go back to your word processing program and save the file as a word only or text file. This eliminates all the formatting but this is OK. You can easily reapply the formatting in the page layout program. An added benefit is that the document will print with fewer problems.

CREATING A MAQUETTE

Before you begin to assemble your book with the computer, you must have a clear idea of the finished product. The Oxford English Dictionary's definition of design begins with the phrase a "mental plan." This strikes to the heart of the matter. Design is not just decorative embellishment, or the desire to make something look attractive. It is an attitude to a task, or in the case of bookmaking, a series of tasks, that involves planning, tolerance of complexity and integrative skills, from conception to final realization. Design, although it includes the understanding of certain conventions and the acquisition of certain skills, is fundamentally a means of clarifying content. This clarification occurs at two levels. Firstly, to yourself, and secondly to another.

The single most helpful design strategy is to commune with your work. Look carefully and patiently at your material to see if a structure suggests itself. To guide this process it is essential to make a simple preliminary copy of your book. This is known variously as a "rough," a "comp" or a "dummy." We will use the word "maquette."

It is helpful to make two maquettes. The first of these will address the editing of your images and text. It is assumed you have a collection of images. In all likelihood they were not produced specifically for a book. In the first instance we will edit these from the perspective of bookmaking, a quite different forum to that of the portfolio or exhibition. After this we will construct a second copy, taking a more integrated approach, considering all of the details of the design process. There is a strong temptation to neglect this step as it is easy to try out various ideas and image/text relationships on the screen. However, it is best to resist because the infinite number of possibilities offered at the click of a mouse can confuse rather than clarify. Also the highly "finished" look of the screen image can often be seductive to the point of distraction, and begin to lead, rather than follow, your ideas.

This book employs the "exquisite corpse" strategy with words rather than images. (See Chapter 1, *p.* 7 for an example using images.)
One Hundred Million, Million Poems. English translation of Raymond Queneau's book, *Cent Mille Milliards de Poèmes,* 1961. Translated by John Crombie. Kickshaws Press, 1983.

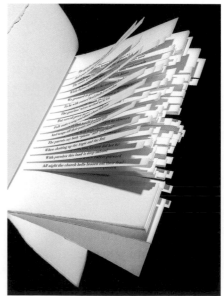

THE PRELIMINARY MAQUETTE: CLARIFICATION OF CONTENT

Paradoxically in creating a book by computer, the best initial approach
is to employ the time-honored simple tools: scissors, paper and glue.

You will need:

- Copies of the images that
  are going to be used in
  the book.
- Text printed in an
  appropriate word pro-
  cessing program.
- Captions and headings set
  in a larger typeface and cut
  into small pieces.
- Scissors.
- Glue stick, or a roll of
  adhesive tape.
- Blank paper.
- A pencil.

Zweig often uses *trompe l'œil* effects
which reference the act of assemblage,
so important in making a book.
Janet Zweig, *Heinz and Judy, a play,*
Photographic Resource Center,
Boston, 1985.

The best way to anticipate the experience of viewing the book is to
lay the images and text in a long line on the floor. The initial maquette
should be seen as the opportunity to attempt to deal with all the data
at your disposal. Do not be afraid to put in more images than you
would use for an exhibition or for a portfolio.

Take the time to say what you have to say. Remember that a book
is a sequential unfolding of experiences that build cumulatively to
create a new, more complex whole. There is no pressure to say
everything at once. A useful strategy is to divide the book into sections
or chapters. It is perhaps a statement of the obvious but the chapter
represents a means of introducing a new but related set of thoughts and
images. Essentially it serves the purpose of providing a pause, or point
of rest, in the experiencing of the work. It allows the inclusion of
images and text that would not be possible to include in other forms
of visual organization. A chapter is best thought of as a self-contained
thought or series of related thoughts.

A useful analogy is that of a night's sleep. Think of each chapter as
a dream, a dream that has its own logical (or illogical) message. Think
of the book as a representation of the entire night's set of experiences;
then structure the book so that one proceeds from one dream to
another, as the night unfolds. The result may be harmonious,
contrasting, or even discordant.

This advice may sound over-explicit or patronizing. However, the point is important. The message is that the book facilitates complexity. Its linear form, and the fact that it takes time to read, permits you to introduce a level of richness and resonance that is difficult to achieve in any other medium, with the possible exception of video or film.

The first maquette should be almost deliberately rough and un-precious. Try to allow your material to speak in its own voice in the hope that meanings you did not consciously intend are revealed. The medium of bookmaking, with its qualities of time and sequencing, will affect and condition your work, often in new and unexpected ways.

The word "medium" suggests there is a process somehow "outside" of ourselves, that helps us find the most appropriate form of expression. For example, often one does not know one's thoughts until one tries to express them through the medium of speech! If this can be true for the most direct link between private, internal thought and the external manifestation of that thought, then how much more should it be true for the more complex ideas one addresses when one begins to order and combine words and images on the printed page.

Do not try to over-edit the work at this point. See what happens when you use all of your images. See what happens when you place images together that you did not originally intend to be in juxtaposition. See what happens when you group images into chapters and subsequently order them to create a more complex experience.

The maquette is the forum where you try ideas before refining your layout. Above is a page from the maquette and below, the finished page when printed. Observe how Zimmermann refined the basic idea by making notes directly on the maquette.
Philip Zimmermann, *High Tension*. Printed and published at Visual Studies Workshop Press for *Montage 93*, Rochester, N.Y., 1993.

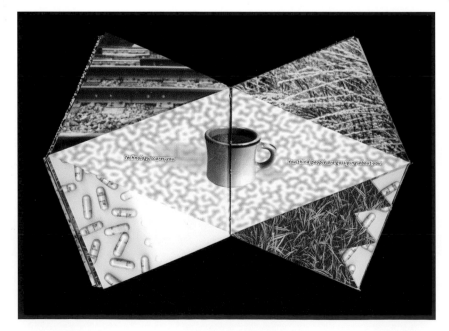

EVALUATING THE
PRELIMINARY
MAQUETTE

When you have finished, read this maquette as if you were seeing it for the first time. Imagine it was written and assembled by someone else. Put your intentions and desires in the back of your mind and look at it objectively. Analyze where the sequencing of the imagery is successful. Pinpoint where it starts to break down. Look carefully at the text, both in its own right and its relationship to the images.

Actively interact with the maquette at this stage. Indicate, by drawing boxes, which images should be bigger, or which ones may benefit by reduction. Consider the possibility of repeating images, much like a chorus in that other linear form of creative expression, music.

Allow time to digest this material. If you are fortunate you will have presented yourself with choices and options previously hidden from view. It is impossible to overstress the value of this initial step. Gaining distance and a sense of objectivity about one's work is one of the most difficult aspects of creative expression.
This point can be illustrated by a comment I once heard made by a friend who managed an art gallery in Sydney, Australia. I remember looking with him at some paintings made by applying paint behind glass. They were lucid, and the best of them were astonishing. But there were some that did not seem quite right. They either addressed different visual and/or conceptual concerns or else they seemed relatively clumsy in execution.

However, the artist (who was not present) did not perceive the dissonances that were so apparent to us. I asked my friend about this and he said, in his typical mixture of profundity and flippancy,

"Douglas, this is why artists have dealers. Only we know how to tell which is the artist's best work."

I am not suggesting that this somewhat disrespectful attitude is correct. However, it does indicate an important truth. It indicates that one can get so wrapped up in the creative process, that one loses all sense of objectivity about one's work. Intentions get mixed up with effects; effort and time spent get confused with results.

The issue of identity, implied in the discussion, is directly addressed in this double-page spread.
Peter Bunce, *Confide In Me,* self-published, Sydney, c. 1995.

The important question to ask is not, "Does the book say what I wanted it to say?" but "Can I take responsibility for what it is saying?" This is a fine but important distinction. It accepts the fact, as discussed above, that the act of assembling, sequencing and ordering the work is a creative act with its own consequences and effects. It is also a reminder that from time to time, one will receive new insights and learn new things when one engages with a medium.

For the skeptical I would like to expand on this thought. Consider what happens when you make a photograph with a reflex camera. One looks through the viewfinder and selects the image one wants. The shutter is pressed. A picture is made. But what happens? Instantly the mirror raises and blacks out the viewfinder, the shutter opens and closes, and the mirror returns to its normal position. Only then is vision through the camera restored. Thus an image is made, and a subsequent judgement formed, on an event that was never really witnessed. The image represents what we saw up to the moment of exposure and what followed it shortly after. Admittedly this time is short, a mere fraction of a second in most cases. However, the intriguing fact remains that a photograph made with a reflex camera, was made while the photographer was literally blind. Yet we continue to make images, and claim authorship for these images, on the basis of statements that to all intents and purposes claim, "This was how I saw it."

The point is that all the time, in many different ways, we take for granted intrusions by our medium of choice, without fully realizing how much it participates in what it is we imagine we are saying all by ourselves. It is the purpose of this discussion to make this point in such a way that the reader is fully conscious of this mechanism and can begin to accept and learn from this process. What we are addressing is essentially a dialog between intention and effect. One takes one's material, and submits it to the construction of context and meaning inherent in the medium of bookmaking. Each decision made on sequencing, pacing, juxtaposition and so on will affect how the book is read and understood, not only by an anonymous reader, but more importantly by oneself.

It is for these reasons that the construction and subsequent appraisal of the maquette is such a critical part of the process.

This example of the often playful, yet always sophisticated work of John Wood, demonstrates how the process of research, note-keeping and collage, intrinsic to the construction of the maquette, can have its own beauty and artistic integrity.
The Olive Tree, John Wood. Iris print, 16″x 24″, 2000.

THE FINAL MAQUETTE

Although the emphasis when making the preliminary maquette was on the clarification of content, rather than the design, the two are in fact inextricably related. If you have taken this job seriously, it is likely you have presented yourself with many design strategies that are particular to your book. In constructing a second version, these embryonic ideas will be focussed and modified by the specific considerations listed below. The more clearly you can visualize the finished book, the better off you will be. Resist the temptation to get on the computer just yet. Planning and thought at this stage will pay dividends in the future.

The following issues require consideration.

- The shape of the book.
- The size of the book.
- The length of the book.
- The printing and binding method.
- Page layout.
- Typographical issues. (See Chapter 3.)

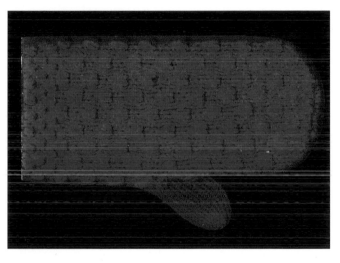

A whimsical example of how the shape of the book can reflect the contents. Tonjia, *The Red Mitten,* Visual Studies Workshop Press, Rochester, N.Y., 1996.

THE SHAPE OF THE BOOK

Most books follow certain conventions with respect to shape. Square or rectangular books are what we are most accustomed to seeing. There is a good reason for this. Circular books, though possible to design and produce, are very tricky to bind. They also have the unfortunate tendency to roll off the shelf!

Even within this limitation there are many choices. It should be apparent from working on the preliminary maquette, that the qualities of your images and text will influence and even restrict, choice. For example, if most of the images are vertical or "portrait" in orientation, then logically the book is best conceived as being portrait as well. Similarly if most of the images are horizontal or "landscape" in shape and orientation then the same should, in most cases, apply to the shape of the book. If there is a mix of portrait and landscape images, these often look good in a square format.

Although most rectangular books are printed in a ratio of about 4:5, other possibilities exist. If for example the book has panorama images, then the book can have the same aspect ratio. Look carefully at your images to see if they present clues to creating other more unusual shapes.

THE SIZE OF THE BOOK

There are a number of practical and aesthetic considerations that govern page size. As in much of bookmaking, you must try to visualize the finished product, including how it is to be printed. For the most part this book assumes you will be using a conventional desktop (most likely an inkjet) printer. These printers make prints of great beauty and elegance but they do force you to accommodate to their limited size.

Most accept only letter size or A4 size paper, or at best legal size paper (8.5″ by 14″). However, the only way to know what yours is capable of is to open a document, go to the page set up dialog box and see what choices are available. Newer models permit custom paper sizes. If there is such an option then you are only limited by the width of the paper that will fit in the printer. The length can be nominated in the software. (This can be 24″ or more.) Otherwise, the largest paper size indicated in the dialog box is the limit.

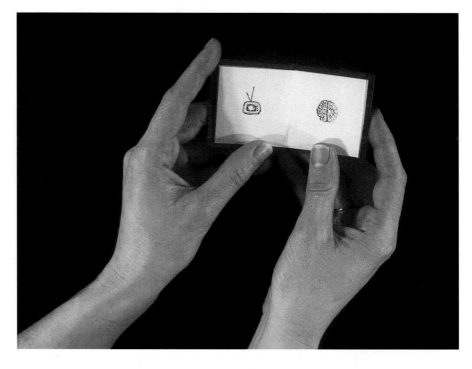

Varying the size of the book can present unusual creative opportunities. Depending on your content, you can make your book either very small, or very large.
Rachel Siegel, *The Random Picture Dictionary of Religious and Spiritual Dichotomies,* Strong Spirit Press, Portland, Oreg., 1998.

If however, you are making a book to be printed commercially, then the choices are greater. If you go to a bureau (such as Kinko's) and ask for help, they will offer useful advice, usually accompanied by instructions and sometimes even software to assist you to set up your document. However, using a commercial printer will add greatly to the cost of production. It also takes away much of the fun. Printing is as much an art as it is a science, and like most things to do with art, practice is essential. It is cheaper, and more beneficial, to work on your own printer at home than to have your book proofed at a service bureau each time you change an image file or alter a page layout.

Usually the size of the book printed at home will be half the maximum size of the paper that the printer will accept. This is because it is often necessary to fold the paper in half to hide the show-through and/or wrinkling.

THE LENGTH OF THE BOOK

The length of the book is mostly a matter of what you have to say and how much time and space you need to say it, but it will affect the final appearance of the work, particularly with respect to the binding system you choose. (See *Binding Issues, p. 29.*)

PRINTING ISSUES

Many of the general issues connected with printing have been covered above. However, there are printing issues specific to the content of the book.

The most obvious of these is whether the book is monochrome or full color. (Conversely the type of printer you have will govern the appearance of your contents.) Modern inkjet printers, even the cheaper models, have the ability to print color images with great fidelity. If you have a laser printer (unless it is a color laser printer) you will be limited to printing in black and white.

The type of printer you select also exerts an influence on your design. Most desktop inkjet printers deposit a thick layer of ink on the paper. This can result in beautiful images with a rich, almost velvety quality—but at a price. Look at the back of an inkjet print from the printer you intend to use. Most likely you will see pronounced "show-through." This term describes the effect where the image or text printed on one side of the paper is visible on the reverse. Often there will be also wrinkling caused by the wet ink distorting the fibers of the paper.

The issue of "show-through" and "back-up" is demonstrated in this beautiful book designed by Christian Ide. Each page shows the position and number of each of the characters in a letterpress type drawer. He allows the following page to "show-through" to indicate the relative position and size of each of the compartments. The precise alignment demonstrates the principle of back-up which requires that any show-through that might occur, lines up logically from page to page. Christian Ide, *Fast 1/2 Minimum,* Alinea Presse, Berlin, 1991.

Detail from:
Christian Ide, *Fast 1/2 Minimum,*
Alinea Presse, Berlin, 1991.

This is especially visible on the back of an image. This may be overcome by using very thick paper, but is usually only successful if the book layout has an image on one side of the page and either nothing, or text on the other. (Text, as it uses less ink, is less likely to show through or distort the paper.)

A laser printer which forms an image by melting, or fusing (usually with heat) a thin layer of plasticized powder to the surface of the paper, minimizes these problems. Unlike ink, the toner does not penetrate the paper but instead remains on the surface.

Also, be prepared to test your printer for alignment if you decide to print on both sides of the paper. Very few machines print to the edge of the document. There is frequently a non-print area of up to 0.25˝. This can cause the front (recto) of the page to print out of alignment to the rear (verso). This alignment is called backup. You will have to experiment with your printer to determine whether this is a problem. There is no easy solution. Usually you have to create different margins for right and left hand pages.

There are also other ways to produce your book. These range from using a high volume black and white or color digital printer to print it in one operation, to using your electronic files to create conventional offset plates so that the document can be printed on an offset printing press.

An example of concertina binding. This method is relatively easy to construct and has the advantage of allowing the book to be read conventionally from page to page, or to be opened (as shown here) to reveal all of the pages simultaneously.
John Crombie, *Overcoated*. Illustrations by Sheila Bourne. Kickshaws Press, Paris, 1982.

The reality is that in learning to make a book, you are also learning some of the skills employed in the commercial printing and publishing industry. Your book, when finished, could quite likely be given to a publisher who could use the files to print your book in commercial volumes, using professional equipment, with little or no further work.

BINDING ISSUES

Binding has a profound effect on design and choice of page layout. Page layout decisions are to a large extent determined by the binding system you will use at the end of the job. This is not as paradoxical as one might first think and is why the development of the maquette is so important. It may come as a surprise to realize how important it is to have a clear idea of one's destination at so early a stage.

Stapling, or saddle stitching a signature, either with metal staples or with linen thread, works best if the book is relatively thin. Thick books do not close satisfactorily if this binding method is employed. Traditionally, thicker books are constructed by stitching individual signatures together to form one unit. This is quite a complex operation for the novice.

Thick books made at home are best sewn together with a stab stitch or bound using the "concertina" method. These methods are effective, can be accomplished with simple tools and are recommended for most self-published books. They also allow your book to grow without affecting the binding process. Using the signature layout for a large book means you will have to sew multiple signatures together. You must also ensure that the book length occurs in multiples of 4. It must be 4, 8, 12, 16 pages, etc., and you will have to know before you begin your final layout, exactly how many pages are in your book. Additionally you will have to print on both sides of the paper.

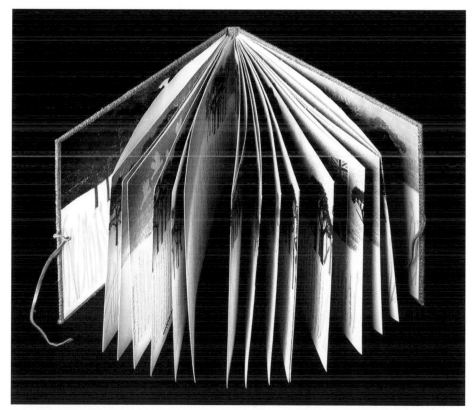

Concertina binding enables you to present your work as sculpture. With the pages fanned in this manner, the book displays its contents so they may be viewed from all angles.
Bound for the Goldfields, Wayzgoose Press, Katoomba, New South Wales, 1990. The text is from *Household Words*, a nineteenth-century English magazine edited by Charles Dickens.

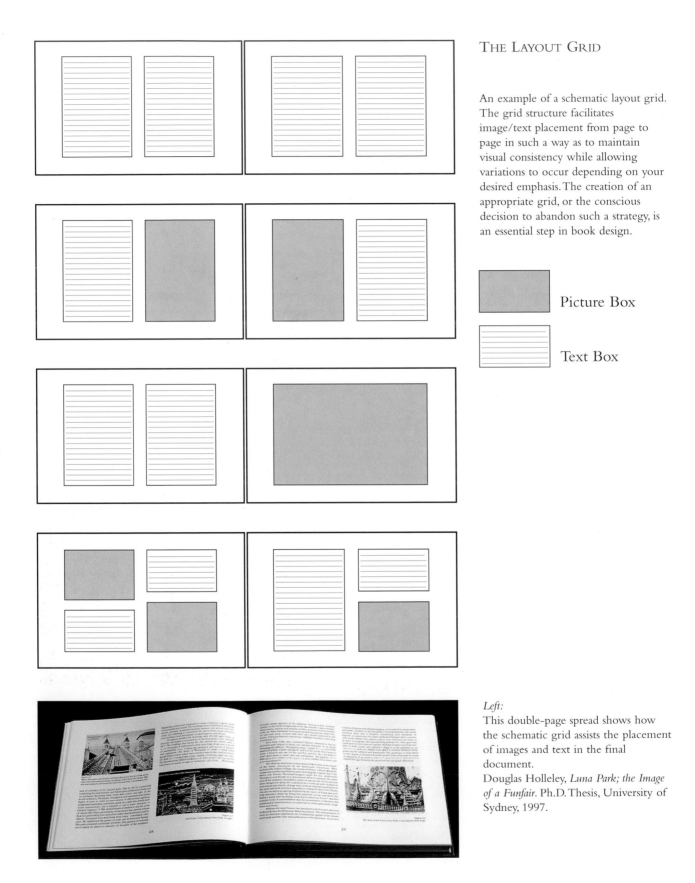

The Layout Grid

An example of a schematic layout grid. The grid structure facilitates image/text placement from page to page in such a way as to maintain visual consistency while allowing variations to occur depending on your desired emphasis. The creation of an appropriate grid, or the conscious decision to abandon such a strategy, is an essential step in book design.

Picture Box

Text Box

Left:
This double-page spread shows how the schematic grid assists the placement of images and text in the final document.
Douglas Holleley, *Luna Park; the Image of a Funfair*. Ph.D. Thesis, University of Sydney, 1997.

PAGE LAYOUT

The page is the fundamental unit of book design. There are two main considerations when laying out your pages.

Thinking across the spread

Think of each double-page spread as a stage where the drama unfolds. The spread is a fixed proscenium, which when held at normal viewing distance, occupies most of the reader's visual field. Gary Frost of the Newberry Library once observed that the picture field represented by the Chicago phone directory is 10″ x 22″.[1] Thus when composing the page layout, work across the gutter, considering the totality of the visual field rather than each page as an isolated visual element.

1. Frost quoted in, Keith Smith, *Structure of the Visual Book*. keith smith BOOKS, Rochester, N.Y., 1995. *p. 9.*

Thinking through the book

Also remember that these pages must relate to each other one after the other. The view of the first spread will be replaced by a view of the second and so on through the book. Therefore it is important to establish a rhythm that connects the pages, not only across the gutter, but throughout the book.

ESTABLISHING A LAYOUT GRID

The traditional way to resolve these issues is to create a template or master grid to assist you in positioning your elements on the page. It determines the margins around your page, the width of text columns, the number of text columns, and the size and placement of images on the page.

Typically a book using images will have three main elements. There may be pages where there is only text, pages where there are only images, and pages where text and images co-exist. Thus when creating your grid you will have to consider how each of these will relate to each other to provide a sense of internal consistency and coherence. Ascertain whether any patterns have emerged from the preliminary maquette. If so indicate them schematically by sketching them as boxes on a blank sheet of paper.

The schema on the opposite page is offered as an example. It is based on the layout of an academic thesis and as such may be too formal for a more expressive book. However, it illustrates the usefulness of such a page layout strategy.

Creating a grid can result in simple but highly elegant solutions. This example is notable for its restraint and sophistication.
Zen. Published by Edition Tiessen, woodcuts by Ian Tyson, 1994.

As you can see, by using a double column it is possible to retain clarity and consistency through the document by simply altering the elements within the basic grid. Observe how the grid allows text and picture elements to be interchanged thus permitting a solution for any contingency. Pages of text, images, or any combination of these two have pre-determined solutions which allow a very tight integration of the visual and textual elements of the book. The result is somewhat mechanistic although appropriate for the nature of the publication. This particular solution may or may not suit your book. However try to see if you can codify your material in this schematic manner.

A grid also addresses the issue of show-through. It is almost impossible to eliminate this phenomenon. It can even occur subliminally, as an optical illusion, when the impression created by the first page is retained in the mind and then superimposed over the new page. This conscious alignment through the page should be exploited as a subtle signifier of coherence and continuity. In saying this, consider contrast rather than direct alignment (this is quite different from simple mis-registration). The operative term however, is "consider."

Once you have established a grid you have created a set of rules. This is both a good and a bad thing. It is bad if you have not thought it through, and it is either inflexible or inappropriate to your content. It is wise to experiment with a variety of ideas before deciding. Once you have started on a particular track it is very difficult to change course.

The good thing is that if you have spent time and effort in devising a solution specific to your needs, then these rules are not constricting, but instead liberating. They allow you to concentrate on the refinement of your ideas because the basic schema for each page is essentially pre-set. Remember that they may be rules, but they are rules of your own making.

The essential principle is to create a rhythmic structure that carries the reader through the book. Good design is perceptible but not obtrusive. It is a device for ensuring that what you are trying to say is communicated to the reader, allowing him or her, for a moment to enter your world, if not your mind.

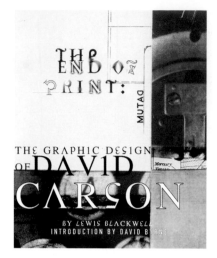

Cover of
David Carson, *The End of Print, The Graphic Design of David Carson.* Text by Lewis Blackwell. Laurence King Publishing, London, 1995.

David Carson, *2nd Sight.* Text by Lewis Blackwell. Laurence King Publishing, London, 1998.

An example of a more free form approach to page layout. David Carson's work systematically questions the assumptions of the grid. His work is notable for its playful and often daring typography, and unusual juxtapositions of word and image. David Carson, *2nd Sight*. Text by Lewis Blackwell. Laurence King Publishing, London, 1998.

THINKING OUTSIDE THE BOX

However, there are times when it is appropriate to question the assumption of the grid. The program Adobe Photoshop allows you to to create a multi-layered image, and combine this with text, permitting a looser, more unstructured approach to page layout. Compared with the notion of "the box" (inherent in QuarkXPress), it allows you to subvert the grid structure, with its attendant assumptions of containment and framing. It is no longer necessary to have images with fixed edges, or have separate boxes for images and text.

Such opportunities have resulted in the expression, *thinking outside the box*. This involves adopting an attitude to the book somewhat analogous to that exhibited by Native Americans and Australians, who construct images in caves and on rock faces without employing the stylistic device of a frame (or grid) to define the edge of the image. The picture simply starts, sometimes in response to a specific geological formation, but as often as not, because it can. These marks often accumulate, sometimes over many years or even centuries, to form a palimpsest of accumulated visual wisdom.

This thinking is perhaps best exemplified by the work of the American graphic designer, David Carson.[2] Carson almost aggressively destroys the grid. Employing multiple typefaces, unusual spacing and curved columns he creates "word pictures" of great graphic interest. Traditional qualities of legibility are replaced by more complex messages which stress the interrelationship of the word and image. The sometimes overwhelming visual intensity of his layouts encourages the creation of new meanings and connections. The reader is forced to decode the message rather than simply read it.

2. David Carson, *The End of Print, The Graphic Design of David Carson*. Text by Lewis Blackwell. Laurence King Publishing, London, 1995.

The computer facilitates layered effects with images and typography. This cover (of a self-published magazine) is notable for its complexity and density. Peter Bunce, *Whatever*, self-published, Sydney, c. 1998.

However, be aware that even these new conventions are still only just that. The fact is that the computer is capable of being used in any manner you choose. It is for this reason that the process of research is so important. Your grid, or lack of it, will reflect your experiences in their totality. It will reflect what you understand a book to be, what you think is the nature of your contents, and all of the influences, conscious or otherwise, that have filtered your perception of these issues. One is tempted to say beware, but better still, be aware.

ADDITIONAL DETAILS

Add the following information to the final maquette:

1. *Title.*
2. *Author's name.*
3. *Colophon.*
The colophon is the term given to the information that describes who created the book, where this occurred, and the details of production. It should also include, if you decide to edition your book, how many copies were printed, or how many copies the edition will be limited to, if printed on demand.

    Not only that, a colophon will remind you where and when it was produced. No doubt it seems at present you will always remember this moment, but it is surprising how quickly such details are forgotten. A book is as permanent a forum for your work as will ever exist. There is a good chance it will be around your entire life and beyond. Do not allow its value to be diminished by uncertainty over its origins.

4. *Acknowledgements.*
An expression of thanks is appropriate if you have used the material of others or if you have received special help from anyone.

David Carson, *2nd Sight.* Text by Lewis Blackwell. Laurence King Publishing, London, 1998.

CONCLUSION

You will observe there has been no need to use the computer in this chapter. The computer is a wonderful device for assembling your document once you have created your overall design plan. Machines cannot think or create, the two qualities you need most at this stage. Simple tools are all you require.

    With the maquette in hand the computer will do what you want. With this roadmap you will quickly translate your thoughts into a finished document.

    Without it, you will be lost.

Although a somewhat Eurocentric view, the vowels may be seen as the basic building blocks of language. In this etching, Petr Herel renders them in an almost architectural manner, investing their newly acquired three-dimensional form with gravity and mystery.
Petr Herel, *Voyelles*. Artist's book (etching and letterpress). Graphic Investigation Workshop, Canberra School of Art, 1988.

CHAPTER 3

TYPOGRAPHY

BEFORE the computer made it possible for anyone to set type, typography was a highly specialized craft. Although Johann Gutenberg's development of movable type in Germany in 1450[1] meant books no longer had to be written by hand, it was nevertheless necessary to set each lead character, one at a time, by hand. Despite the labor-intensive nature of this process, books set this way, at their best, exemplify the highest standards of printing. Many contemporary artists and craftsmen (sic) still set type in this manner because of the precise control it offers over letter placement, and the quality of the finished product. Metal type, printed on a letterpress press,[2] imparts an almost three-dimensional quality to the page, producing a tactile, as well as visual, impression.

For almost four and a half centuries, the procedures for the manufacturing and setting of type, changed very little. However, things speeded up in the nineteenth century when the Linotype machine was invented by Ottmar Merganthaler in 1884. The operator entered the text on a keyboard and the device produced whole lines of metal type, known as "slugs." Compared to the hand-setting of individual letters, this was a revolution in speed and efficiency. This system persisted for a good eighty years, even after many books were no longer printed by letterpress. As late as the 1960s offset-printed[3] books were being produced with text set on the Linotype machine.

However, the the most important development in the 'Sixties was photo-typesetting. This process employed either a photographic negative or cathode ray tube to image text onto photo-sensitive paper. The characters could be enlarged or reduced in varying degrees so it was no longer necessary to have metal type characters or matrices for each size. This process made things both faster and cheaper. However, there was a price to pay for this convenience. Previously, with cast metal type, the letter proportions varied slightly for each size of type, even in the same family. Smaller sizes usually had slightly wider characters with a larger x-height. Photo-typesetting's "one size fits all" scaled type meant the loss of these subtleties. Additionally the characters were seldom as sharp or as well defined as those printed from freshly-cast, metal characters.

An example of contemporary letterpress printing from hand-set metal type. Typesetting and printing by Mike Hudson and Jadwiga Jarvis, *Private Impressions,* Wayzgoose Press, Katoomba, 1995–96.

1. This is only true in the West. Movable type was in use in the Orient in the 11th century.
2. The letterpress process requires placing the lines of type on the "bed" of a press. The raised type is inked, the paper is placed in position, and then pressed in contact with the type with a cylinder or platen.
3. Offset printing is still the most common form of printing. A plate is made and the ink adheres to the areas of the plate that are to be printed. This ink is then transferred, or offset, to a master cylinder covered with a rubber blanket which transfers this impression to the paper.

There were also other developments in the 'Sixties. Letraset introduced the dry transfer system[4] which enabled a variety of type faces to be produced and distributed relatively cheaply. These were often quite whimsical and/or adventurous.

Regardless of the method, typesetting was a craft practiced by specialists, using expensive equipment that could only be afforded by large printing houses or specialty typesetting houses. Above all, the highly trained operators were familiar with the history and conventions of typesetting, and for the most part, imparted to their work qualities of legibility, harmony and proportion. Gaucheries and obvious errors were usually not present.

However, the development of the personal computer, especially the graphics-oriented Apple Macintosh in the 1980s has completely revolutionized the practice of typesetting. Now anyone can set type. Good quality fonts produced by the same companies that used to make cast metal type matrices, give the lay person tools once reserved for highly trained professionals. In many ways, this access to typographic tools is reason enough for the invention of the personal computer. It is difficult to imagine a greater development in the history of printing since Gutenberg. However, tools, no matter how sophisticated, do not grant the user the education and training that traditional typographers possessed.

It is worth making the effort to be aware of traditional typographic practice. At first glance it seems sufficient to be able to nominate a particular typeface to give your document a superficially "finished" or even "professional" look. However, there is more to typography than simply selecting a typeface. At minimum, letter size, leading, and the relation of these variables to column width can radically change the appearance and effect of the page, and even the "look" of the typeface itself.

It is true that it is appropriate to question and challenge some of the traditional ways type has been used. However, as discussed often in this book, challenging assumptions carries more weight when it comes from a position of knowledge, rather than one of inexperience.

4. Type characters were attached to paper backing sheets which were then burnished onto the finished artwork.

An example of a pair of Linotype "slugs." In this photograph you can see there are three distinct lines of lead. Two contain the actual letters and a third acts as a spacer to govern the distance between the top and bottom lines. This use of lead spacers between lines gives rise to the term "leading" which describes the distance between lines of type.

The Evolution of the Typeface

Mechanical type was originally based on letter forms once created by hand. The characteristics of the first writing tools influenced the shape of the individual characters. In Classical times writing was performed using either a brush or reed pen. The "Roman" typeface was first written on stone with brush or pen and then subsequently incised with a chisel.

After the invention of movable type in the fifteenth century, this basic letterform of the Latin alphabet was modified in response to changes in cultural and aesthetic values and the increasing sophistication of typecasting and printing machinery. As printing became more mechanized and separated from its origin in hand-written script, so the typeface designers experimented with new forms. The following categories are used by typographers to indicate the main changes in the evolution of the roman typeface.

Old Style

THIS category of roman typefaces originated in Europe in the fifteenth century. They are characterized by a lack of contrast between the thick and thin strokes of the letters. The serifs are oblique. These attributes combine to present a very even impression when the text is set in blocks on the page. The lighter faces such as Garamond and Bembo are popular choices for book design. The style is best exemplified by the work of Claude Garamond (1480–1561), a Parisian typeface designer of the French Renaissance. The initial letter of this paragraph (as is this book) is set in Monotype Bembo.

Transitional

THIS term is reserved for typefaces that were designed in the mid-eighteenth century. The contrast between the thick and thin strokes is exaggerated, starting a trend that would culminate in the Modern style of the nineteenth century. In comparison to the oblique stress of the old style, here the accent is on verticality. The typographer best exemplifying this style is John Baskerville (1706–1775) who used it when he printed Virgil's *Georgics* in 1757.[5] Baskerville also designed an italic typeface to accompany the roman variation.[6] The initial letter of this paragraph is set in Baskerville.

Old Style eg. Garamond
abcdefghijklmnopqrstuvwxyz
abcdefghijklmnopqrstuvwxyz
ABCDEFGHIJKLMNOPQR
STUVWXYZ

Transitional eg. Baskerville
abcdefghijklmnopqrstuvwx
abcdefghijklmnopqrstuvwxyz
ABCDEFGHIJKLMNOP
QRSTUVWXYZ

Modern eg. Bodoni
abcdefghijklmnopqrstuvwx
abcdefghijklmnopqrstuvwx
ABCDEFGHIJKLMNOPQR
STUVWXYZ

Sans Serif eg. Univers
abcdefghijklmnopqrstuv
abcdefghijklmnopqrstuv
ABCDEFGHIJKLMNOPQ
RSTUVWXYZ

Slab Serif eg. Rockwell
abcdefghijklmnopqrstuv
abcdefghijklmnopqrstuvw
ABCDEFGHIJKLMNOPQR
STUVWXYZ

5. Rob Carter, Ben Day and Philip Meggs, *Typographic Design: Form and Communication,* Van Nostrand Reinhold Company, New York, 1985. p. 205.
6. Alan and Isabella Livingston, *Encyclopædia of Graphic Design and Designers,* Thames and Hudson, London and New York, 1992.

Modern Style

MODERN Style capitalized on the improvement in type casting methods that permitted ultra thin serifs. The style retains the vertical stress of Baskerville but the appearance is more severely geometric, breaking the connection between printed type and its origins in written script. The serifs are straight lines, and the strokes vary greatly in weight from bold, thick strokes to fine hairlines. The master of this style was Giambattista Bodoni (1740–1813), a printer and type designer who spent the majority of his career in Parma, Italy. The initial letter of this paragraph is set in Bodoni Regular.

Sans Serif

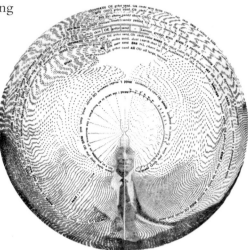

THE other innovation, associated with the Modern Style is the sans serif face. The first was designed by William Caslon IV in 1816. He called it Egyptian. It was not used widely until 1832 at which time Vincent Figgins placed it in his catalog and called it sans serif. In the United States it was originally referred to as Gothic.[7] Sans serif, literally "without serifs," is a face stripped of all decorative embellishment. Despite its origin in the nineteenth century it has been most commonly employed during the twentieth century, where its directness and unadorned appearance epitomized twentieth century ideals of design simplicity and functionality. The initial letter of this paragraph is set in Univers, a family of sans serif typefaces designed in the 1950s by Adrien Frutiger.

Bonnie Gordon, a book artist whose work blurs the boundary between type and image, literally "stretches" the medium of typography by printing her text on a transparent substrate and distorting it before printing.
The Anatomy of the Image Maps, Visual Studies Workshop Press, Rochester, N.Y., 1982.

7. W. Turner Berry and H. Edmund Poole, *Annals of Printing,* Blandford Press, London, 1966.

Other categories

The above four type styles are complemented by other letterforms. Of these, faces with slab serifs (eg. Rockwell) are sometimes regarded as a separate category. Defying categorization however, is the plethora of contemporary display faces designed since 1960, first to be published in dry transfer form, and more recently, on disk. A significant type designer of this period is Neville Brody (b. 1957).

It is also appropriate to mention the work of calligraphers and graphic artists who draw letters freehand. This is perhaps the most elegant and expressive means of making a typographical statement. Eric Gill (1882–1940) and Hermann Zapf (b. 1918) are notable practitioners. More recently, Martin Sharp (Australia) and Wes Wilson (USA) approach typography with a freedom and appreciation of its graphic qualities that will inspire anyone who makes the effort to research their work.

THE TERMINOLOGY OF TYPOGRAPHY

You will observe that computer programs refer to typefaces as fonts. In the printing trade this term traditionally describes a complete set of characters (alphabets, punctuation marks and numerals) for one size of typeface. Because computers re-scale type from a master matrix, rather than have separate designs for each size, the term has lost much of its original meaning. As far as digital typesetting is concerned, you can use the two terms interchangeably.

LETTERFORMS

The following terms will allow you to identify the components of typographical characters and styles to assist you to discriminate between different typefaces.

Capitals or Upper Case: The larger letters in a font. The term "capital" comes from their use on the capitals of Roman columns.
Lower Case: The small letters of the alphabet.

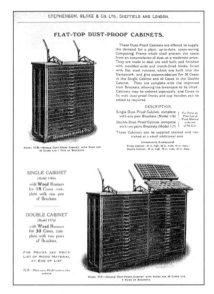

This page from the catalog of an English manufacturer of type furniture illustrates the origin of the terms, upper and lower case. As you can see, on top of the rack of cases there is a support which holds the individual typecases while in use. There are two levels to this support. The top one for the capital letters is called the "upper case" and the other, the "lower case." These terms subsequently became applied to the characters of the font themselves.
Catalog, Stevenson, Blake & Co. Ltd., Sheffield and London, 1924.

Baseline: The imaginary line upon which the base of each letter rests. However, sometimes letters such as o, v and w, drop minimally below this line to appear optically correct.
Capline: The line that runs along the tops of the capital letters.
Meanline: The line that runs along the top of the body of lower case letters.
x-height: This is the size of the lower case letter "x," a letter with no ascenders or descenders. It is the distance between the baseline and the meanline.
Ascender Line: The line that runs along the tops of the ascenders.
Descender Line: The line that runs along the bottom of the descenders.

Below: An example of justified text.
The Bishop's Brothel, Wayzgoose Press, Katoomba, New South Wales, 1994.

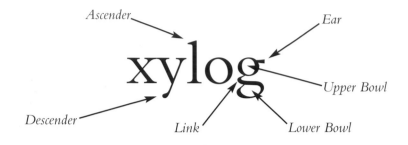

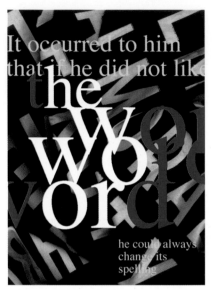

Ascender: The part of certain lower case letters (such as bdfhklt) which extends above the x-height.

Descender: The part of certain lower case letters (such as jpqy) that drops below the x-height.

Stroke: Any of the linear, as opposed to curved, elements within a letterform.

Hairline: The thinnest strokes within a typeface.

Above:
The Word, Douglas Holleley, 1994.
These two images combine text with collage. In both cases the collage was scanned directly into the computer using a flatbed scanner, and the text placed on the image in Photoshop.

Bodoni
Hairline serif

Baskerville
Bracketed serif

Below:
Tragediæ, Douglas Holleley, 1994.

Serif: The terminal stroke at the top and bottom of the main strokes of letters in a roman style typeface. Different typefaces use different styles. Bodoni uses a hairline serif, while Baskerville and Times Roman use a bracketed serif.

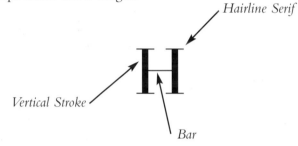

Bembo   *Bodoni*

Stress: The degree to which the thicker parts of the stroke are angled. The Bembo type above is stressed obliquely, while the Bodoni typeface has a perpendicular stress.

TYPEFACE SIZE

The size of type is not the actual size of the character itself, but the height of the lead body on which it was originally positioned. Size is expressed in points, of which there are 72 to an inch.

The biggest influence on apparent size is the x–height of the type relative to the size of the ascenders or descenders. For example Univers has a large x–height and very short ascenders and descenders in comparison with other typefaces. (See below.) All the following typefaces are set in the same size (36 pt.). Notice how the x–height of the lower case characters changes from one typeface to another in proportion to the length of the ascenders and descenders.

xylo   xylo   xylo

Univers   Times New Roman   Bembo

This single lead letterpress character "A," shows how the size of a typeface is measured. It is not, as you might think, the size of the character itself, but is instead the height of the "body" of the block on which the character is placed. The dimension "x" is the body size of the type and is expressed in points.

SPECIAL TYPE STYLES

It is essential to understand that the type styles described below are separate fonts. Thus for example, in the Univers family there is a separate (designed) font for each of the variations. Thus there is a font called Univers Oblique (Italic), Univers Light, Univers Bold, etc. It is correct practice to select the specific variation from the Font menu.

This screen image of the open Font menu in QuarkXPress illustrates how each variation of a typeface is in fact a separate font. It is essential to select the variation from the Font menu rather than applying the *italic* or *bold* variations in the Style menu.

Do not apply the generic italicizing, emboldening, etc. command in the program. This is a distortion (and can also cause printing problems). Sometimes you will have no choice if the face you select has no designed variations. Try to avoid such fonts wherever possible.

In the digital domain there are two main classes of font. TrueType and PostScript. PostScript is the best choice, having specific designed styles for each typeface. However, these will not print on an inkjet printer unless you have a program like Adobe Type Manager (ATM) installed. This program is invariably bundled with Photoshop, and it is almost certain you have it in your system. Check the ATM "Read Me" file for instructions on how to adjust the control panel if you have screen display or printing problems.

Bold type: Type that has thicker strokes, giving the typeface emphasis.
Condensed type: Condensed type is proportionally narrower than regular type, taking up less space on the line.
Italics: Angled type with a form change in some of the characters.
Light: Type with thinner strokes than normal.
Small Caps: Capital letters, usually the size of the x-height of the lower case letters. Like the italic or bold commands, they are best selected from the Font menu, if available, rather than use the QuarkXPress small capitals command.
Dingbats: Various decorative signs, symbols and bullets used for emphasis.
Old Style Figures: Numbers compatible with lower case letters. e.g. 1234567890.
Ranging Figures: Numbers that are the same height as the capital letters.

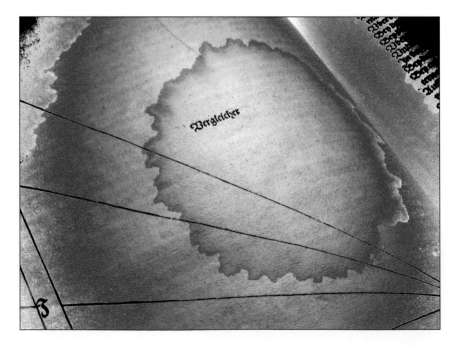

Type can assume an almost abstract quality when photographed. Using letters, not simply as written symbols, but as elements in an image, changes their familiar function as communicators of abstract thought, and instead persuades the eye and the mind to see them as shapes on a two-dimensional surface.
The Map of Time, Douglas Holleley, 2000. Photographed from Albrecht Dürer's, *Hierin sind begriffen vier Bucher von menschlicher Proportion,* Nurenberg, 1528.

Another example of type as image. Like the photograph on the facing page, this image was made in the first instance by photographing text printed in a book. Compare these images to those of the same book photographed in a more conventional manner, *p. 47, overleaf. Z*, Douglas Holleley, 2000. Photographed from Albrecht Dürer's, *Hierin sind begriffen vier Bucher von menschlicher Proportion*, Nurenberg, 1528.

SETTING TYPE

There are many variables that affect the appearance of the text on the printed page. Certainly the typeface you select is important. You should choose a typeface on the basis of how it will look set as a body of type on the page. Do not simply consider the individual letterforms. Fonts look very different when printed as a block than they do as individual letters. Additionally, the appearance of the font can be considerably altered by how it is spaced and set. (These variables will be discussed shortly.)

Appreciate the fact that the computer allows you to learn typographic skills relatively quickly. It is a very simple matter to change the typeface by simply highlighting the text and trying another font. Do not jump to the first solution, but print many tests. To learn typography, in addition to understanding its conventions and nomenclature, you must spend a lot of time setting type and evaluating the finished work. With hand-set type this would have meant spending a whole day setting the page and pulling a proof print. An expensive and time-consuming task. Now it is quick and inexpensive to make a test print. Evaluating a range of printed pages of type is the best and fastest way to learn. Do not make judgements based on the screen image. Do not settle for the first solution. Test, test and test again.

There are no simple rules for selecting a font. Some authorities argue that serif faces are easier to read. The reason proposed is that the

The Drop Cap option provides points of emphasis in a document by enlarging the initial letter of a new paragraph. As this example shows, the dropped letter does not necessarily have to be a capital.
Douglas Holleley, *Past and Future Tense,* Rockcorry, Rochester, N.Y., 1998.

serifs create a subliminal horizontal line that facilitates the scanning of the text, guiding the eye to the next line. Similarly it is argued that sans serif typefaces can be more difficult to read for the same reason. Decisions however, cannot be made on the basis of a simple formula. The font you choose (and how you set it) should be, above all, appropriate to the nature of your document.

TYPESETTING STYLES

The way you arrange the type on the page will have significantly more effect on how your document is perceived than perhaps any other variable. At the simplest level you have to consider the shape of the block of type and its apparent "weight" or visual emphasis. A block of type forms an image on the page. Thus you must first consider its external qualities of shape and proportion. Secondly, you can then proceed to refine its internal qualities. These include—sensitive spacing, the logic of the line breaks and the elimination of distracting internal flaws. (See *Common Errors, pp. 55–56,* later in this chapter.)

All of these choices affect legibility—a quality prized in traditional typography. Legibility is of paramount importance if your book contains a large amount of text and you wish the reader to concentrate on the sense and meaning. You can make your text easy to read and understand if this is what you want. However, there may be times when expressive issues will be more important than legibility. You can make the reader pause, even struggle, if this suits your purpose. How you set your type controls legibility and flow. Do not allow it to "just happen," or worse, not happen at all.

Opposite Page
Two double-page spreads from Dürer's treatise on the proportions of the human figure. These pages show his ideas on the subject as related to typography. Designing letterforms is perhaps one of the most complex arts. Not only must the individual letterforms look harmonious, they must also be designed to work in combination to form the myriad words of language. Many great artists have devoted much of their lives to their study.
Albrecht Dürer, *Hierin sind begriffen vier Bucher von menschlicher Proportion,* Nurenberg, 1528.

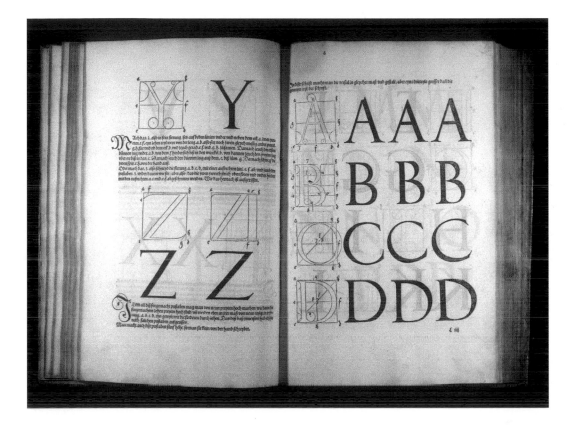

There are four main ways to set type. They are Justified, Ranged Left, Ranged Right and Centered.

JUSTIFIED type sets the columns so that the left and right margins are straight and parallel. This setting produces neat, regular columns of type, each line having a standard length. This is the style most frequently employed in books of text, where regularity of impression from page to page is a design consideration. The main drawback is the formation of "rivers" (blank spaces connecting vertically through the body of the text) which can often occur if you rely entirely on the logic of the program to determine the line breaks and hyphenation.

FLUSH left (sometimes called ragged right) setting produces a straight left margin but the line length varies, usually within a range of about plus or minus one word (about 5 or 6 characters). It is sometimes argued that this method facilitates legibility, as the eye perceives clear visual clues as it scans from one line to the next. This method can be very elegant. There should be little or no hyphenation.

FLUSH right (sometimes called ragged left) setting reverses the position of the straight line. In this case the straight margin is on the right hand side of the column. The lack of an aligned left hand column can slow reading speed as it is more difficult for the eye to locate the beginning of the next line. It is best used with restraint, with small amounts of text.

Centered text is seldom used for extended narratives.
It is most useful for title pages, poetry
or other specific
tasks.

An unusual effect can be employed by using the forced justification tool (found in the Style, Alignment menu) in QuarkXPress.

T   h   i   s
s   p   r   e   a   d   s
w   o   r   d   s
t   o   f i t   t h e   t e x t   b o x

Paul Zelevansky's typesetting shows a profound understanding of the importance of harmony and balance on the printed page. He uses rubber stamps, hand-lettering and other techniques to create his typographical layouts. In *The Case for the Burial of Ancestors, Book 2,* (not illustrated) Zelevansky uses a group of typefaces generated by various manual typewriters.
Paul Zelevansky, *The Case for the Burial of Ancestors, Book 1,* Zartscorp Inc. Books/ Visual Studies Workshop Press, New York, 1981.

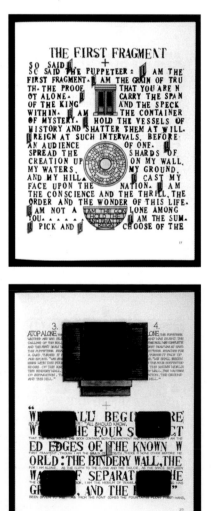

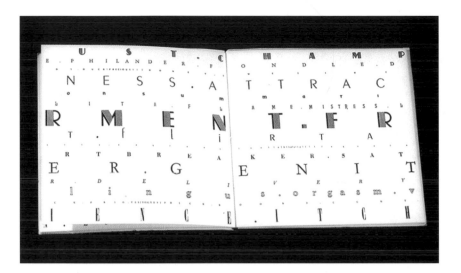

An example of forced justification, in this case printed by letterpress.
John Crombie, *Spreading the Word,*
Kickshaws Press, Paris, 1987.

Finally, be aware that the shape of the text box can be altered to form new and expressive shapes on the page. (See *Altering the Color of the Text,* overleaf.)

As the reader progresses through this book by John Crombie, the pile of words at the bottom of the page diminishes as the words are seemingly drawn up from it to be incorporated into the text.
John Crombie, *Untitled Book,*
Kickshaws Press, Paris, 1983.

ALTERING THE COLOR OF THE TEXT

As mentioned before, a block of text forms an image on the page. This black and white shape can appear spacious and light gray, mid-gray or solid and heavy, almost black. The word "color" is used to describe this effect. The color affects not only the overall visual impression, but also the legibility of the text.

The following variables will affect the color and legibility. Each is important but in practice you will need to assess their interrelationship rather than each in isolation.

Line Length

Excessively short, or excessively long lines are difficult to read. There are no hard and fast rules on line length. About a dozen or so words seem to optimize ease of reading. The implications for type size and letter spacing (tracking) are obvious. Shorter lines are best set with smaller type.

Type Size

Type size greatly influences how a text is read. It may seem a statement of the obvious but a large typeface grabs attention, both visually and sonically, and a small typeface seems very quiet in comparison.

Even though the text below is written in another language, the principle of legibility and reading effort relative to line length is illustrated vividly. Note how the longer bottom lines take longer to scan, even if you do not know how to read German.
Die Nibel Ungen, Gerlachs Jugen Bucherie, Gerlach & Weidling, Vienna and Leipzig, 1920.

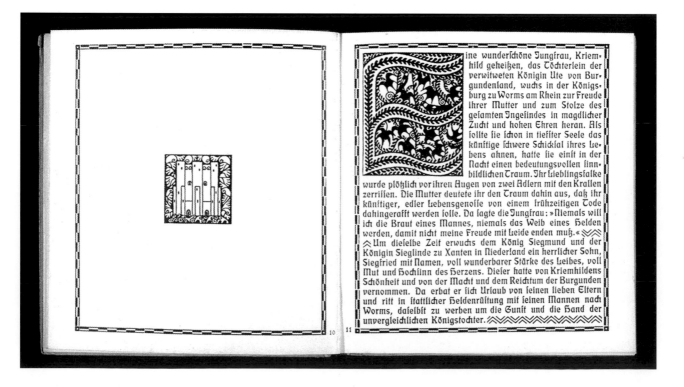

A variety of type styles are exemplified in this double page spread. Note the use of color, shade, varying type size and overprinting.
Werner Enke, *ABC Buechlein,* Harrisfeldwegpresse, Germany, 1985.

Size, as the previous paragraph also demonstrates, is relative. The context plays a significant role. A few lines of very small type can have considerable impact if that is all there is on the page. Apparent size can also be altered by using bold, condensed or italic fonts.

Letter Spacing: Tracking and Kerning

Most typefaces will print from the computer with letter spacing as the designer intended. However, letter spacing can be altered, either for functional reasons, say squeezing in an extra letter to avoid a clumsy hyphenation, or for expressive reasons, such as putting in either more or less space to darken or lighten the color. Computers use the term tracking to describe letter spacing. Extra tracking is particularly useful for headings, especially when capital letters are being used.

Closely related to tracking is kerning. Kerning is the adjustment of the space between individual characters. Often certain pairs of letters do not look "correct" together if you rely on the program's default settings.

John Crombie uses color and shape in his book, *Lapse and Collapse.* Kickshaws Press, Paris, 1985.

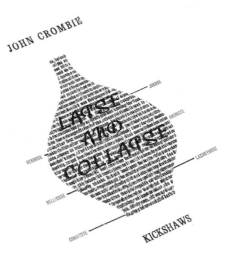

MAW   MAW

In this example, the default positioning of the A and W is too widely spaced. This looks clumsy and out of balance. Kerning so the gap is narrower improves the appearance of the pair.

Inter-line Spacing: Leading

Leading is the term which describes the space between the lines. It originated when traditional letterpress practitioners created extra space by inserting strips of lead between the lines of type. (This is also the clue to its pronunciation.) Leading is frequently not considered with computers as most page layout programs default to a setting (auto) that works quite well. However, be aware that by using the auto setting, the leading will often be expressed as a percentage. (QuarkXPress uses a default leading of 20% of the type size. Thus the auto leading setting for 9-pt. type is 10.8 pts.) This can cause an awkward underlying line-spacing grid.

There are conventions for the use of leading. Text that is set "solid," producing a tight and compact visual impression, uses a value the size of the typeface. Thus if using 12-pt. type set solid, the leading should be set to 12 pts. Maximum legibility usually comes by adding about 20% to the size of the type and then rounding the result to a whole number. As a general rule, more leading is required for type with a large x-height. If you wish to create an even more "airy" and open impression, try a leading value double the point size.

Also interesting is to apply leading values smaller than the type size. In this way lines of type can actually overlap each other. This is an effect you may wish to try. It tends to work best in small amounts, in headings and other points of emphasis. The legibility of the type is reduced but sometimes, and somewhat perversely, legibility, a prized quality in traditional typography, is not necessarily the same thing as clarity, a more indefinable quality that can sometimes come in strange (dis)guises.

The Shape of the Text Block

Text is commonly set in a rectangle. However, page layout programs allow you to alter the shape of the text to complement or contrast with other design elements, such as images, on the page. There are two main ways to do this. QuarkXPress allows you to create polygonal shaped text boxes with irregular boundaries. Alternatively you can create extra boxes around the main (usually square) text box, and using these, with the runaround option selected, to force the type into new and unusual shapes. (See Chapter 5, *Runaround, pp. 102–103.*)

He had noticed in the past that there was an aspect of his personality that remained almost wickedly objective, even when he was deeply moved by either ecstasy or fear. It was like a little hard kernel that travelled around and through his body, sometimes lodging in his brain, sometimes in his eyes. At worst it would end up in his mouth. This kernel he had always suspected hid something that was deeply inimical to his wholeness as a human being.

There is a writer who once observed that it seemed that traumatic events, and the sum total of the perceptions that occurred at the time of this event, can remain in the body where they become encysted. A thick protective layer forms around this nexus of pain and experience which attempts to keep these dangerous aspects hidden within its hard shell. It is said that this tightly constrained ball of pain can grow until it actually becomes a physical object, possessing real weight and dimension. This particular weakness of his was something that came and went with serendipitous indifference to the circumstances in which he found himself. He had always maintained a fairly old fashioned idea about beauty, and sometimes he surprised himself with his quite definite views about how a woman should dress. Not that he was ever in a position to be particularly choosy about such matters. He was hardly the model of impeccable fashion himself. In fact if he was honest he would have to admit that his sense of dress was, at best, merely adequate.

The woman came closer and closer.

He could feel her heat. He was filled

with desire. As she got closer her

stomach almost touched his face. She

smelled the way he imagined opium

might feel.

Above, right: The first paragraph is set 9 pt. with 9-pt. leading. The second paragraph is set 9 pt. with 13-pt. leading. The last paragraph is set 9 pt. with 18-pt. leading. Text from the author's book, *The Frock,* Rockcorry, Ithaca, 1999.

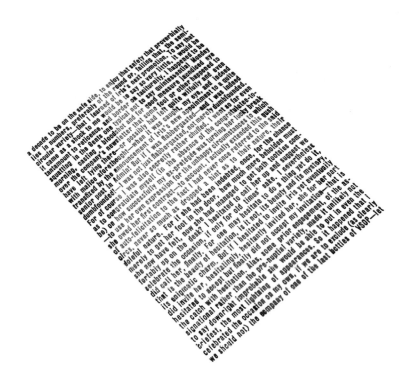

Another example of John Crombie's use of color to create an image within a text block.
Lapse and Collapse, Kickshaws Press, Paris, 1985.

Colored type

This is quite different from the use of the term "color" to describe the tonal weight of the block of type. As the examples show, selective use of color can add visual interest, and alter meaning, in a most effective manner.

Jas H. Duke, *Dada Kampfen um Leben und Tod,* Wayzgoose Press, Katoomba, 1996.

COMBINING TYPE AND IMAGES

As discussed in Chapter 1, the computer facilitates combining images and text in new and interesting ways. You can do this by either using the text tools within Photoshop (see illustration *p. 194)* or add words after importing your picture into the page layout program. The former method permits the greatest amount of creative freedom as many type effects are possible. However, as the images need to be "flattened" before importing them into the page layout program, there is little or no opportunity to modify the text once it is in place in your document. It is often better, therefore, to add the text in a program like QuarkXPress after the image has been corrected. This way you can modify the text easily at any time.

In this series of four essays presented in four separate volumes, the type is set ranged left. Of particular interest is the strategy of using typography to visually connect each book by using the large, colored initial letter to spell out the word "type" when the four volumes are juxtaposed.
Mike Hudson and Jadwiga Jarvis, *Private Impressions,* Wayzgoose Press, Katoomba, New South Wales, 1995–96.

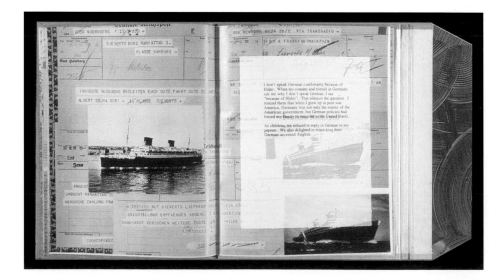

It is not necessary to restrict yourself to classical typesetting methods when combining type and images. In this example, Laurie Snyder has scanned hand-written and hand-typed letters in addition to other family memorabilia, to create a collage of words and images.
Laurie Snyder, *The Book of Letters,* self-published, 1997.

COMMON ERRORS

Rivers

Rivers are caused by (usually excessive) spaces between words, produced when text is justified. Sometimes these spaces can align vertically from line to line, forming the distracting appearance of "rivers" running through the text block. They can be eliminated with careful hyphenation and tracking or kerning adjustment.

Misaligned Backup

In Chapter 2, *p. 28,* backup was mentioned as a layout/printing issue. Most of the problems are created at the typographical stage when insufficient consideration is given to column width, and the positioning of this column on the page. Both sides of the page must align correctly so that any show-through is cancelled out, or at least correctly defined, by the text or image so affected. Blocks of type and images need careful positioning so that their shape on one side of the page, defines the position of elements on the obverse. The essential principle is to ensure that both sides of the page relate to each other.

Poor Hyphenation

Most programs hyphenate words automatically. For the most part they do a good job. However, check that the breaks occur sensibly, so both parts of the word more or less stand alone. Be careful to ensure that breaks do not occur leaving one character hanging on a line all by itself. Most adjustments are best made manually in the final proof read, but QuarkXPress offers control over global hyphenation decisions. (See Chapter 5, *p. 113.*) A useful rule of thumb is to apply little or no hyphenation at all to text that is ranged either right or left.

Widows and Orphans

Widows are very short lines (usually one or two words) that appear at the end of a paragraph, column, or page, or at the top of a page when a line is left over from a preceding page. These short, isolated lines should be reunited with the text from which they have been separated. Often minute changes to the tracking or judicious editing is sufficient.

Closely related are orphans. An orphan is an indented line of a new paragraph that begins at the bottom of a column, or worse still, a page. Although not as visually offensive as widows, avoid their presence in your document.

An example of "found typography." In this image a book cover has been torn up and otherwise mutilated, scanned with a flatbed scanner and further manipulated in Photoshop, primarily by using the cut and paste commands to repeat elements through the picture plane.
In War, Peace, Douglas Holleley, 1994.

Misaligned Baseline

This refers to lines of type not being at the
same level across the gutter, either of individual
columns or from page to page. This problem
can often occur when the auto leading feature
is selected. It also results in poor backup when
lines of type printed on one side of the page
show through in between lines on the obverse.
Lines of type should be superimposed over each
other when printed on both sides of the page.

FINAL THOUGHTS

It should be clear by now that typography is a
complex and challenging art. It is essential to
appreciate the principles discussed to use type
sensitively and well. However, all the rules in
the world are no substitute for patience, practice,
and creativity. Typography is not an end in itself,
but a means of clarifying and communicating
content. As such, be open to the consideration
of more abstract ideas when designing your
book.

Recently, a friend pointed out that
Shakespeare was typeset very differently when
first published in Elizabethan times, than it is
now. It was originally set to reflect how it was
to sound. Spaces and line breaks were employed
to reflect the pauses and emphases of the spoken word. Conventional
punctuation was kept to a minimum, de-emphasizing the words as text
and reinforcing the obvious fact that they were to be spoken out loud.

Consider such thoughts when setting your text. Do not simply
appropriate current conventions. Ascertain whether your text may have
a musical quality, and if so, how may this be communicated. Consider
also the visual qualities of type. Unusual shapes, varying sizes and
widths, and all the variables discussed in this chapter, can radically
influence the appearance of your book. Imagine type as an image.[8]

You may also find it useful to make note of unusual typographic
arrangements that occur in "real life." Billboards, factory signs, and
ephemeral notices can provide clues for new ways of arranging
conventional type or can be used to make photographs that can be
incorporated into your layout.

In this example words were typed onto
an image which was perforated with a
needle and then torn into pieces. The
fragmented paper was then scanned
with a flatbed scanner and further
manipulated in Photoshop using the
cut and paste commands.
All Thoughts Fly, Douglas Holleley,
1994.

8. See the work of poets such as
Apollinaire and other Dada typesetters
of the early twentieth-century.
Additionally the work of contemporary
concrete poets such as Richard Tipping
is of interest.

These images demonstrate how examples of "found typography" may be collected from life. These images, made in Mexico, are from the author's book, *Past and Future Tense,* Rockcorry, Rochester, N.Y., 1998.

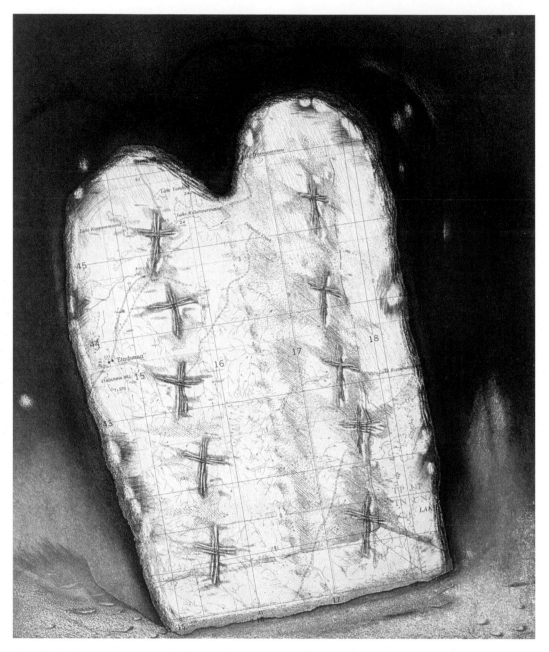

Petr Herel often creates images which question the nature of language and thought. The abstract signs and symbols in his work suggest and infer messages which seem to manifest the qualities of order and symbolic logic that we expect to find in language, yet at the same time the nature of the message remains tantalizingly inscrutable. Image by Petr Herel from his *Hymne to God, my God, in my Sickness,* Labyrinth Press, 1986. Artist's book, color etching and aquatint with chine-collée.

CHAPTER 4

SETTING UP
Preparing your document for page layout.

WHEN you come to the computer to create your book, you have to *Open* a *New Document*. This simple step involves the consideration of many factors. It assumes you have a clear idea of what you are trying to say. It assumes you have a well thought out maquette. Above all, it assumes also you have a clear idea of what your finished book will look like.

There is no point in simply selecting a conventional letter sized page and hoping that things will somehow "work out." Once you open your document you have, to all intents and purposes, decided what your final product will be. It is for this reason you must consider at this stage, not only the work you have already put into your maquette with respect to content and page design, but also events that will necessarily occur in the future. In particular you must consider:

- The final shape and size of the book.
- The length of the book.
- The printing and binding method.

Easter 1998, Douglas Holleley.

All these factors will influence how you "set-up" your book. In this chapter we will examine some sample page set-up schemes while at the same time considering how these will impact on the binding and presentation when the book is finished. These sample set-ups will use QuarkXPress as the exemplar. This is so because this program enjoys considerable industry support and as such is widely used. If however, you are unfamiliar with it, please read Chapter 5 for instructions on its use, or adapt your knowledge of a program with which you are already familiar to the examples herein. All programs will require a similar thought process at this stage of the work.

It is also important you understand the terms *recto* and *verso*. The recto is the page you see on the right-hand side of a book when opened at a double-page spread. It should always have an odd number (1, 3, 5, etc.). The verso is the page on the left-hand side of the spread. It should always have an even page number (2, 4, 6, etc.).

The *recto* is the page on the right-hand side of the book when opened. The *verso* is the page on the left-hand side of the spread.

The Single-page Set-up

With the single-page set-up, you design one page at a time. Because each page is self-contained, it is easy to change the page-order whenever you wish. Production is simple. First, print the recto, and then place the same sheet upside-down in the printer, and print the verso.

However, because you are printing on both sides of the sheet, you must consider *how* the book will be printed. If you are using an inkjet printer, you may have "show-through" problems. (See *pp. 27–28.*) To minimize this effect you may have to use very thick paper and/or keep your layout simple. For example, placing an image on the recto and a caption on the verso. However, if you have a laser printer, which uses toner rather than ink, show-through will be less of an issue, and you will have more success when printing on both sides of the sheet.

Books set up this way, and printed on either an inkjet or laser printer as single sheets, can be successfully bound with a stab-stitch *(p. 227–228)* or a coil *(p. 226).* If this is your first book, you may have more success using the double-page set-up, described on *p. 62.*

If you desire a more sophisticated product, you can take the book to a service bureau (such as Kinko's) where you can find fast and relatively inexpensive volume (laser) printers such as the Xerox DocuTech and/or DocuColor. These machines can print on both sides of the paper, sequence the pages, and even proceed to bind the finished book, all in one operation. If this is how you intend to print your book, see also *Saddle-stitching, pp. 71–73.*

Setting Up a Single-page Document

When you select the *New, Document* option from the *File* menu in QuarkXPress the dialog box at right will appear. This illustration shows a horizontal page document. The *Automatic Text Box* is not selected. This means you will have to draw text boxes where and when you require them. The *Margin Guides*, which will appear on the page when the document is open, are, in this example, set to 1″ on the top and each side. The bottom guide is set 10% higher to visually center the artwork on the page. If you were to set equal values for all four margins, the layout would appear to be slightly low on the page when the book was printed.

Also, be aware you are not restricted to a standard paper size. Simply enter the height and width of your intended page size (e.g. 8.5″x8.5″ for a square book) and then trim the pages after the book has been printed.

Below:
Whether you use QuarkXPress, Pagemaker, InDesign, or even a simple word processing program, you will have to decide the orientation and size of your page. This example shows a horizontal, letter-sized document in QuarkXPress, set up to be designed, printed and bound, one page at a time.

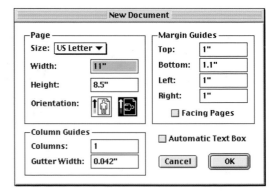

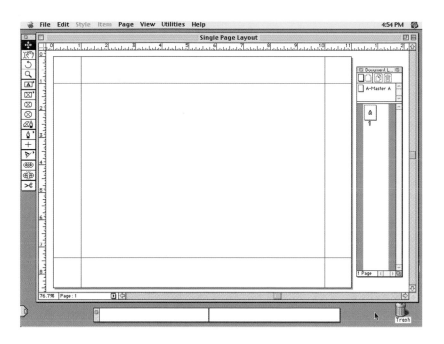

Left:
The page view of a single-page set-up in QuarkXPress.

1. NOTE: All keyboard commands in this book are for Macintosh computers

Below:
This book utilizes commercially available comb-binding which is inexpensive, and in the right context, perfectly acceptable.

The image was made by Sonia Sheridan and students during a Summer Workshop where the participants used a Xerox 6500 color photocopier as an imaging tool. Direct color photocopying is the pre-cursor to the use of a scanner as a first generation imaging device as discussed in Chapter 8.
Yony #7, Vol. 1, July 1976. Generative Systems Journal. Produced at the Visual Studies Workshop, Rochester, N.Y., by Sonia Sheridan and students of the Visual Studies Workshop Summer Institute.

Click OK and the computer will display Page 1. Press Command Zero[1] (to show full page view) and it will look like the diagram above. See *pp. 106–107* for instructions on how to add new pages and change their order within the document.

The advantages and drawbacks of this set-up include…

Pros
- Easy to set-up and view.
- Easy to change the page order within the book (if necessary).
- Can be easily bound at home using a stab stitch or coil. If printed commercially, automatic signature binding is an option.
- When printed at a commercial printshop, the pages will appear in the correct order.
- Uses the full size of the paper. (It does not have to be folded in half.)

Cons
- Show-through with inkjet printing may be a problem.
- Does not give you a view of the double-page spread as you lay out your page.

The Double-page Spread

This page set-up is particularly suitable for the first-time bookmaker because one of the fundamental issues in book design is to produce a coherent and satisfying appearance *across* the double-page spread. It is essential to consider how pages relate to each other, rather than design each one as a single, isolated unit. With this set-up, facing pages appear side by side on the screen, much as they will appear when printed in your book.

It is also especially useful if you are using an inkjet printer as you print on only one side of the paper.

Double-page spread books are also easy to bind. However, the binding method will of necessity be some-what unconventional. Because the "gutter," the space or crack between the two pages, is in the middle of the sheet, it will be necessary to join each spread together on both the right and left edge of each printed sheet. The diagram on the opposite page will give you an idea of how this occurs.

When printed you will have two pages on each sheet. This will halve your paper size. If you are printing on landscape oriented, letter-size paper, which is 11″ wide, the finished dimension of your book will be 8.5″ high by 5.5″ wide.

The double-page spread set-up is an excellent way to make your first book. You simply fold a piece of paper in half to form the two facing pages. Page design is facilitated as your screen view closely resembles how the spread will appear when it is printed.

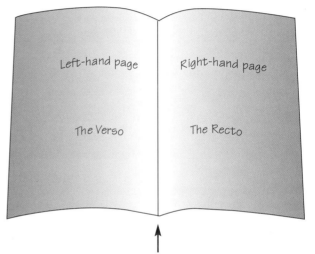

Fold

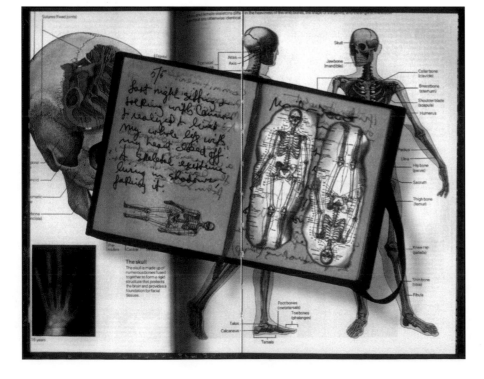

Although not strictly illustrative of the double-page spread set-up in the sense that the gutter here is stitched rather than simply folded, this marvelous layout teases the viewer with an image of a spread, within a spread, within a spread. Carl Sesto, *Ordinary Events,* SMFA (School of the Museum of Fine Arts) Press, Boston, 1994.

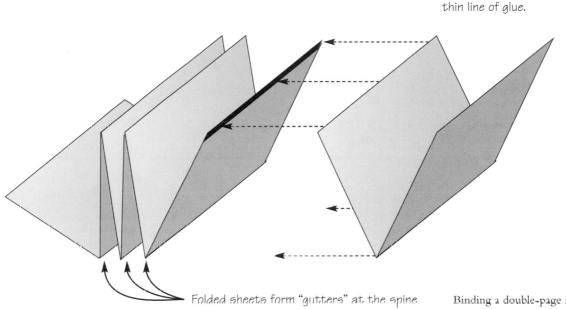

Join edges of page together with
thin line of glue.

Folded sheets form "gutters" at the spine.

Although this set-up requires somewhat unorthodox binding, it has some elegant properties that cannot be achieved with more conventional books. The fact that the "gutter" is a single folded sheet, rather than a joint where two pages meet, means images and text can be arranged and printed across the entire width of the spread. This can provide unusually coherent design opportunities. Often, when using other, more common forms of binding, the layout on facing pages can misalign, or even disappear, where it meets at the gutter of the book.

A small refinement to this set-up will allow the book to be opened like a giant concertina. You can set-up your page with a little extra margin on either the left or right-hand edge of the spread. This "tab" can then be used to join each of the printed pages together. This is a very elegant solution as the book will lie perfectly flat when fully opened. The internationally respected private press, Wayzgoose,[2] has used this method of binding in some of their recent books. The only disadvantages are the slight bulk that the glue tab adds to the edge of the page, and the fact that the view on the screen is not exactly identical to the finished appearance of the book. In practice this means that each time a page is displayed you will have to disregard the small tab that will be used to join the sheets together. However, the ease of binding and structural integrity of the finished product makes this set-up worthy of serious consideration.

The following pages show how to set up a straight double-page spread and a double-page spread, with tab.

Binding a double-page spread book is simply a matter of folding the printed sheets in two and (carefully) joining them together at the edges with a glue stick. There is no need to physically join them at any other point. You will find that the book forms itself naturally when the folds meet at the spine. The only difficult aspect of construction is ensuring that the pages are aligned squarely when you paste them together. It is recommended you use an archival glue stick for this task.

2. The Wayzgoose Press is located in the Blue Mountains west of Sydney, Australia. The two principals, Mike Hudson and Jadwiga Jarvis, produce limited edition letterpress books of great beauty and technical sophistication. I am grateful to them for showing me this binding method and allowing me to share it in this book.

SETTING UP THE DOUBLE-PAGE SPREAD (STRAIGHT)

Because we are creating two pages on one sheet, the guides have been made correspondingly smaller to suit the reduced scale of the page. As each page of the finished book in this example is actually 5.5˝ x 11˝, the guides have been set at 0.5˝.

Layout will be further facilitated if extra guides are included to make it clear that we are looking at two pages not one. Rather than draw them on each page of the document by hand, we can draw them on the *Master Page*. In this way the guides will appear on each new page automatically. To access the master page, double click on the *Master Page* icon labeled *A–Master A* in the *Document Layout* palette. (See the diagram below.) For further details on this procedure and other master page functions, refer also to the discussion of the Document Layout palette, *pp. 106–107*.

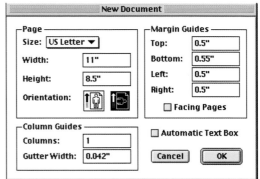

The master page of the document is now displayed. Any changes we make, including any items (such as picture and/or text boxes) we might place here, will appear on each and every page of the document created using this master page. In this case we have placed a guide to define the mid point (5.5˝) of the double-page spread. We have also made two other guides (at 5˝ and 6˝) which frame each single page.

To make these guides first go to the *General Preferences* in the *Edit* menu. This can be easily accessed by pressing Command Y.

Unless you plan on making a tall, thin book (and why not?) you will have to ensure that the page is oriented horizontally on the screen. The *New, Document* dialog box will look like that above if you are using letter size paper. The *Margin Guides* will give you a framework with which to work with to assist you in positioning your layout on the page.

Be aware however, that you will have to draw more guides directly on the master page once the document is open. You access the master page by double clicking on the master page icon in the *Document Layout* palette.

Place the guides as shown at left to clearly indicate that what you are working with is a view of two facing pages.

You will also observe in the *Column Guides* window (illustration above), that even when working on a single column document, you will always have to set a minimum *Gutter Width*. This value will usually appear by default. If in doubt, type in a value of zero. When you click OK a warning will display a minimum and maximum *Gutter Width*. Choose the minimum value, type it in the *Gutter Width* field, and press OK.

You are now ready to go.

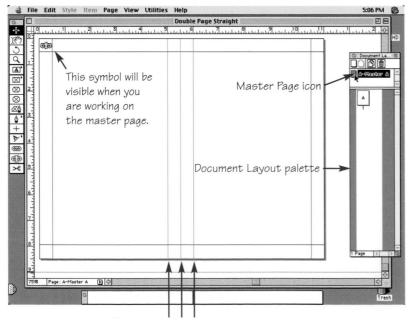

Guides placed on master page

When you do, you will see you have the choice of whether you wish your guides to appear in front or behind any items you may place on the page. Select *In Front,* and return to the view of the master page.

To create the three guides, place your mouse in the ruler on the left hand side of the screen. Press the mouse button and the cursor will change to two small vertical lines with arrows pointing left and right. Drag the cursor to the right. As you do you will see that a vertical line is created that follows the movement of the mouse. You will see that the distance of the line from the left hand side of the page will be displayed in the *Measurements* palette at the bottom of the screen. You will notice how this changes as you drag the line across the page. Move the line until the value is half the width of the page. In this case this will be 5.5″. Release the mouse button and you have created a guide. You may find you let go of the guide at the wrong spot. If so place your cursor over the guide, press the mouse and drag it back to the ruler at the edge of the page. The guide will disappear. Then try again. You can also create horizontal guides by dragging guides down from the ruler at the top of the page.

Create two additional guides, 5″ and 6″ from the left hand side of the (double) page. To see the effect of this, double click on the first page of your book (the icon with number "1" underneath it in the *Document Layout* palette). You will see that the guides you have drawn appear automatically on this page. To create further pages, click on the *A–Master A* icon and pull it down the *Document Layout* palette until it is underneath Page 1. A new page will be created labeled "2." You will also notice it has a small "A" on it to indicate that it has the properties of the master page, *A–Master A.* Do this each time you wish to add a new page to your book.

Document Preferences for Double Page Straight

General | Paragraph | Character | Tool | Trapping

Horizontal Measure: Inches ▼   Points/Inch: 72
Vertical Measure: Inches ▼   Ciceros/cm: 2.197
Auto Page Insertion: End of Story ▼   Snap Distance: 6
Framing: Inside ▼   ☑ Greek Below: 7 pt
Guides: In Front ▼   ☐ Greek Pictures
Item Coordinates: Page ▼   ☑ Accurate Blends
Auto Picture Import: Off ▼   ☐ Auto Constrain
Master Page Items: Keep Changes ▼

Cancel   OK

In *Preferences* you can customize your copy of QuarkXPress. The keyboard command to access them is Command Y. The most important choices are the units of measurement, and the position of your guides. Quark v.4 defaults to placing the guides in front of the boxes whereas v.3 places them behind. Usually you will find *In Front* to be the most useful.

The drawing at right shows how the double-page spread set-up looks when finished. For the purposes of clarity the drawing shows the book in a somewhat expanded form. You will find however, that books made this way lie flat and are easy to read.

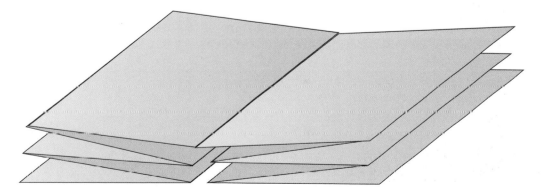

SETTING UP THE DOUBLE-PAGE SPREAD (WITH "TAB")

Creating a "tab" on your document will enable you to more easily join the successive pages together when it comes time to bind your book. Such a book is said to be bound as a *concertina*.

To demonstrate the setting up of such a page we will choose a larger paper size. Be aware however, that this assumes that you have a printer that accepts tabloid size paper. If you haven't, there is a "work around" for this limitation which enables you to set up a page of this size and print it on a small printer, but at the same time allows you at any time to take the document to a friend's house, school, or bureau that may have a larger device where you can print it full size. It is worth remembering this simple but effective strategy.

A concertina binding as you might use with the double-page spread set-up. *A Catalog of Japanese Plants, Bulbs and Seeds.* Published by L. Boehmer & Co. Yokohama, no date. It appears this beautifully designed and printed catalog was to publicize the Japanese seed inventory of a German company with an office in Japan.

In the *Page Setup* dialog box of your printer you can re-scale your document. In other words you can print a tabloid-size document on letter-size paper by simply stipulating a degree of reduction when it comes time to print. To find this value, simply divide the length of the paper you intend to print on by the length of the paper size of your document. If your book is designed with a page length of 17″ for tabloid, and you wish to print it on letter-size paper, you divide the 11″ of the letter paper dimension by the 17″ of the document layout. If you do this you get the value of approximately 65%. Type this value into the *Page Setup* dialog box. Your large document will now print on smaller paper, giving you a scaled-down version of your book which will suffice until you have access to a larger printer.

To return to the page set-up with "tab." In this example the dimensions are 11″ high by 17″ long. However, we need an extra 0.5″ at the edge of each double page to form a hinge so that the pages of the book can be glued together, but lie flat when open.

Below:
A concertina binding for the double-page set-up with tab. As you can see the pages joined together in this manner allow the book to be read either as a conventional book, or the contents unfolded so the book may be seen as a continuous series of images. Douglas Holleley, *Bizare* (sic), Rockcorry, Woodford, New South Wales, 1999.

Enjoy the fact that although you may be using a computer to make your book, you will nevertheless employ from time to time, techniques which have been used for centuries. This illustration is from the book, René Martin Dudin, *L'Art du relieur-doreur de livres*, L.F. de la Tour, Paris, 1772.
Courtesy of the Cary Graphic Arts Collection, Rochester Institute of Technology. Rochester, N.Y.

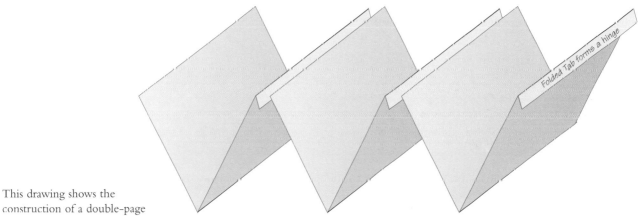

Folded Tab forms a hinge

This drawing shows the construction of a double-page spread book with tab. You can see how the tab acts as a hinge to join the spreads together.

The *New, Document* dialog box for the double-page spread with tab will look like the box at right.

The margin guides are set off-center so there is an extra half-inch on the right-hand side of the document. We will again place additional guides on the master page to indicate the center of the double page. We will also create, and shade, the "tab."

New Document

Page
Size: Tabloid ▼
Width: 17"
Height: 11"
Orientation:

Column Guides
Columns: 1
Gutter Width: 0.042"

Margin Guides
Top: 1"
Bottom: 1.1"
Left: 1"
Right: 1.5"
☐ Facing Pages

☐ Automatic Text Box

[Cancel]   [OK]

To the right is the view of the master page with all the guides in place. The effective double-page width is now 16.5″, not 17″. You will see that the new center of the spread has been defined by a guide at 8.25″ from the left hand edge of the paper. Additional guides have been placed an inch either side of this new "gutter."

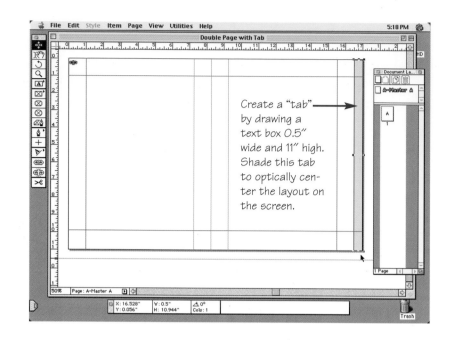

Note the gray box forming a "tab" on the right hand side of the spread. This box was created by first drawing a guide at 16.5″. A text box was then drawn 0.5″ wide by 11″ tall in the space between the guide and the right hand side of the spread. This box was then shaded a neutral gray by going to the *Item, Modify* menu. The background color was set to black and the shade set to 50%. It is shaded so that when you layout your book your eyes will not be distracted by the extra space on the right hand side. When the layout is finished, but before you print, you will go back to the master page and use the *Item, Modify* box to set this tab to either white, or none, or simply delete the box altogether. This will turn off the gray shading on all of the pages in your book. There is little point in having ink where you wish to apply glue. It is only an on-screen visual aid to assist with layout.

The advantages and drawbacks of this set-up include...

Pros
• Facilitates layout by allowing you to view the double-page spread as you work.
• Allows you to print across the gutter.
• Concertina binding allows the book to be read conventionally, or unfolded to be seen as a linear sequence.
• No show-through problems.

Cons
• The tab can bulk up on the outside edge of the page(s).

A view of the desktop with a tabloid sheet marked out with guides. Note how the guides are off-set to the left by the width of the tab. The tab has been shaded to match the desktop to compensate for this visual eccentricity. In this way you can view a symmetrical screen image as you work.

Below:
This book has been printed using a French-fold set-up and bound with a stab stitch.
Douglas Holleley, *Love Song*, Rockcorry, Woodford, New South Wales, 1995.

THE FRENCH-FOLD

This page set-up is named after the way it is folded and bound after printing. This method can produce books of great beauty and elegance but it is a little more difficult to work with on the screen.

The illustrations indicate in diagrammatic form what the page layout will look like.

This set-up addresses the problem of show through by printing on only one side of a sheet of paper. You then bind the edge of the pages at the spine so that the rear of the printed sheet is completely hidden from view.

As the illustration shows, the half of the paper that forms the left-hand page, the verso, will appear on the right-hand side of the screen. Similarly, the right-hand page, the recto, will be to the left of the screen. This can be confusing because although it appears you are looking at a spread, you are really looking at both sides of the same page.

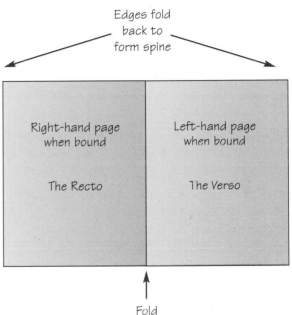

Edges fold
back to
form spine

Right-hand page
when bound

The Recto

Left-hand page
when bound

The Verso

Fold

Fold the edges of the
sheet back to meet at
the spine

Left-hand side of
page layout
forms the Recto,
the page which
appears to the
right in the book.

The Recto

The Verso

Right-hand side
of page layout
forms the Verso,
the page which
appears to the
left in the book.

Fold forms outside edge of page

The two diagrams on this page show the construction of a French-fold book. Such a book can either be bound as a concertina, using the same joining methods as were used in the double-page set-up, or joined with a stab stitch. Although using a stab stitch produces a book that does not open completely flat, it is still a useful and elegant way to construct a book. It is recommended for its ease of construction, and strength.

By hiding the rear of the printed page you can use coated, single-sided, specialty inkjet papers which reproduce images with great fidelity and beauty. Many of these papers, especially Epson's "photo quality matte" inkjet paper, possess a delicate tactility. Books produced in this manner, with this paper, can feel as valuable and as reassuring as an old family heirloom.

Setting up the page for the French-fold is identical to the double-page spread. Like the double-page spread you can choose to set up your page symmetrically or you can use a "tab." In both cases you simply fold the pages in the opposite direction. Thus the pages are joined in the

gutter, not at the edges. As the diagram at left shows, the concertina binding, although workable, is not ideal. The gutter interrupts the spread plus you have the added difficulty of perceiving the layout as a cohesive whole on the screen. It is for this

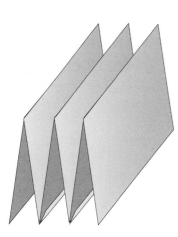

reason that the concertina is not the binding of first choice for this set-up. In Chapter 11, *p. 232*, you will find instructions on *butterfly binding*, a method you may decide is preferable.

However, an easier method is to *stab stitch* together the sheets at the spine as shown above right and below. This forms a book with great strength and is easy to bind with either a hard or soft cover.

Strictly speaking, the "French-fold" set-up has its origins in the orient rather than Europe. This example shows a refined version of the stab stitch René Martin Dudin, *L'Art du relieur-doreur de livres*, L.F. de la Tour, Paris, 1772. *Courtesy of the Cary Graphic Arts Collection, Rochester Institute of Technology, Rochester, N.Y.*

The advantages and drawbacks of this set-up include...

Pros
- Show-through is hidden.
- Book may be bound a variety of ways.
(See Chapter 11, *Butterfly Binding, p. 232*.)

Cons
- Concertina binding retains the presence of the gutter.
- It is easy to be distracted by a screen image that looks like a spread, but is in fact displaying both sides of the same leaf.
- Stab stitching results in a book that does not open flat.

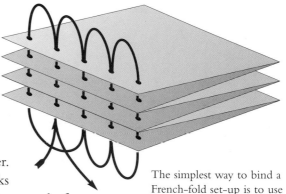

The simplest way to bind a French-fold set-up is to use a stab stitch. For further instructions see *pp. 227 and 228.*

Saddle Stitching

Although this is perhaps the simplest and most common binding it may come as a surprise to realize it is one of the most complex to set up. The reason for this is that you must know in advance exactly where each page will appear in the finished book so when printed, folded, and stapled, everything is in exactly the right position.

   For such a book an additional (structural) maquette must be made to determine which pairs of pages will be printed together on the same sheet.

The steps to follow are as follows:

1. Determine the exact number of pages in the book. This must be a multiple of 4, which may mean you will have to leave one, two or even three pages blank.

2. Get some blank typing paper and fold it in half to form a blank maquette. Let us assume that the book is 16 pages long.

A saddle stitched book is easy to bind but relatively difficult to set up. After you have made your maquette, you will need to make another blank maquette to assist you to position your pages in such a way so that when they are printed they will appear in the correct order within the book.

   The only time this will not be necessary is if you are using a commercial digital printer at a service bureau. If this is the case you can give the printer the files, and the machine can be programmed to create the imposition.

   Even if you are able to do this it is essential that you give the printer a proof copy of the document with all pages pasted in their correct position.

You will need 4 sheets of folded paper. Each when printed will have two pages on one side and two pages on the other. A total of four pages on each sheet. Place these 4 sheets inside each other to form the maquette. It will look like the accompanying diagram. Write the page numbers on each of the pages starting at the front of the book.

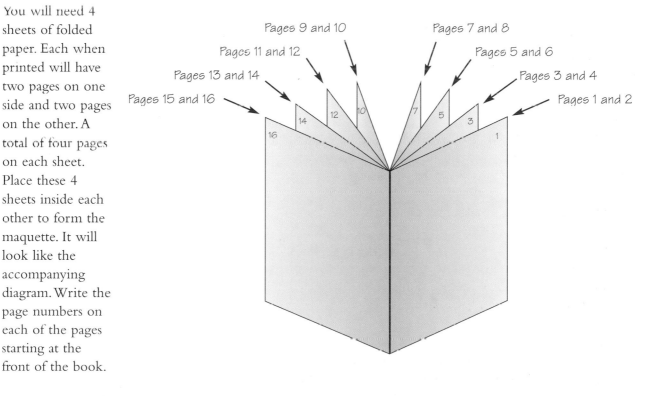

3. Now disassemble this maquette. You will have four sheets of paper with numbers written on each page.

These numbers will show you where you have to place each page, so that when the book is assembled and bound, everything will appear in its proper place. For example the sheet with the pages 16 and 1 printed on one side will require that you print pages 2 and 15 on the other side. This form of document preparation is called an imposition. It will look like the following diagram.

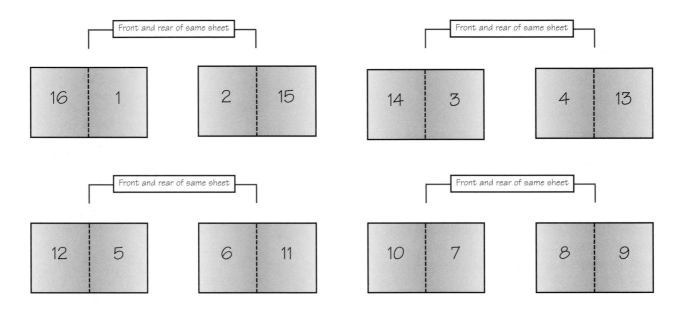

This procedure can be repeated for any number of pages as long as it is a multiple of 4. To check for accuracy you will notice there is always an even number on the left hand side and an odd number on the right. You will also observe when added together the total is always the number of the pages in the book, plus one. Thus in this example, the page numbers on each double-page always add up to 17.

Each such set of pages is called a signature. You can create a longer book by sewing several signatures together. If each of these signatures consists of 16 pages, the book can be 16, 32, 48, 64, etc. pages in length. Obviously such a book requires that you have a well planned maquette. Books have been traditionally bound in this way in the past.

If your book is 32 pages in length, then instead of making a blank maquette of 32 pages you can make two maquettes each of 16 pages. The first of these starts with page number 1 and continues to page 16. The second starts with page 17 and finishes with page 32. The binding involves sewing together the signatures at the spine, joining them with cloth tape. This requires some skill and practice. If you wish to try this method you will need to refer to a specialized book binding text, or get a professional bookbinder to help you.

If you intend to bind with a saddle stitch you will first need to determine the number of pages in your book.

Then make a blank maquette with this number of pages as shown on the previous page, and mark each page with its page number. Disassemble the maquette and you will have a series of sheets with two pages on each side. There will be two page numbers on each side of each sheet.

These numbers will show you where you have to place each page, so that when the book is assembled and bound, everything will appear in its proper place. For example, if you have a 16 page book, you will have to print pages 16 and 1 on one side of the sheet and pages 2 and 15 on the other.

In practical terms, the easiest way to construct such a book is to use the single-page set-up and lay out your book a page at a time in linear sequence. Then, when you have finished, you can use the *Document Layout* palette to rearrange the single pages so that, in the case of a 16 page book, page 16 is adjacent to page 1, 2 adjacent to 15, etc.

Having rearranged your document in this manner you can then set the *Print* dialog box to print two adjacent pages on one sheet at a time by checking the *Spreads* box. (See *pp. 195–197*.) The problem of imposition virtually disappears if you use a commercial printer such as Kinko's. Their highly automated printers will place your images in the correct position, assuming you have remembered to keep your book to page multiples of 4. (It is also good practice to give them a properly paginated mock-up of the finished book.)

The advantages and drawbacks of this set-up include…

>   *Pros*
> •   Simple to bind if a single signature.

>   *Cons*
> •   Complex task of establishing imposition.
> •   Difficult to bind if there is more than one signature.
> •   Cannot use an inkjet printer because of show-through unless the book has blank pages (or minimal text) behind the images.

This book was set up as a saddle stitched signature and subsequently printed on a Xerox DocuTech machine. Going to a commercial (digital) printing house enables the printing, folding and binding operations to be performed in one series of operations.
Camila Mesquita, *Journeys on Diverse Times, Through the Eyes and Words of Past, Present and Future Travellers,* Visual Studies Workshop Press, Rochester, N.Y., 1996.

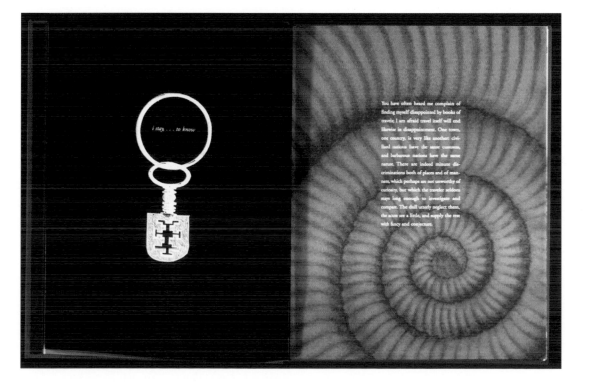

Using the
Automatic Text Box

The simple page set-up schemes
discussed so far have guides
which only indicate the broad
outline of the page. They work
best for picture books which
usually have small amounts of
text. You lay out your book page
by page, inserting the text
manually where needed. The
guides will suffice to accurately
position the picture and text
boxes. However, if you have a
large amount of text you will
find it useful to use the *Automatic
Text Box* option.

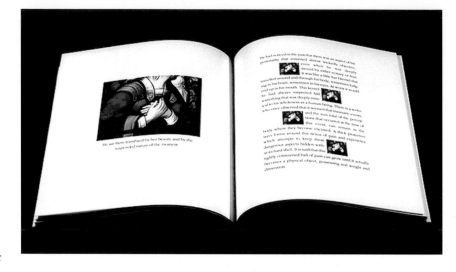

An example will show this at work. The following assumptions will
be made.

- The book will be square.
- The book will be bound using the French-fold with stab stitch.
- Tabloid paper will be used.

The diagrams illustrating this set-up are from a book called *The Frock*.[3]
The set-up uses the double column option to create two, active, linked
text boxes on each spread. Each
column thus forms a single text box
on each page, when the sheet is
folded in two before binding.

The diagram at right shows the
master page and *New Document*
dialog box. By experimenting with
the margin guides and the gutter
width (here the gutter refers to the
gap between the two columns) it has
been possible to allow text to display

Right:
A view of the *New, Document* dialog box for
The Frock. This book uses the *Automatic Text
Box* as the content is a continuous short
story, with images inserted on appropriate
pages. Using this feature causes the text to
flow through the book, moving to the next
page automatically when a picture is inserted.

This book is bound with a stab stitch
using the French-fold set-up. Although
there is only a single column on each
page, it is formed by creating a double
column set-up with the gutter set
sufficiently wide to create a single text
box on each page.

3. Douglas Holleley, *The Frock*,
Rockcorry, Ithaca, N.Y., 1999.

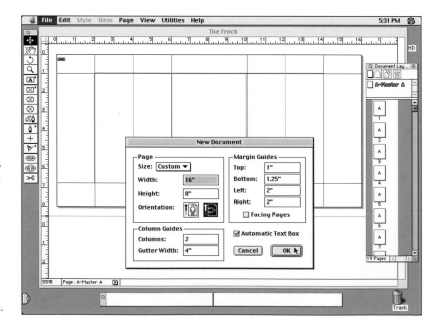

in the middle of page (each side of the sheet). You will notice that the position and size of the text boxes is determined by the margin values. Allocating 1″ on the top, 2″ to either side, and 1.25″ for the bottom guides defines the edges of the box. The gutter value of 4″ has been chosen as it places each box 2″ from the center of the spread, mirroring the *Left* and *Right* margin of 2″ when the paper is folded in half.

The *Automatic Text Box* option has been checked. To import the text, go to Page 1 of the document (you will see a blinking cursor in the text box) and select from the *File* menu, the command *Get Text*. (Keyboard shortcut Command E). The story is then imported into the two column layout. (See pp. 89–90 for more details.) Pages will be created automatically until the whole story is imported.

The diagram below shows the text in place. You will observe how the text flows into the two column layout. Notice also how the shape of the automatic text boxes have been altered by inserting (blank) picture boxes of various shapes. Leaving the *Runaround* set to *Item* allows them to force the text to flow around their shape. A sample page view of the printed book is shown on the opposite page.

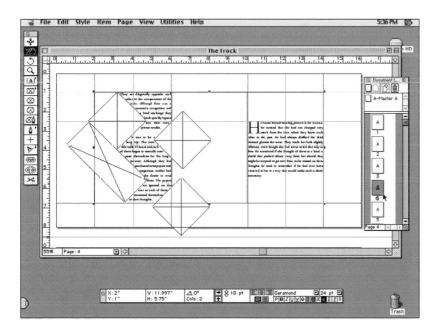

CONCLUSION

This chapter reinforces the reality that each step in bookmaking is dependent on another. It assumes you have a basic knowledge of QuarkXPress and possess some bookbinding skills. If not, read Chapter 5, *The Page Layout Program* and Chapter 11, *Binding the Book*. It is normal to feel somewhat overwhelmed at this stage if this is your first book. However, a patient approach will overcome all obstacles.

PLACING PAGE NUMBERS IN
YOUR DOCUMENT

1. Go to the *Master Page* icon in the *Document Layout* palette, and double click on this icon to view the master page.

2. Draw a *Text* box on the master page where you would like the page numbers to appear on each page of the document.

3. With the *Contents* tool selected, type the keyboard instruction, Command 3.

4. A symbol will appear in the text box that looks like this: <#>

5. Treat this symbol as if it were the actual page number. Highlight it, and assign the font, size, color and horizontal and vertical alignment you desire.

6. Go back to the *Document Layout* palette and drag the *Master Page* icon over Page 1 of the document. (This operation transfers changes made to the master page to the document as a whole.)

7. The numbers will now appear automatically on each page when you return to the document.

Left:
A view of the open document with the imported text in position. Note how the shape of the text has been altered by placing other blank boxes partially inside the main text box. On these boxes the *Runaround* has been set to *Item*. As a result the words have been forced to conform to the presence of these shapes. (See Chapter 5, *pp. 102–103*, for more details on the *Runaround* control.)

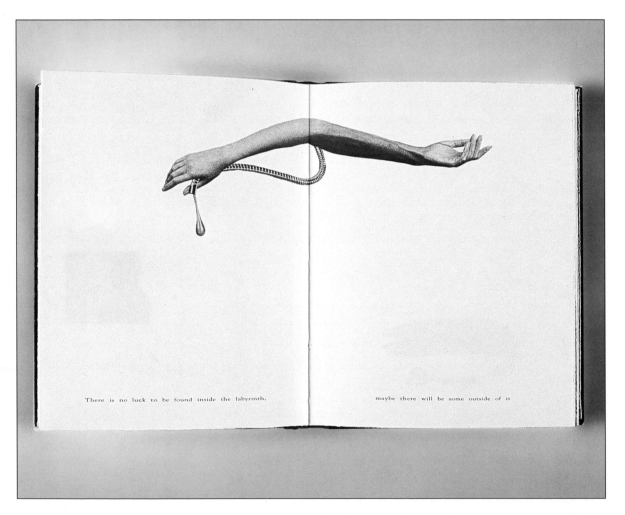

Peter Lyssiotis, (Text and Photomontages). *Feather and Prey.*
Self-published in an edition of 10, Melbourne, Vic., 1999.
Other contributors include design by Errol Ellis, offset
printing by Burnie Rackham, and binding by N. Doslov.

CHAPTER 5

THE PAGE LAYOUT PROGRAM

ACQUIRING fluency with a page layout program lies at the heart of computer bookmaking. Such programs are used because they allow you to integrate your text and images to create layouts on the page. They also offer supreme control over your text, giving you the ability to set type as well as any professional typesetter. Additionally, they are designed to help you manage large and often quite complex documents. This chapter introduces the use of the page layout program QuarkXPress.™ However, there are other excellent programs available which do much the same job, for example Adobe Systems' Pagemaker,™ and more recently, InDesign.™ The general principles discussed here, if not the specific keystrokes and nomenclature, will facilitate the learning and use of these other programs even though they are not specifically discussed.

Also be aware that different versions of QuarkXPress exist concurrently. Version 3 (an outstanding program), although now superseded by version 4, can still be found on many computers. This chapter uses "screen images" from version 4. Do not be fazed by these changes in appearance if they look different from the copy of the program you are using. The main difference between versions of QuarkXPress, other than the appearance of the dialog boxes, is the degree to which extra features are present or not. The core functions, however, of setting up a page and placing type and images on the page remain much the same from version to version. The mastery of these essential functions is all that is required. Setting type thoughtfully, placing and sizing images and controlling the interaction of these two basic elements is the essence of the task. This will never change. All versions of QuarkXPress as well as other page layout programs, will facilitate these measures.

Make the effort to understand the principles embodied in the specific examples and you will quickly find you can sit down in front of any computer loaded with any version of any page layout program, and with little difficulty create work as sensitive and as thoughtful as you are yourself.

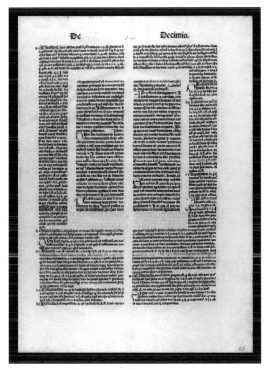

One of the fundamental principles of using QuarkXPress is the fact that any page element, be it text or image, is contained within a box. This concept relates directly to traditional letterpress practice which itself evolved from conventions of page layout developed by medieval scholars.
Michael Wensslar, *Plate 23*. Page from a book printed at Basle, 1478. *Courtesy of the Cary Graphic Arts Collection, Rochester Institute of Technology, Rochester, N.Y.*

Similarly, this chapter will discuss only those aspects of QuarkXPress that you need to know to get started. Not all of the features will be explained. As you acquire fluency through practice you will find that knowledge of the other functions will come almost automatically.

USING QUARKXPRESS

There are a number of basic principles to keep in mind when using QuarkXPress for the first time. Although not listed below, the first and most reassuring is that it is logical and simple to learn. There are six basic concepts you have to know to use QuarkXPress.

You have to know...

- that QuarkXPress works on the principle of placing text and images in *separate boxes*.

- how to *set up* a document for the kind of book you want.

- the nature and function of the tools in the Tool palette and especially which tool lets you move the boxes and/or work on them from the *outside* and which tool lets you work *within* them.

- how to put *text* in your document.

- how to put a *picture* in your document.

- how to move these boxes around and change their attributes using the *Runaround* and *Modify* options.

These of course are the basic operations. As you gain proficiency and confidence, these operations can be supplemented by more sophisticated choices. However, even with what at first glance might seem to be a limited repertoire, one can create documents with great style and flair by simply combining images and text on the page.

Above and Below:
Warren Lehrer, *GRRRHHHH: A Study of Social Patterns.* Based on weavings by Sandra Brownlee Ramsdale, with chants and stories by Dennis Bernstein. Ear/Say, New York, 1989.

THE PRINCIPLE OF BOXES

QuarkXPress is easiest to understand if you
have seen a letterpress printing press. You
have perhaps noticed one in an old western
movie. Letterpress works on the principle
of positioning a cast lead alloy "block," or
box, for each element to be printed on the
page. In the case of pictures, each image, or
in a commercial publication each
advertisement, was cast as a single element
and occupied its own "block." In the case of
type, individual letters were placed in line(s)

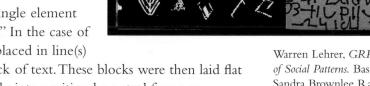

and combined to form a block of text. These blocks were then laid flat
on the press and locked tightly into position by a steel frame or
"chase."

Warren Lehrer, *GRRRHHHH: A Study
of Social Patterns.* Based on weavings by
Sandra Brownlee Ramsdale, with
chants and stories by Dennis Bernstein.
Ear/Say, New York, 1989.

QuarkXPress works in a similar manner. Each element, be it an
image, block of text, or headline, has its own electronic box
corresponding to the letterpress block. These boxes may then be moved
around the page to create a layout. Additionally, they can be made to
overlap or overlay each other to create more complex effects.

OPENING AND SETTING UP A NEW DOCUMENT

The very first task one must perform is to open and set up a new
document. Chapter 4 described how in order to do this successfully
you will need a clear idea of what your book is going to look like
when finished, printed, and bound. This is because the first thing you
need to know is the size and shape of the
page.

A view of the *File* menu showing how
you set up a *New, Document* in Quark-
XPress. The *New, Library* option allows
you to create files which store
frequently needed resources such as
logos, etc. The *New, Book* option allows
you to combine separate (pre-existing)
document files into chapters of a book.
Do not worry about these last two
options at this stage.

After launching QuarkXPress elect from
the *File* menu, a *New Document.* (Ignore the
option of opening a new *Library* or *Book*.)
When you do so the dialog box shown
overleaf *(p. 80)* will open. It will become
immediately apparent that you have to know
from the start what the size and shape your
document will be as you will have to enter
this information in order to proceed. For the
purposes of simplicity we will begin using the
one page set-up as discussed in Chapter 4.
(pp. 60–61.) We are going to construct a
landscape book of letter size and shape.

You will observe there are a number of requests for information about your document. Although this window looks different to that in version 3, you will see that in both cases the same information must be entered.

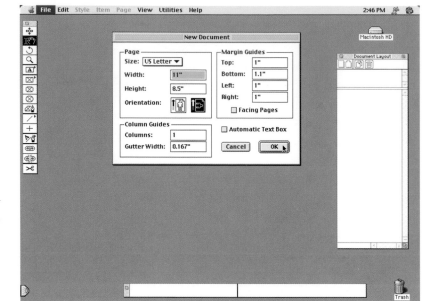

The first box is the *Page Size* box. There are five choices within the box labeled size. They are *US letter, US Legal, A4* and *B5 letter* (used in countries with the metric system), and *Tabloid*. If you wish the orientation of the book to be landscape, check the icon as indicated in the accompanying diagram. If none of these choices suit your book you can nominate a custom page size simply by typing in the desired dimensions where the width and height are indicated. The box will then automatically label itself *Custom*.

The next box allows you to choose how many *Columns* you want on each page. The term *Gutter Width* in this case refers to the gap between the columns. You might wish to experiment with this feature to see if you like the appearance of a document with more than one column per page. You may also use it to set up two columns for a French-fold book as discussed in Chapter 4, *pp. 74–75*. However, to keep it simple for now, we will select one column.

Next, look at the *Margin Guides* box. This sets guides to assist in positioning your text and images on the page. (These guides will also define the size of your automatic text box if you decide to create one.) In this case we have selected the top and side guides to be one inch from the edge of the paper. In accordance with general practice, both in matting and framing prints for exhibition and laying out pages for publication, the bottom margin has been made slightly bigger (10%) to optically center the layout. Exactly centered margins often present the illusion that they are arranged slightly lower than the center even though nominally they are correctly placed.

Underneath this is the *Facing Pages* box. We will not select this feature. If selected, the document would open with master pages for the left and right hand sides of a double page spread.

The final choice is whether you would like the document to open with an *Automatic Text Box* in position. If your book has a substantial text component then this is a valuable feature because it allows you to

When you open/create a new document, a dialog box will appear and you will be required to enter the various details of your book. To do this successfully you will need your maquette so you know what size and orientation your pages are. The maquette will also indicate the proportion of text to images. This will help you to decide whether or not to select the automatic text box feature.

Some readers may have version 3 of QuarkXPress on their computer. If so the dialog box will look a little different. However, the information that must be entered is identical. Accept the fact that there will always be modifications to the interfaces of software. Being patient, and carefully understanding what is really being asked for, will equip you to work on any computer platform, using any page layout program.

import your text from a word processing program in one simple operation. QuarkXPress will fill the first box with the text and then continue to create new pages, with automatic text boxes, until the whole of the text has been imported. Thus with one operation one can bring a twenty page document into QuarkXPress. The program will continue to create pages and format the text, until it comes to the end of the word processing document. (See Chapter 4, *pp. 74–75* for an example of a page set-up that uses this feature.)

If your document is mostly images with small amounts of text to be inserted at particular places through the book, you may find it easier to leave this option turned off and simply create text boxes where and when you need them. For now we will leave it turned off while we work on a simple sample page and learn the basic tools and operations of this program. Select OK and your document will open at page 1.

Carl Sesto, *Ordinary Events,* SMFA Press, Boston, 1994.

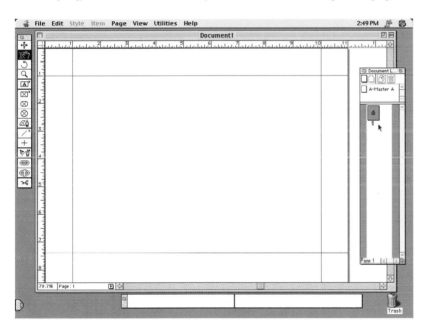

The very first keyboard shortcut you will find useful is Command Zero. This will allow you to see the page you have created so that it fully fits the monitor. You can find other choices for viewing your document under the *View* menu. You will find that you can select options that magnify or reduce the view of your document. However, this command is handy to remember, as it quickly produces a full page view of your work. Next look at the palettes and tools on display.

The small, thin, vertical palette on the left side of the screen is the *Tool* palette. At the bottom of the screen is the thin, horizontal *Measurements* palette. To the right of the screen is the *Document Layout* palette. They are useful for creating, modifying and navigating through your document. We will look at the *Tool* palette first.

Left:
This illustration shows the new document, with its guides visible, as specified in the dialog box on the opposite page. You will also see there are three palettes visible. The small, thin, vertical palette on the left side of the screen is the *Tool* palette. At the bottom of the screen is the thin, horizontal *Measurements* palette. To the right of the screen is the *Document Layout* palette. They are useful for creating, modifying and navigating through, your document. The role of each of these palettes is discussed in this chapter.

THE TOOL PALETTE
Creating and Modifying Text and Picture Boxes

As discussed earlier, QuarkXPress works on the principle that each element of the page is contained within a box. The *Tool* palette reflects this principle in the sense that each of the tools has a direct bearing on how these boxes can be created or manipulated. There are two kinds of boxes. *Picture* boxes and *Text* boxes. There are no prizes for guessing their respective contents.

The first tool is the *Item* tool. The word "item" is used to describe any self contained page element. An item is usually a picture box or text box but can also be a line, more correctly called a rule. (If you are working with QuarkXPress version 4 or later it can also be a text path.) The symbol for this tool is a little box with an arrow coming out each of its sides. This tool looks at boxes from an exterior perspective rather at their contents. Whether the item is a picture or text box, the item tool allows you to move it around the document to any position, or even delete it completely.

You use it by clicking on its icon in the tool palette and then selecting the box you wish to move, modify or delete. The cursor will change to the same symbol that is on the tool palette. Now you can move the selected box in any direction by clicking on the box and while holding down the mouse button, dragging it around the page. When this tool is selected you can also use the arrow keys on the keyboard to nudge the selected box in small increments to fine tune its position on the page.

Item tool selects, re-sizes and re-shapes items.

Contents tool imports and edits text and images.

Rotation tool alters the angle of items on the page.

Zoom tool magnifies or reduces the view of the document.

Rectangular Text Box tool (with access to other text box shapes).

Rectangular Picture Box tool.

Rounded Corner Picture Box tool.

Oval Picture Box tool.

Bezier Picture Box tool.

Angle Line tool (with access to other line tools).

Orthogonal Line tool draws horizontal and vertical lines.

Line Text-Path tool (with access to other text-path tools).

Linking tool creates text chains to flow text between boxes.

Unlinking tool breaks links between text boxes.

The second or *Contents* tool is used when you wish to work inside the box directly on its contents. The two symbols are intended to remind you of the function of this tool. When you are working with the contents of a text box the cursor will be in the shape of an "I" beam, just as it would in any word processing program. You use this tool to import or type in text or to highlight text when you change typeface, character size, color, tracking, etc. as permitted in the *Style* menu.

When working within a picture box then the cursor will be shaped like a hand. If you place the cursor over the image and press the mouse button, you will find that you can "grab" and move the picture around within the box. You may also change its magnification, or otherwise alter it according to the choices available in the *Style* menu. There is a discussion of the choices available to modify text and images in the *Style* menu later in this chapter.

The next tool is the *Rotation* tool. Its symbol is a little circular arrow which graphically represents the ability to rotate any item on its axis. Using this tool, the whole box and its contents can be oriented at any angle. In this way type or images can slope across the page. To use it you first select the item you wish to rotate. Now select the rotation tool. The cursor will turn into a circle with cross hairs. Place it over one of the active points on the corner of the box you wish to rotate. As you move the mouse while holding down the mouse button, the box will rotate.

The next tool is the *Magnification* tool symbolized by a magnifying glass. This tool allows you to alter the view of your document on the screen. After selecting the tool your mouse pointer will turn into a small circle with a "+" (plus) sign. You then click on the screen over the section you would like to magnify. You can also use it to "draw" around the part of the document you would like to see more clearly. The area thus described will then fit the viewing area of the screen. If you hold down the Option key, the cursor displays a "–" (minus) sign, and again by clicking the mouse the document will reduce in size. Remember that after any such operation you can quickly return to the full page view by using the keyboard shortcut Command Zero. Toggling back and forth between detail view and overall view is so common that this keyboard short cut should be committed to memory immediately. It saves much time.

The next five tools create the boxes that enable you to put text and images in the document. Different versions of QuarkXPress will display slightly different choices. The main difference is that version 4 (or greater) offers a Bezier drawing tool which can be used to create text boxes, picture boxes, lines and text paths.

In this chapter this feature will not be discussed in any detail as using it well is a skill in its own right. It is unlikely you will need it for some time. Should you have version 4 or later, refer to your manual for instructions on its use.

MEMORY LAPSE

Clifton Meador, *Memory Lapse*.
Produced and printed at the Center for Editions, Purchase College, SUNY, Purchase, N.Y., 1996.

The Text Box Tools

Icons with the letter "A" inside are, as you would expect, the boxes you select when you wish to place text in your document. To use this tool, click on the icon and move the cursor to the document. The cursor will change to a cross hair symbol. Place it where you want the top left hand corner of the box to be, press the mouse button and draw the mouse to the right and down to create a box. When you have done this, a cursor will appear, usually in the top left hand corner of the box and will flash on and off, indicating that the box is active and ready to accept typed in text or have text imported from another program. Remember when working within a box you need to select the *Contents* tool. Type in a word or two to see how this works.

Re-sizing the box, or giving it a vast range of attributes is easy so you do not have to be too accurate at this stage. Try moving the box. Select the Item tool and place the mouse cursor over the box. Click and hold down the mouse button and move the box around the page to get a feel for how this tool positions your box on the page. You can also re-size the box by grabbing any of the active points, located on the corners or in the middle of each of the sides, and click and drag them. When an active point is selected, the cursor will change into a hand with a pointed finger.

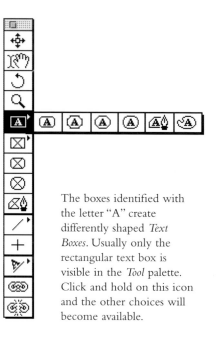

The boxes identified with the letter "A" create differently shaped *Text Boxes*. Usually only the rectangular text box is visible in the *Tool* palette. Click and hold on this icon and the other choices will become available.

The Picture Box Tools

The next four icons represent four different types (shapes) of picture boxes. Additionally, there are another three choices in a sub menu within the rectangular picture box tool. You will notice that each symbol is again a diagrammatic representation of a box but instead of containing the letter "A," they are differentiated from the text box by having the diagonals delineated to form an "X" within the box.

To see this, select the first (rectangular) one, and just like you did with the text box tool, draw a picture box on your open page. You will see that the box is different to the text box in the sense that it does not contain a flashing cursor bar, but instead is indicated by the diagonal lines. You can move and re-size this box easily by following the same procedures as described for the text box above. Again, like the text box, you can give this box a host of differing attributes, and we will discuss them later.

It is enough to realize that already you can begin to set type and place an image anywhere, and at any size on the page. You can also change the size and spatial relationships between text and image with only the few tools we have discussed already.

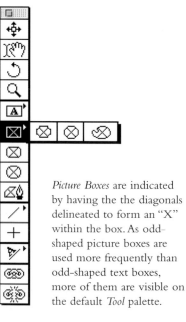

Picture Boxes are indicated by having the the diagonals delineated to form an "X" within the box. As odd-shaped picture boxes are used more frequently than odd-shaped text boxes, more of them are visible on the default *Tool* palette.

CHOOSING THE SHAPE OF A TEXT OR PICTURE BOX

You will observe that you can draw both text and picture boxes in a variety of shapes. Notice that the rectangular text box contains a small arrowhead pointing to the right of the palette. If you click and hold this icon you will see there are other shapes available. These choices are also available for drawing picture boxes but are arranged in the tool palette somewhat differently, probably as it is more common to have an unusually shaped picture than text.

The boxes have the qualities that their miniature iconic shape suggests. The following discussion of these shapes applies equally to text and picture boxes.

The *Rectangle Text* and *Picture* box tool for drawing rectangular or square boxes. To draw a perfect square, hold down the Shift key as you draw the box. The Shift key is the general key for constraining proportions for a variety of actions so you should try it to observe how it also will assist you to draw a perfectly circular text or picture box when the Oval box tool is selected.

Rounded Corner Text and *Picture* box tool for drawing rectangular boxes with rounded corners.

Concave Corner Text and *Picture* box tool for drawing rectangular boxes with the corners rounded inward.

Beveled Corner Text and *Picture* box tool for rectangular boxes with beveled edges.

Oval Text and *Picture* box tool to draw either elliptical or circular boxes. As mentioned above, hold down the Shift key while drawing the box if you wish to create a perfect circle.

The *Bezier Text* and *Picture* box tool allows you to draw a box any shape you might choose using the Bezier pen tool. (Consult your manual for more details on this feature.) You use this tool by selecting it and then moving the cursor over your document. The cursor will look like a cross hair. Click and release the mouse button where you want your shape to start. Now move the mouse. Select the second point and again click and release the mouse. You can do this indefinitely, putting in as many points as you require. To finish your shape you must return to your starting point. As you place the cursor over the point where you started the cursor will change to a small

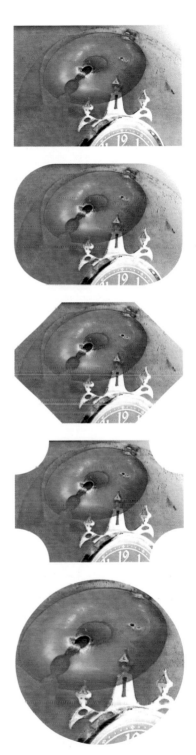

Photograph from the author's book, *Past and Future Tense*. Rockcorry, Rochester, N.Y., 1998.

square, indicating that the starting point has been recognized by the program. Click the mouse for the final time and you will have an irregularly shaped, polygonal picture box. It is important to close the path by returning to the start. You have to wait for the little square to appear and then click.

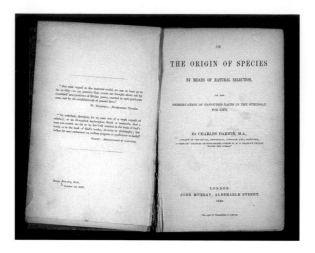

The *Freehand Text* and *Picture* box tool enables you to draw a shape as if you were using a pen or pencil on paper. Simply place the cursor where you wish to start and begin to draw. You will have to complete the path by returning to the starting point and waiting for the little square to appear that indicates the program recognizes the starting point. When this happens click the mouse.

Note: Both the Bezier and Freehand boxes can be edited after completion. You select the Item tool and then go to the Item menu and ensure the Edit, Shape box is checked. Again, refer to your manual for further information on this procedure.

IN ALL CASES to re-size boxes and maintain their proportions hold down the Shift and the Option key while you drag a corner handle. You will see that the box remains the same shape but simply gets bigger or smaller.

THE LINE TOOLS

The *Line* tool is for drawing lines at any angle. Like drawing boxes, the line does not have to be drawn with total accuracy. Its position can be altered with the Item tool. Also its length can be altered by grabbing the active point on either end and moving it either in or out. Its thickness and other attributes can be also altered by accessing choices in the Style menu in the same way we have discussed before for the text and picture boxes.

The *Orthogonal Line* tool will draw lines that are either perfectly horizontal or vertical. To use it place the cursor, which will look like a cross hair, over the point where you wish to start the line. Click on the mouse button and keep holding it down. While keeping the button depressed[1], drag the cursor to where you want the line to finish and release the button.

In a sub-menu under the Line tool are found a *Bezier Line* tool and a *Freehand Line* tool. Again, refer to the manual for instructions on how to best use these tools.

If the going sometimes gets a little tough as you work your way through these details, remember that if a job is difficult it usually means that it is worthwhile. Besides, a book can have a profound effect. Illustrated above is a first edition copy of Darwin's *Origin of Species*. Whether you agree or not with the conclusions derived from his series of acute observations, even the most diehard objector would have to concede that since this book was published, the world has never been the same.

Charles Darwin, *Origin of Species by Means of Natural Selection, or the Preservation of Favoured Races in the Struggle for Life,* John Murray, Albemarle Street, London, 1859.

Courtesy of the Elmira College Archives, Gannett-Tripp Library, Elmira College, Elmira, N.Y.

1. If you feel guilty about keeping the mouse depressed you can tell it jokes to keep its spirits up!

TEXT-PATHS

Text-paths are present in QuarkXPress version 4 or later. Essentially they enable you to draw a line on which you may type in text. This line can be straight or curved. By now the icons should look familiar.

The *Line Text-Path* draws diagonal text paths. To use the text-path tool click where you want the path to begin and then again after moving the mouse, click where you would like it to finish. A flashing cursor bar will appear on the line and you can either type in the text, or import it from another program.

The *Orthogonal Text-Path* tool constrains the lines so they are either perfectly horizontal or vertical.

The *Bezier* and *Freehand Text-Path* tools permit you to type text on curved paths.

THE LINKING/UNLINKING TOOLS

The final tools on the *Tool* palette are there to help you connect one text box with another so that your text can flow through your document. The icon in both cases is a chain, either linked or broken. As you would surmise, the linked chain connects one box with another. If you use this tool any "overflow" of text will flow from the end of the first text box in the chain to the second and so on.

The best way to appreciate this feature is to draw two text boxes on one page. Select the linked chain icon and click on the first box. The edges of the box will seem to turn into one of those signs you often see outside movie theatres where the lights are programmed to look like they are chasing each other. Then move the cursor to the second box. It will look like an arrowhead. Click on the second box.

When you do this an arrow will appear to indicate that when text reaches the end of the first box, it will now flow to the beginning of the second box.

Most often you will be linking text boxes from page to page rather than simply from box to box. To do this you will need to reduce the page view of your document so you can see more than one page at a time. To do this go to the small box at the very bottom of the open QuarkXPress window. (Indicated by a small red arrow on the illustration below.) Type in a value, try around 40% and press the Return key. You will see that now you can begin to get an overview of your document. Experiment with other levels of magnification to find the one that is most helpful for your needs.

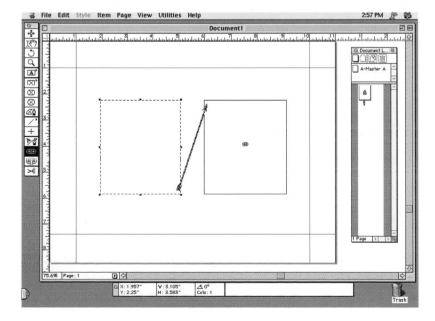

If you wish later to remove this link, again select the chain link icon. The document will now show the arrow between the two text boxes. Now select the icon of the chain with a broken link and click on the arrow head where it enters the second box. The two boxes will now be unlinked. Before using these tools in earnest, be sure to save your document. Often these links connect text across separate pages and it is very easy to click on the wrong box. This can create a nightmarish collection of idiosyncratic links, trapping your text in a carousel ride that seems like it will never end. If this happens, and you have saved your document, you can always choose the *Revert to Saved* option in the *File* menu and try again.

This concludes the discussion of the *Tool* palette. Open a document and practice working with these tools. Draw a picture box and a text box and try using the *Item* tool to move the boxes around the page. When you select a box with the *Item* tool you can then delete it by pressing the Delete key. Place the boxes in various configurations and try putting them on top of each other to get the "feel" of the program. This is of course more interesting if there is some text in the text box and there is a picture in the picture box.

Bill Burke, *Mine Fields,* Nexus Press, Atlanta, Ga., 1995.

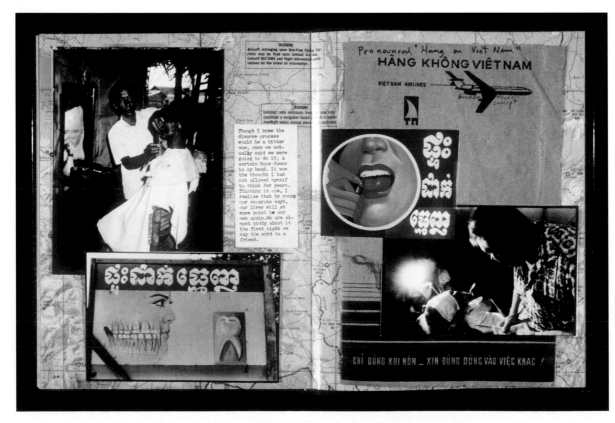

PLACING TEXT AND IMAGES INTO THE DOCUMENT

TEXT

Create a text box by selecting the *Rectangular* text box option from the *Tool* palette, and then size and position it on the page.

There are three ways of placing text in the box. The first and most direct is to simply type your text in, just as you would if you were writing in a word processing program. The second is to import the text using the *Get Text* command. Thirdly, you can *Cut* or *Copy* text from another document and *Paste* it into the text box.

Try typing in some text. It will start where the flashing cursor is located and the line width is a function of the width of the box. To make the lines longer, simply make the box wider and vice versa. Like a word processor, but with infinitely more precision and control, the attributes of this text can be altered by accessing the choices in the menu at the top of the screen. A full discussion of these will follow shortly but you may wish to experiment at this stage just to see what happens when you try various options. Remember that when you wish to work on the type, you are working within the box and therefore you must have the *Contents* tool selected.

Highlight your text, just as you would with a word processing program, and try some different fonts and sizes. You will see other choices in the *Style* menu. Try a few options and see what happens. Also try changing the size and proportion of the boxes and see how this affects the appearance of your text.

To import text from a word processing program, select the *Contents* tool and then select the box where you want the text to go by simply clicking on it. Having done so the flashing cursor will appear in the box. Now go to the *File* menu at the top of the screen. You will see the command *Get Text*. (The keyboard shortcut for this command is Command E, another useful one to remember.[2]) When selected, a dialog box will appear on the screen. It will ask you to locate the text you wish to import. After finding the appropriate word processing file select *Open* and the text will flow into the text box.

The text will appear in the text box, in the typeface and size used in the document in the word processing program.[3] If there is more text than there is room in the box, then the text will stop when there is no more space and a small, red, square symbol with an X inside, will be visible after the last word. Should this occur you have the choice of making the text box bigger, by dragging the "handles" on the corners

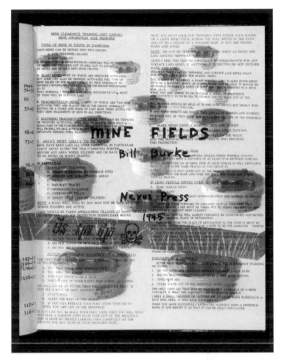

Bill Burke, *Mine Fields,* Nexus Press, Atlanta, Ga., 1995.

2. It is worthwhile remembering this (Mac) command as it also works for importing images. When a picture box is selected, the *File* menu automatically changes to reflect the nature of the box. Instead saying *Get Text,* in the picture box mode it will say *Get Picture,* which also has the keyboard shortcut Command E.

3. Please refer to Chapter 2 and read the section on preparing your *Text* for the page layout program.

and sides of the box or creating another box and linking it to this first box to create more room. Alternatively you can also make the type smaller and change the "leading" or space between the lines.

The third method of placing text is to move text from another program or elsewhere in QuarkXPress. Highlight it and then simply cut and/or copy this text and paste it into the text box.

IMAGES

To import an image you follow a procedure very similar to getting the text. First you create a picture box by selecting one of the picture box tools. Draw the box approximately the size you would like the image to be when you import it into your document.

Then select the box with the *Contents* tool. (The tool you always use when you want to do something *within* the box you have created.) If you now go to the *File* menu you will see that the options have changed. Because you are working with a picture box, instead of saying *Get Text*, the option will say *Get Picture*. The keyboard command for this operation is again Command E.

Brad Freeman, *MuzeLink, The Tours,* New Haven, Conn., 1997.

Select this option. A dialog box will appear asking you where the image you wish to import is located. Work your way through the options until you find the image file you wish to access. When you have found it, select *Open*. The image will then be imported into the document and appear in the box.

When the image appears in the document you may notice a number of changes. Firstly, it will not look exactly as it did when you viewed it in Photoshop. QuarkXPress does not actually place the file itself in the document. What it does is create a low resolution rendition of the image which you use to position and size the picture. So if your picture looks grainy or otherwise not as you imagined, do not worry. When it comes time to print, the program will instruct the printer to look for the original image file and the document will then print from this original file. That is if it can find it. Read the following paragraph carefully:

Understanding this paragraph is crucial to using QuarkXPress successfully. When you have finished your book or project, it is essential that the image files are placed in the same folder as the QuarkXPress file itself. If you do not do this, the program will not be able to access the original image files and will be forced to print from the lower resolution screen image of the file. This will result in poor quality. It is good practice to create a folder each time you use the program and put the QuarkXPress file and copies of all the image files in this folder, as you proceed. In this way the program will have all the data it needs to be able to print the book successfully.

Bill Burke, *Mine Fields,* Nexus Press, Atlanta, Ga., 1995.

The next thing you will notice is that the image may not fit the picture box exactly. The image may be too big or it may be too small. In Chapter 6 where scanning is discussed, you will be advised that ideally the image file should be sized in Photoshop so that it is the size it will appear in your document. This is not always known in advance so the rule of thumb is to size your image so that the longest side of the image is the length of the longest size of the page. If you have done this then the image is probably too big. As a result when you view the image in the document you are seeing only a portion of the whole image. This is because when QuarkXPress imports the image it imports it at 100%. In other words, it does not (automatically) scale the image to fit the box.

To fit the box you have to change the scale of the image. The easiest way to do this is to remember a simple keyboard command. This is a command that is used so frequently, and is so useful, that its memorization is to all intents and purposes mandatory. To fit the image in the box hold down Shift, Option and Command and while holding down these three keys press the "F" (for Fit) key.

The image will now be reduced to fit the smallest dimension of the picture box. In doing this you also retain the correct proportions of the image. Now adjust the box to fit the image exactly by dragging the sides of the box so that they are barely overlapping the image. If after doing this the size of the image in the corrected picture box is inappropriate you can re-size the box, and the image within in it, by again selecting Shift, Option and Command and then while holding these keys down, place your mouse cursor on one of the corners and drag the corner either in or out. As you do so the box and the picture will change size keeping the proportions intact. This is an extremely useful procedure as it very quickly allows you to change the relative proportions of the image to the text and to the dimensions of the page. You can now select the *Item* tool and move this box around the page to try out different locations for the image.

You will notice in the *Measurements* palette at the bottom of the screen that the percentage reduction values are displayed as you re-size the image. You can also re-size the image within the box by highlighting these values, typing in new ones, and pressing the return key. In this way you can frame your image with great precision.

The discussion to this point has assumed that the image is too big for the picture box. However it may be that your image when imported is smaller than the picture box you wish it to occupy. You may be tempted to try to re-size the image by using the Shift, Option, Command F shortcut. You will find that this works but is very bad practice because it will result in poor print quality.

Never, I repeat never, enlarge an image in QuarkXPress. Should this happen to you then you have not properly prepared the image in Photoshop. It may be that you have scaled the image at a small size but with high resolution, thinking that this is the same as a larger image at less resolution. This is a legitimate, even logical, mistake. However, it will print poorly. If this happens, you must return to the original image file in Photoshop and use the *Image Size* command to change the size of the picture so that it is either the exact size as it will appear or a little larger. (See *p. 163.*) Save the image at this new size, ensuring that the resolution is at minimum 225 dpi and then go back to QuarkXPress and re-import the image.

The other thing you will notice is that with the *Contents* tool selected, your cursor will change to the little "hand" symbol depicted in the icon on the *Tool* palette. When the hand is visible, if you hold down the button on the mouse you will see that you can move the image around inside the box. In this way you can re-position your image within the box and crop the picture to suit your layout should you so desire. It is good practice to enlarge your view of the picture box. Fit the box to the image so there is no white space visible between the edge of the image and the boundaries of the box. Return to the full page view after using the *Magnification* tool by pressing Command Zero.

It is appropriate at this stage to try this out on your document. Create a picture box and import and size an image. Create a text box and type in some text or try importing text as discussed above. See what happens when you move these two boxes relative to each other and how you can alter the appearance of you page. You will find you can re-size text in a box in exactly the same manner you re-sized an image by holding down the Shift, Option and Command keys and dragging the corners either in or out.

Above:
A pioneering example of early Macintosh typography. Drucker has capitalized on the appearance of jagged type to emphasize the edgy nervousness of her story. As well as being an accomplished book artist she has also written extensively on the history and theory of artists' books. (See the *Bibliography.*)
Johanna Drucker, *Simulant Portrait*, Druckwerk, New York, 1990.

CHANGING THE ATTRIBUTES OF YOUR IMAGES AND TEXT

The options in the QuarkXPress menu at the top of the screen provide many ways to alter the appearance of your document. Open a page in QuarkXPress with a picture box containing an image and a text box with some words. We will experiment with these options so that you will get an appreciation of the creative possibilities available to you.

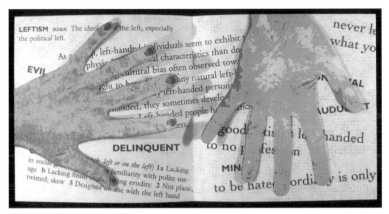

Above.
Anne Martens, *Leftisms,* Visual Studies Workshop Press, Rochester, N.Y., 1994.

You will find that the choices in the menu change according to what tool you have selected and what kind of box you are working with. Sometimes the alternatives may seem a little overwhelming. However, if you have a document open and apply each of the choices in turn, you will quickly learn how simple it really is.

The attitude to adopt is one of open minded experimentation. Don't feel you have to remember everything, or have total control to proceed. It is best to think of this as a kind of computer game and the prize, instead of the destruction of some ugly alien, is the creation of something beautiful, or at least appropriate, to what you want to say. You may well find you need remember only one or two things that you will use with any regularity. Mastery will come as a function of what you have to say, not by learning every little thing the program can do. Already you have the ability to import words and images into a page and alter their size and relative position. This is itself a powerful tool. Only a few short years ago you would have had to have access to a typesetting machine, a reprographic camera and a layout table to do even this.

The first task you will most likely wish to attempt is to alter the appearance of your text to take advantage of the typesetting capabilities of QuarkXPress. Similarly you may also wish to alter the appearance of images in document. The greatest amount of control over the appearance of your text and images in their respective boxes is exercised in the *Style* menu.

THE STYLE MENU

The *Style* menu is used to alter the characteristics of the item, or box, you are working on. Simply clicking on the item with the contents tool selected will be sufficient to tell the program to display the appropriate options for the kind of item that is active.

If you click on a text box you will see in the *Style* menu the options for modifying the appearance of the text. Clicking on a picture box will change the options in the *Style* menu to image adjustments. This menu will also change if you should wish to alter the characteristics of the *Line* (or *Rule*) tool. If the latter is selected you can change the thickness of the line, make it appear as a single or broken line or even ask it to put arrow heads on the line should you so desire.

THE STYLE MENU FOR TEXT

With a text box selected the following choices are available. Please note that most of the choices in the Style menu (for both text and pictures) can also be accessed in a "shorthand" manner in the *Measurements* palette. Details of this palette can be found immediately following this explanation of the *Style* menu for both text and images.

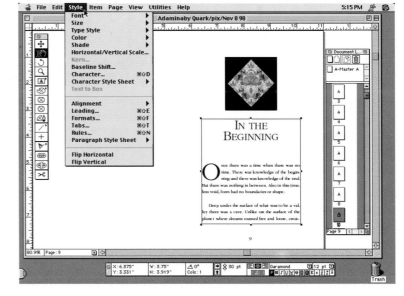

The *Font* option allows you to select a typeface from the fonts installed in your computer. The reader is reminded (wherever available) to select from the *Font* menu not only the font by name but also, if the option exists, by style. For example, if the name of the font has a little arrow to the right, follow this arrow to see if an italicized version is available. If so choose this rather than selecting the plain type and then using the italicize option in the *Type Style* option. The same holds for bold. If no choice exists then by all means use the *Type Style* option to alter your type but do this as a last resort rather than by choice. In this way you will minimize printing errors.

This is a view of the *Style* menu when a text box has been selected. Note how the options reflect the attributes of text only. When a picture box is selected the menu changes to reflect choices that control the appearance of images.

The *Size* option allows you to scale the type to a fixed size.

The *Type Style* option allows you to assign various attributes to your type. As well as the usual choices such as bold, italics and underline, there are other options you may wish to explore. For the most part these are self-explanatory and best learned by practice.

The *Color* option changes the color of the type.

The *Shade* option allows you to control the intensity of the ink that defines the type when you print your document. You will see that you have the option of allowing the color selected to be fully saturated at 100% or you can choose to reduce the intensity of the color by selecting a lighter value such as 50%.

This is useful as many colors, such as
pink and pastel blue can be obtained by
simply altering this value. Gray type,
obtained by selecting the color black
and applying a lighter shade, can lend a
sophisticated air to many documents.
You can add to the color choices in this
palette by referring to the section on
the *Edit* menu and reading the section
on the *Colors* option.

The *Horizontal/Vertical Scale* option
allows you to stretch your type
horizontally and/or vertically. This is
useful if you wish to make a line of
type, usually a headline, fit a pre-
determined width, exactly. The dialogue
box will ask you to enter a percentage, either greater or lesser than
100% to change the proportions of your type. Use this with caution as
it can greatly affect the character of the font you have chosen,
sometimes to the point where it no longer resembles the original
typeface.

The *Kern/Track* option allows you to alter the space between
letters. This alters the appearance of the type and helps to fit a line of
type in a particular space. The tracking is usually set at zero which is
the amount determined by the font manufacturer as suitable for a
particular typeface. If you want to change this, select the type and enter
a new value. To make the type tighter select negative values. (Up to
minus 100.) To stretch the space between the characters enter positive
values. (Up to plus 100.) A little goes a long way. You can also change
tracking "on the fly" by selecting the type you wish to adjust and
click on the small, horizontal, hollow arrows in the *Measurements*
palette. Extra tracking in headlines can often provide effective emphasis.

Baseline Shift moves your selected character up or down. This
feature is similar to the *superscript* and *subscript* option in the *Type Style*
menu. You will seldom need to use this option.

Character allows you to access, in one central place, all of the
options discussed above. This is a kind of universal dialog box where
many changes can be made from one place. It is appropriate at this
stage to be aware that most of these commands are also accessible on
the *Measurements* palette.

The *Character Style* sheet allows you access to predetermined text
styles if you have created any. Don't worry about it for now.

The *Alignment* option is similar to that found on most word
processing programs. It allows you to set your type ranged *Left*

Joan Lyons, *The Gynecologist*, Visual
Studies Workshop Press, Rochester,
N.Y., 1989.

Janet Zweig, *Heinz and Judy, a play*,
Photographic Resource Center,
Boston, 1985.

(in other words with a vertical left-hand side and a right-hand side that finishes where each line ends on a whole word), ranged *Right* (where the opposite occurs), *Justified* or *Centered*. There is also an option which enables you to *Force* justify your text so that the final line of justified type stretches to fit the width of the text box. This last option is sometimes useful for special type effects as often quite novel spacing occurs as the program stretches a small amount of type to accommodate a long line.

Leading is a term that comes from the days of letterpress printing. It refers to the space between lines of type. Once this was altered by placing strips of lead between the lines of type to physically move them apart the desired distance. The term has been retained but now instead of using lead of various thickness to space the lines, we nominate a value expressed in the units of the typeface, i.e. in "points."

The *Formats* menu option controls the attributes of paragraphs within your document. As you can see from the illustration, there are a number of settings you may find useful. Most are self-explanatory but the reader's attention is drawn to the option *Drop Caps* which has been selected by checking the box for this option. When checked, you can assign an enlarged, "dropped" capital letter or word to the paragraph. This is a useful device for laying out your document. It announces breaks in the text quietly but emphatically and is an excellent way of injecting variety into large amounts of text that can otherwise monopolize (monotonize?) the appearance of a page.

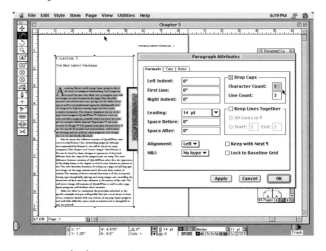

It is possible to apply this option to either a single character or a whole word. You can also "drop" the desired character or word any number of lines for dramatic effect.

Rules draws a line above and/or below a selected paragraph.

Tabs can be inserted and positioned with this option. Usually the default setting is suitable but this option allows you to fine tune their position and insert more if necessary.

The *Paragraph Style Sheet* option here allows you to select and apply any *Style Sheets* you may have created. These enable you to save formatting choices such as font, leading, tabs, etc. if you use them often. This is something you will grow into and you most likely do not have to worry about it now. (For more information see the discussion of the *Edit* menu, *pp. 111–113,* later in this chapter.)

As you would expect the *Flip Horizontal* and *Flip Vertical* options perform these variations to your text. These options are also available on the *Measurements* palette and are indicated by small, solid arrows.

This is a view of the *Formats, Paragraph Attributes* dialog box. To apply a "drop-cap" to the beginning of a paragraph, highlight the paragraph text and open this box. As you can see you can specify how many characters will be "dropped" and how many lines they will occupy.

This screen image will differ slightly from what you will see on your computer. This image is a cut and paste composite. In reality when the box is open the highlighted paragraph text will return to its normal color. It will return to the highlighted state, with the drop cap inserted, when the OK is given and the box closes.

THE STYLE MENU FOR IMAGES

When you select a picture box with the *Contents* tool you will see the options described below. You can apply a number of relatively simple transformations to your images such as inverting the image, posterizing the image or altering its contrast. These transformations are relatively crude. Far more control can (and probably should) be exercised in Photoshop to the original image file if these changes are seen as necessary.

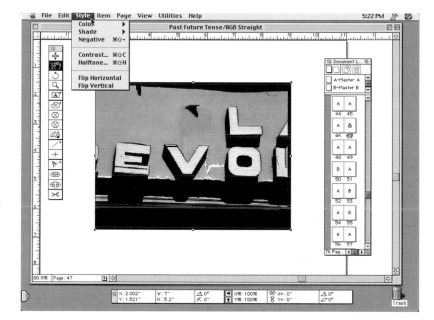

A view of the contents of the *Style* menu when a grayscale image occupies a picture box. If a color image is in the box, *Color* and *Shade* will be grayed out and unable to be applied.

More useful is the ability to use the *Color* and *Shade* options to change these qualities in the page layout program. These options will only apply if the image is monochrome. These two controls can very quickly alter, often helpfully, the nature and character of your page. The shade option is especially convenient if you are placing type over an image as it can quickly and easily reduce the contrast of the image making the type more legible.

The *Negative* option simply inverts the image tonally to appear as a negative.

The *Contrast* option is a simple version of the *Curves* control you find in Photoshop. (See Chapter 7, *pp. 146–148.*) Again, such variations are best made in Photoshop to the original file.

The *Screening* (v.3) or *Halftone* (v.4) options are best ignored at this stage. QuarkXPress automatically sets (halftone) screen values when it prints and these almost always work well. However, you can experiment with coarser screen values in this menu for (occasional) special effect.

The *Flip Horizontal* and *Flip Vertical* options allow you, when the *Contents* tool is selected, to alter the orientation of the image in the picture box.

The rule of thumb to follow with respect to images is similar to the caution when selecting type styles. You will recall the advice to select type variations from the *Font* menu rather than apply these styles to the type in QuarkXPress. That is, if the font permits an italic or bold choice in the *Font* menu then select this option rather than applying *Type Styles* to plain type. A similar general rule applies for images.

Wherever possible make your modifications in Photoshop rather than in QuarkXPress. Your document will print faster and is less likely to have printing errors if the image file need only be accessed, rather than modified, "on-the-fly" as it prints, by QuarkXPress.

THE MEASUREMENTS PALETTE
Shorthand Access to the Style Menu (and Other Useful Tools)

Before going any further take the time to understand the function of the *Measurements* palette. This is the long thin horizontal palette at the bottom of the screen. If it is not visible you will have to go to the *View* menu and select *Show Measurements* palette. This palette will display information about any item, be it a picture box, a text box or a line you may have drawn and selected, enabling easy access to many ways to alter the appearance of this item. For example, with a text box selected the *Measurements* palette will display the following information.

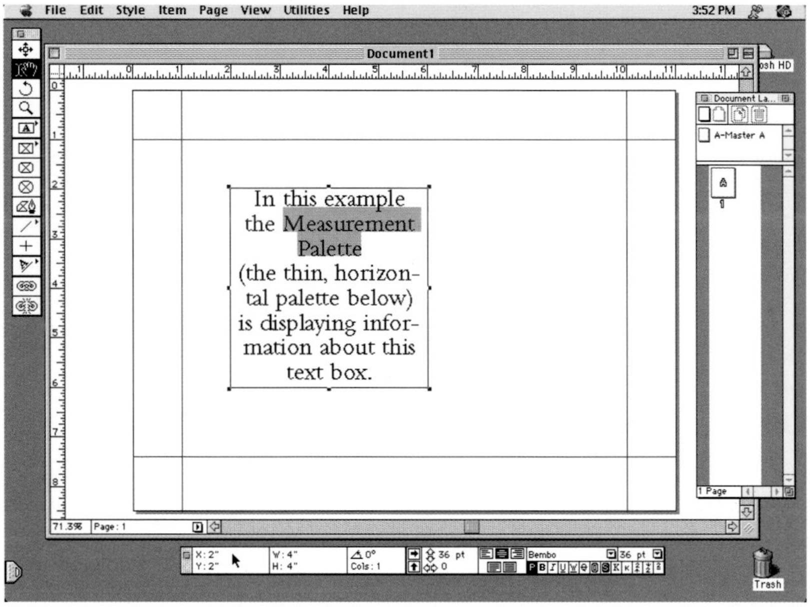

The first box on the palette shows the point of origin of the text box, in this case two inches across on the X axis and 2 inches down on the Y axis. The next box displays the actual size of the text box which in this case measures four inches square. If you highlight these values and type in new ones, after pressing the Return key, the box will change size and shape accordingly.

The next box contains the *Rotation* indicator. In this case the box set to 0° is square to the page. Try highlighting the value of zero and changing it to say 15° and press the Return key. You will see that the box will now be at this angle to the page.

The remainder of the controls provide shorthand access to the options in the *Style* menu. The little arrows in the boxes flip the contents horizontally or vertically. The hollow arrows next to these control the leading (in this case see how it has been set to 36 pt.) and the kerning. (The value 0 shown here indicates that the horizontal spacing between the characters is set according to the manufacturer's suggestion.)

The *Measurements* palette is the long, thin, horizontal palette at the bottom of the screen. It permits you quick access to information about the size and location of a selected item. In this example we can see that the selected text box is four inches square and located two inches across and down from the top left-hand corner of the page.

Additionally you can quickly access most of the items in the *Style* menu relevant to the type of box you have selected, in this case a text box. You will see on the right-hand side of the palette that you can quickly change *Fonts* and their *Style, Leading, Tracking* and *Kerning.*

The final set of controls enable you to adjust the *Alignment* (here centered), select a *Font* (Bembo), change the *Size* of the typeface (here 36 pt.) and finally assign various attributes to the type such as *Small Caps*, *Bold* or *Italics*. (Use with caution as previously advised.)

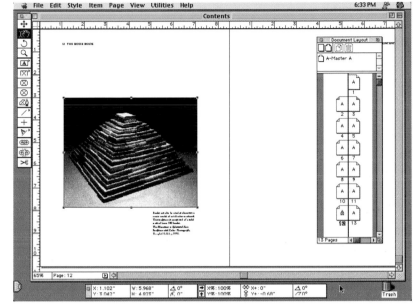

When a picture box is selected, the *Measurements* palette alters to reflect the *Style* menu for images. As for a text box the first two sub-boxes display information about the size and position of the box. In the third box the top figure permits control over the rotation of the box itself. Underneath this is a control that allows you to alter the corner radius of the box. Changing the values to more than zero will give you a box with rounded corners.

The two arrows that come next will flip the contents of the box vertically or horizontally. More importantly is the following box which shows the magnification or reduction of the image file in the box. Ideally this will display at 100%. If the value is greater than 100% then it means the picture is being enlarged in QuarkXPress. This is NOT recommended as it will result in inferior image quality. It is OK to reduce the image but ideally not less than about 75%. Try to get it as close to 100% as you can.

At this stage ignore the last two boxes, the first of which tells you how much of the image is hidden by the box. The last two controls change the angle or skew of the image within the box.

The essential principle to remember is that the *Measurements* palette has two main functions. Firstly, it allows you to accurately size and position any item that you have selected. Secondly, the palette provides shorthand access to most of the controls in the *Style* menu for the kind of item you have selected. If it is a text box you are working with, then the palette will contain the tools necessary to alter the attributes of the text. If it is a picture box then the controls will represent the contents of the *Style* menu for pictures.

Now that we have learned how to create and change the attributes of text and picture boxes, the next step is to learn how they can interact to create a layout. A layout is created by placing the boxes on the page in various configurations. This can be as simple as placing a caption underneath an image, or it can become extremely complex as boxes are stacked over each other to create more sophisticated effects.

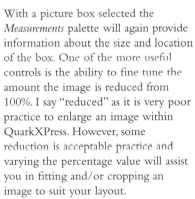

With a picture box selected the *Measurements* palette will again provide information about the size and location of the box. One of the more useful controls is the ability to fine tune the amount the image is reduced from 100%. I say "reduced" as it is very poor practice to enlarge an image within QuarkXPress. However, some reduction is acceptable practice and varying the percentage value will assist you in fitting and/or cropping an image to suit your layout.

THE ITEM MENU
Creating a Layout

Depending on which version of the program you have, the *Item* menu will look like one of the accompanying diagrams. Within the menu are tools you will find essential when you begin serious work. As the diagrams show, the essential functions remain the same. (This is likely to stay true for future versions of the program.) Do not be put off by the differing options and appearances of the display. *Modify, Runaround* and *Frame* will always be necessary. They may however, over time, be found in different places, and accessed in different ways. For the purposes of this chapter we will use version 4 to discuss these functions. Be patient and try to understand the principle. You will find it easy to adapt.

Item
Menu
version
4.1.

The two most powerful and useful are the *Modify* option and the *Runaround* option. The third option in the first group *Frame* is self-explanatory. When selected, a dialog box appears asking you to select a width, color, and shade for a frame which will appear around the text or image box you are working on. You will also see a series of frame styles in another window within this dialogue box. You can scroll through the

A view of the *Modify, Frame* window.

diagrammatic list of choices, make a selection, and then evaluate your decision when you see the frame appear in your document.

Now let us return to the *Modify* option. When you select this option, a box will appear with a considerable amount of detail about the item you have selected.

In this case a text box has been selected but similar information will appear if you are working on a picture box. Most of the information is self-explanatory and to a degree superfluous. Notice that within the *Modify* option there are sub menus accessed by selecting "tabs" on index cards.

Below:
This screen image shows the *Text* tab within the *Modify* dialog box. Most commonly you will wish to change the vertical position of the text within the box. (For example this caption is aligned to the *Bottom* of the box so that the bottom line of the caption is aligned with the body text adjacent.)

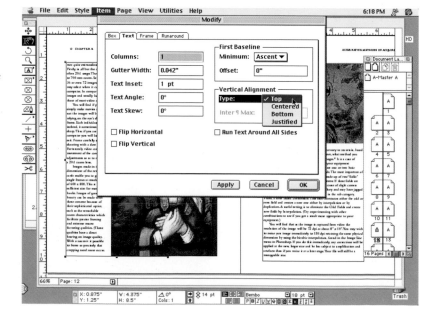

These enable you to access the *Frame* and *Runaround* without having to return to the main menu. You can see that in the case of a text box there are four categories of modification indicated by these tabs. They are *Box, Text, Frame* and *Runaround*.

Within the *Text* option the most important control is the *Vertical Alignment* box. This allows you to control the alignment of your text vertically within the box. You will see that it can be aligned to the *Top*, the *Center*, or the *Bottom* of the box. This is something you may use frequently when you start to place text on the page. Remember that it is here you access this control. Also, remember it is quite different to the other alignment control in the *Style* menu which controls horizontal alignment styles such as ranged left, ranged right, justified or centered.

If you now switch to the tab labeled *Box,* you will see the control *Background*. This controls the color and the opacity of the box you have selected. By accessing these choices you can control the background of your image or text. You will see that as well as being able to control the color of the background, you can also control the lightness or darkness of this background color by altering the shade value. So if you have black selected, you can obtain a light gray by selecting a shade value of say 30%.

However, there is also one further choice which is extremely useful. This is the option that allows you to select *None*, or no background color at all. When this option is selected it is as if you are typing on a sheet of transparent acetate. The applications for this are obvious. You can type your text into the document and by selecting the *None* option, place this text over an image so that the image is visible under the text. You can then alter the color and shade of the text itself by highlighting it and going to the *Style* menu and create a variety of effects.

Unlike using the *Type* tool in Photoshop (where once you have "flattened" the image the type is there forever) this feature enables you to experiment with a variety of type styles and colors and change them easily without altering your image in any way.

Item Menu version 3.32.

Below:
If you select the tab labeled *Box*, you can change the background *Color* and *Shade* of an item. Be aware of the option *None*. This permits you to place text as if on a transparent sheet of plastic or film and then subsequently overlay it on an image or on other text. If you try this you may have to set the *Runaround* to *None* so that the boxes do not try to repel each other's contents when placed in close proximity. (See overleaf.)

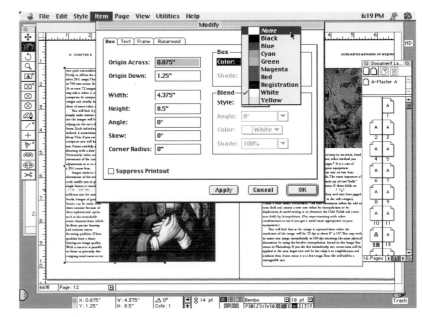

RUNAROUND

This capability of being able to "stack" boxes over each other leads us to the next option which is the *Runaround* option. It is essential that this feature is fully understood. The *Runaround* control affects how boxes behave when they are placed either in close proximity or over each other. If you select the *Runaround* option you will see a variety of choices. There are only two you need memorize at first. They are item and none. The *Runaround* feature, when set to item, creates a kind of force field around the box.

Notice how the body text flows around the image below. Compare this to the overlapping image/text relationship on the facing page. Read the text, and the other captions on this spread, for details on how to control this effect.
Images below and opposite are from the book, *Past and Future Tense,* Rockcorry, Rochester, N.Y., 1998.

The best way to explain this is to cite an example of two possible ways you might want a picture box to interact with a text box. If for example, you were working on a document with a lot of text, you might wish to enliven its appearance with an image. With the *Runaround* set to *Item*, when the image is placed in the text, the words will "wrap" around this picture box because the setting *Item* causes the picture box to repel the text from its borders. You will notice in the *Runaround* dialog box that you can alter the amount of this repelling force by typing in values (in units of points) for each of the sides of the box.

The image on this page is an example. Observe how the text flows around the image. Contrast this to the image on the top of the opposite page. Read the captions carefully for more details.

Notice how the image on this page is forcing the text to "runaround" its border. To the right, the *Runaround* dialog box for this picture box is shown. As you can see this dialog box provides the opportunity to set the "force field" around the picture box. To do this ensure that *Runaround* is turned on by selecting *Item* in the *Type* field.

Next, insert the distance you wish the text to be repelled from the picture box. In this case the top and bottom has been set to 7 points and either side to 14 points. The preview window shows how this will look when applied.

Contrast this with the top image on the facing page.

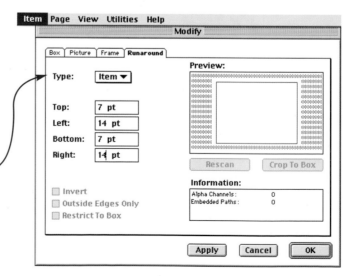

On other occasions you may want the text to be superimposed over an image. The text and image combination you are reading now is such an an example. In this case you do not want either box to repel the other. Instead you will want them to co-exist in the same space.

To allow this, go to the *Item, Runaround* option and select the *None* option for both boxes. In this way each box is independent of each other and they can be placed in any configuration without altering the position of the text within the box. It is essential you understand the nature of this option and how to control your choices. The ability to place boxes on top of each other is one of the great tools of this program. It is essential to realize that the boxes will interact differently depending on whether the *Runaround* is selected or not.

It is to all intents and purposes mandatory to understand these two options. In contrast the following *Item* menu choices, although useful, are not nearly as frequently needed.

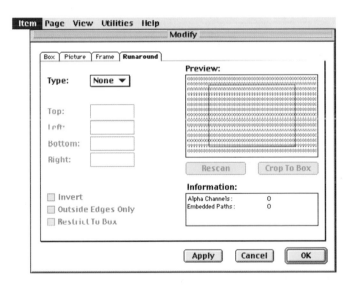

Above and Left:
The image above shows what can be achieved by turning the *Runaround* off. Now the type and the image are coexisting in the same space. The dialog box is shown to the left. You will observe that in this instance the runaround *Type* choice is set to *None*. In the dialog box is a preview of how this will look in the document. You can see that the stylized "text" is superimposed over the box.

If you choose to do this you will also have to ensure that the boxes are "stacked" in the correct order over each other by using the *Send to Front* or *Send to Back* choices also in the *Item* menu (discussed overleaf). Additionally you will have to set the background color in the *Item, Box* tab, to *None*. This ensures the type will not have an opaque (usually white) background.

This is not as hard as it might sound. Try it with a document and you will quickly get the hang of it.

Right:
The *Runaround* control is particularly useful when placing text boxes in close proximity. The top two boxes have the *Runaround* set to *Item*. As you can see the text of the second box has been forced out of the box as indicated by the small red square with the "X" inside.

If however, you set the *Runaround* of both boxes to *None*, then the text on each is visible. In this case this has been used to create a "drop-shadow" effect. However, it is useful any time you wish to put text close together for emphasis or other layout imperatives.

As before, you will have to ensure the background color in the *Item, Box* tab is set to *None*.

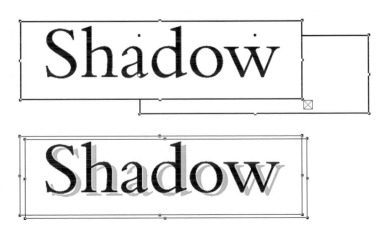

Item menu, continued …

The *Duplicate* option allows you to create an identical copy of a box and its contents. With the *Item* tool active choose *Duplicate*, and the selected box will reproduce itself. This is useful if you wish to repeat certain motifs or images through your document. The *Step and Repeat* option can be ignored at this stage. It gives you the ability to control where the duplicated box will appear relative to the original. You can also specify how many copies of the original you would like. It is unlikely you will ever use it.

Clifton Meador, *Long Slow March*. Co-published Clifton Meador/Nexus Press, Atlanta, Ga., 1999.

The *Delete* command, when the *Item* tool is chosen, simply deletes the selected box. Be careful!

The *Group* command can be used to group together boxes so they can be moved or copied and pasted without losing their position relative to each other. To use this command, hold down the Shift key and with the *Item* tool, select by clicking on each of the boxes you wish to group together. With the Shift key held down each selection is added to the one(s) before. When all the boxes you want to group are selected, select the *Group* option and they will be joined together as one unit. If you wish to un-group them select the *Ungroup* option and they will again be able to be moved independently of each other.

At this stage ignore the *Constrain, Lock, Merge* and *Split* commands.

You use the *Send to Back* option if you have one box layered over another and wish to work on the box that is behind the front box. This control and its opposite the *Bring to Front* control simply change the "stacking order" of the boxes on the screen. Changing their order can also affect the appearance of the page by altering the relative position of image and text boxes.

Space/Align allows you to precisely space and align multiple boxes. Using the Shift key, select the boxes you wish to either space or align and then apply the various options. They are a little confusing at first. You are advised to check your manual, or at minimum ensure your work is saved before you try this feature. Even with practice you can make the wrong choice and items can disappear off the page very easily. If this happens, don't worry. They are still there somewhere. If you have saved your work, and you get lost, simply select the *Revert to Saved* option in the *File* menu.

Item Menu, version 3.

The final five choices within the *Item* menu will be passed over quickly in this chapter. Essentially *Shape, Content* and *Edit* give you the ability to alter the shapes of your text or picture boxes. This is useful particularly if you are using the drawing tools that come in version 4 of QuarkXPress. For the most part you will not likely need these tools at this stage. It is enough to be aware that you can change the shape of the selected picture or text box by selecting *Shape*. (*Box Shape* in version 3.) *Content* allows you to change a picture box to a text box, or vice versa. It even allows you have no content at all if you just wish to use the box as part of a drawing. *Edit* permits you to change or constrain a box shape.

Item Menu version 4.1.

The last two choices *Point/Segment Type* and *Super Step and Repeat* will not be discussed. You are unlikely to use *Super Step and Repeat*. However, if you are interested in using the drawing tools that come with version 4 you will have to read the manual for advice on how *Point/Segment Type* can help you modify Bezier boxes and lines.

In conclusion, remember that the most frequently needed tools in the *Item* menu are those which control:

- the color of the boxes and their level of opacity *(Modify, Box)*.
- the vertical alignment of the text *(Modify, Text)*.
- the thickness, shape and color of a frame *(Frame)*.
- how the items (boxes) interact with each other using *Runaround*.
- the stacking order of the boxes *(Bring to Front, Send to Back)*.

Brad Freeman, *MuzeLink, The Tours*, New Haven, Conn., 1997.

The Document Layout Palette
Master Page and Document Page Control

Until now the discussion has focussed on using QuarkXPress to layout single pages. However, most books are composed of many pages. The most useful way to exercise control over a multi-page document is through the *Document Layout* palette, usually located to the right of the screen. It enables you to create new master pages or edit existing ones, navigate through your document and create new pages with the attributes of the master page.

You can see that the *Document Layout* palette has two main windows. The first of these displays the master page icon. *A master page is created automatically when you set up a new document.* By double clicking on the icon labeled *A–Master A* you can view the master page and make changes to this page that will then appear on each page of your document.

The advantages are obvious. If, for example, you are creating a book with an image in the same place on every page, you can draw this picture box onto the master page and then each time you create a new page it will appear with this box in position. This works for any item. Thus repeating motifs such as rules, text boxes or any other attributes, can be set up in the master page.

You can create any number of new master pages. To create new master pages put the cursor of the mouse over the first of the four little icons at the very top of the *Document Layout* palette. This icon is a blank rectangle signifying a new page. Hold down the button and drag the icon into the master page box underneath the page labeled *A–Master A.* A new page will be created and will automatically label itself *B–Master B.* If you then double click on this new icon, the new master page will be displayed on the screen. You can then draw on this page any items you may wish to appear on subsequent pages created by this master page. This is useful if your book has, for example, mostly pictures on some spreads, and mostly text on others. If this is the case then make a master page for each style. You can create almost any number of master pages. In practice however, you will most likely have only one or two. However, as your skill increases and your document grows, you may find it helpful or necessary to create several.

If your book is text based and you have chosen the automatic text box option, when you import your text, the pages necessary to contain this text will be created automatically.

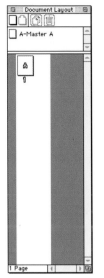

Left:
The *Document Layout* palette enables you to easily navigate through your document. The master page labeled *A–Master A* is created automatically when you create a new document. At the same time a single document page will also appear with the same guides that were stipulated on the master page. To view either the master page or the document page(s) double click on the appropriate page icon in the palette window.

Below:
It is a simple matter to create a new master page. Simply drag the blank *Master Page* icon from the mini menu at the top of the palette into the *Master Page* window as shown below. This new page will have the same guides as the existing master page. (These can be changed if you wish by double clicking on the master page icon and going to the *Page* menu and selecting *Master Guides.)* You will do this if you have any pages with recurring layouts. For example you may have a layout where the recto is simply a single image, and the verso may have only text.

Drag

However, if you are approaching the layout of your book one page at a time, you will need to create new pages as you go.

To make new pages based on the master pages you click and hold on the *Master Page* icon and drag it into the bottom box where the page icons are labeled with a number indicating their position within the document. As you do so a new page is created with all the attributes of the selected master page already drawn upon it. You can put this new page anywhere in the document you so desire. You can put it in front, underneath, or to either the left or right hand side of an existing page. This is how you add new pages to your document as you construct your book. (When you add new pages like this, any text boxes that are present will not be "linked" to the prior page. Revisit the discussion of the *Tool* palette to be reminded how you create links between text boxes.)

Another useful function of the *Document Layout* palette is to help you navigate through your document. As your pages mount up you will see them appear as numbered page icons in the main window of the palette. To view any page simply double click on its numbered icon and it will appear on the screen.

You can also change the order of pages within your document by moving the icons in the *Document Layout* palette. Grab a page by placing the cursor on one of the page icons. You will find you can move it and place it before or after other pages in the palette. As you do so an arrow will appear indicating where the page will be positioned. Be aware that this palette mimics many of the choices available in the *Page* menu in much the same way the *Measurement* palette enables easy access to the choices in the *Style* menu.

You should be aware that this palette may be hidden from view. If it is not visible go to the *View* menu and you will see the command, *Show Document Layout*. If it is visible you can select *Hide Document Layout* to remove it from view. All palettes can similarly be hidden or displayed, by selecting the *Hide/Show* option appropriate to each.

Right: Jonathan Williams and Keith Smith, *(April 19) Lexington Nocturne.* Published and printed by Keith Smith at the Visual Studies Workshop, Rochester, N.Y., 1983.

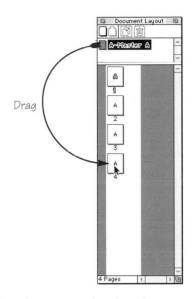

Drag

To make new pages based on the master page you click and hold on the *Master Page* icon and drag it into the bottom box. The palette also enables you to navigate through your document. Simply double click on the icon of the page you wish to view on screen. Finally you can alter the order of the pages of your book by changing the position of the page icons in the *Document Layout* palette. When you try this a little arrow will come out of the page to indicate where it will appear, relative to the page it is being placed adjacent to.

A poem by Jonathan Williams   as interpreted by Keith Smith

OTHER MENU OPTIONS

By now you should have sufficient knowledge to begin to use the program. However, be aware of the function of the other menus available within QuarkXPress. For more details please refer to the documentation that accompanied your program or else consult a detailed handbook for more comprehensive explanations.

THE FILE MENU

We have already used the *New* option. When you select this you have the choice of whether to set up a new *Document, Library* or *Book*. Ignore the *Library* and *Book* option.

 The *Open* option is used to open a previously saved QuarkXPress document.

 Use *Close* to close your document when you have finished working on it.

 Use *Save* to save your document. Use *Save as* to re-name your document or save copies with other names or version numbers if you feel that you may wish to experiment with differing layouts for the same material. Save your document frequently as you work. It is surprising how quickly your work can change and evolve, especially if you are experimenting with unusual text styles or box sizes and shapes. Sometimes you can either go too far with a particular idea or you can make an error that for some reason you cannot undo. If you save your work frequently you minimize the chances of losing too much progress if something goes wrong. You can also set up QuarkXPress to automatically save your work as you go by selecting the appropriate box in the *Preferences/Application* dialog box under the *Edit* menu. However, it is better practice to remember to save frequently and often.

 Use the *Revert to Saved* command if you make a mistake that will not undo or if you have completed a few operations that have proved to be unsuccessful for any reason. As the name suggests, the document will revert to how it was the last time you saved it.

 As discussed before, the *File* menu will enable you to import text or images depending on what kind of box is active on the page. In this case a text box is active and the option reads, *Get Text*. If a picture box was active this command would be replaced by the option *Get Picture*.

 The *Save Text* command allows you to take any text you may have in the QuarkXPress document and export it to another program. When you select this option a box will open asking you to select a name, a destination and a format for this text. You will see that you can

The File Menu, v. 4.1.

choose a simple ASCII or text-only format, or you can save the text in the format of your word processor of choice.

This option is useful if you have written your text in QuarkXPress directly and would like it to appear in another document in another format. It is also useful if you have made significant changes to your text and would like to use the specific word processing program features such as footnoting and spell and grammar checks to process your document. You can then re-import the text if you so desire after having made the appropriate corrections.

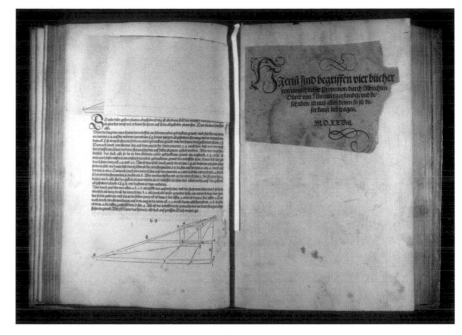

The *Save Page as EPS* option allows you to save a PostScript "image" of your document so you can import it into other programs that support this format.

The *Collect for Output* option is extremely useful. As mentioned before, QuarkXPress does not physically contain your images. For your document to print it is essential that all the image files are in the same folder as the master QuarkXPress file. Using this command ensures that this will occur. This command when selected asks you to nominate a destination folder or disk. This is particularly helpful when you are transferring your document to some sort of external storage media to either take your file to a printer or to archive it for the future. The command will collect the main QuarkXPress file and re-write all of your image files to a separate folder.

It will also analyze your document and list, in a report created in the destination

Above and Below:
A simple way to introduce interactivity into your book is to create flaps which either conceal or reveal information. Albrecht Dürer, *Hierin sind begriffen vier Bucher von menschlicher Proportion.* Nurenberg, 1528.
Courtesy of the Cary Graphic Arts Collection, Rochester Institute of Technology, Rochester, N.Y.

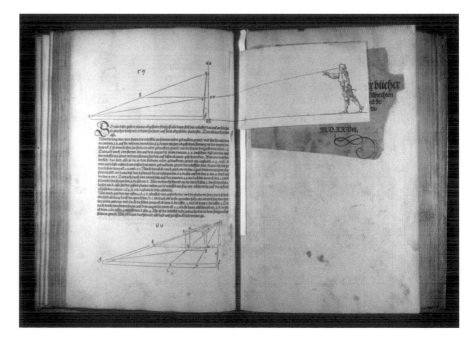

folder, all of the fonts you have used in your document. Like the image files, the fonts you use in the document must be included along with your document if you anticipate they will not be installed in the font folder on the computer that is handling your printing. Because these fonts are copyrighted, QuarkXPress will not collect the fonts in the same way it will collect the image files. It will however name them in the report. You may then, if you choose, go into the font folder and copy the fonts onto

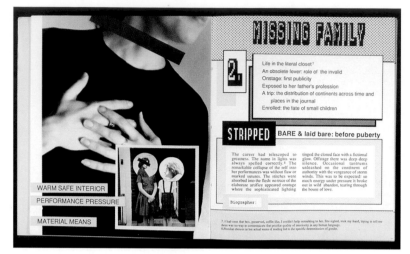

your destination disk or folder. Bear in mind these fonts are copyright protected so you may wish to check with the place where you intend to print your work about the legality of such an activity.

The next three commands are usually employed when you are about to print your document. The *Document Setup* command is seldom used. It enables you to change the page size and dimensions if you decide to change the size and shape of your book either after you have begun to work on it or even if you have finished. It is however, not to be used lightly as it simply changes the size and dimensions of the page. It does not center your layout on the new page size. As such you will find you have to re-do much of your work if you select this option. Use with caution. It is no substitute for a well-planned book.

The *Page Setup* and the *Print* commands are common to all programs and there is no need to explain them at this stage. However, in Chapter 9, *Printing the Book*, these will be explained in considerable detail. There are choices here that can exert considerable control over the finished quality of your work when printed.

Select *Quit* to close the program when you have finished your work.

Above:
Johanna Drucker, *Simulant Portrait,* Druckwerk, New York, 1990.

Below:
Deborah Muirhead, *Practical Speller.* Self-published at the Visual Studies Workshop, Rochester, N.Y, 1998.

THE EDIT MENU

The first command is the *Undo* command. This command usually, but not always, undoes the last operation you performed. The illustration indicates that the last operation was a style change. However, some changes to your document will not be able to be undone. It is for this reason the advice was given earlier to frequently and periodically save your work as you proceed.

The next five operations are common to most computer programs and you probably know them. The *Cut* command eliminates selected text and/or images from the document and places them in that zone of cyberspace known as the clipboard. In other words the images and text have not gone forever but are instead held in the short term memory of the computer and are waiting to be transferred or pasted elsewhere, either in the same document, another document or in another program altogether.

The *Copy* command performs a similar operation in the sense that the contents are transferred to the clipboard but the original selected and copied text or image, remains in place.

Paste allows you to place the text or image in the clipboard back into the same (or another) document in a new position determined by where you place the cursor. QuarkXPress allows you to perform these operations to the entire box as well as its contents. Thus with the *Item* tool selected one can cut, copy, delete or paste entire boxes (Items) and their contents anywhere within the document.

The *Clear* command will delete the item or contents of the item depending on which tool (Item/Contents) is selected. Delete means gone forever. They are not on the clipboard. As a Monty Python fan would say: "they become an ex-item, bereft of life, they have ceased to be."

The two choices *Subscribe To* and *Subscriber Options* create "live links" to other programs and data. You will find the *Subscriber Options* useful if you make changes to your images during the course of constructing your book but keep the same file names. This option allows you to reimport the new version of the image into QuarkXPress and not have to re-size it or change any attributes already assigned to it. The best way to access this option is, with the *Contents* tool selected, to double click on the image in the picture box. The *Subscriber Option* dialog box will appear and you will be asked if you want to update the image to the latest edition. This option is also useful for tables and charts that may have to be updated periodically.

The *Show Clipboard* selection permits you to view the item or box contents you may have cut or copied to be pasted elsewhere.

The Edit Menu, v. 4.1.

Nancy Chalker-Tennant, *Secret Wing,*
Visual Studies Workshop Press,
Rochester, N.Y., 1991.

The *Find/Change* option is common in a word processing program. It finds, and if you command, changes text. It is particularly powerful in QuarkXPress as it not only finds and replaces certain words or phrases, but also finds and changes specific attributes such as text styles.

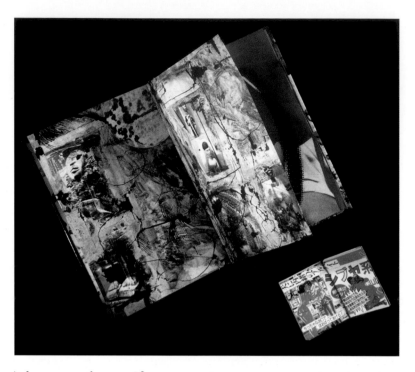

The *Preferences* file gives you the ability to control how your document appears and behaves on the screen while QuarkXPress is running. The pre-set preferences are defaults that will suit most needs. However there are a few choices within the *General Preferences* that you may wish to alter. One of these is the units of measurement your document uses. There are three choices, inches, centimeters and the traditional printer's unit known as the em. If you have a background in printing you may wish to stick with the em (but if so please consult the manual as the program has two ways of calculating this value.) However, most will be happy to select either inches or centimeters, depending on what you are most accustomed to and comfortable working with.

A particularly handy preference to consider altering is the way the guides are displayed. QuarkXPress allows you create guides to help you lay out your pages to accurately center your boxes on the page. The guides can be either behind the boxes or in front. The default is behind so try moving them to front to see if this suits you better. (Refer also to the *View* menu, *pp. 115–116*, discussed later in this chapter.)

As advised before, consult your manual for further information on the other choices available to you. However, it makes more sense to accept the factory defaults in the first instance, with perhaps the exception of the two suggestions mentioned above. Please note that preferences, as the name suggests, are a very personal thing. It is extremely bad manners to alter the preferences if you are using a computer that belongs to someone else, or is in an institution to be used by many people. For the most part the best advice is that if you don't know exactly what you are doing, and do not have the ability to re-set any or all changes you might make, keep out.

Style Sheets are a way of saving attributes, such as font, font size, leading, tracking, etc. that you use often. The default setting is usually

It may come as a surprise to learn that Ohtake not only did not use a computer to design his complex layered pages, but in fact actually dislikes computers. His books are created as collages, and then photo-mechanical separations are made from the finished, hard-copy artwork. Bill Burke, whose book *Mine Field* is also pictured in this chapter, works in a similar manner. The point is this: look at all these works as exemplifiers of excellence, not as literal models to be emulated. As these artists have demonstrated, hybrid forms of book construction can create works that reflect a singular, expressive perspective, and not simply manifest an obsession with process for its own sake.
Shinro Ohtake, *Atlanta 1945–50,* Nexus Press, Atlanta, Ga., 1996.

plain Helvetica type face with no special formatting. *Style Sheets* are best ignored if you are beginning to use the program. Most of the text formatting you will be doing in bookmaking at this stage will be specific to the nature of the particular document you are working on. As such the formatting is unlikely to need saving for future books if for no other reason that one would like to think each book, even each document you create, will have needs specific to that book or document only. However, the *Style Sheets* will become useful as you become more familiar with the program. For now it is sufficient that you know that you can store the attributes of your text by highlighting a portion of the text and selecting the style sheets option. When you do you will see that the font and its attributes are listed, and can be named and stored as a master template, for future use.

The *Colors* option allows you to add extra colors to the choices that come standard with the program. As with many of the menu items we are discussing, it is enough to be aware of this option for the future. Most of the colors you might need can be successfully created by using the color and shade options in the *Style* menu. See your manual for more information. If you try this, and add new colors, you can easily delete these colors by returning to the *Colors* option, highlighting the color you have added and selecting *Delete*. It is useful to mention again the advice given when working with the text linking option earlier in this chapter. When ever you decide to try anything, save your document first. Then if you make a mistake simply choose the *Revert to Saved* option.

The option *H & J's (Hyphens and Justification)* allows you to exercise control over where the program decides to insert a hyphen in a word if it is too long for a particular line. The default settings usually work well but these can be altered as you gain proficiency and experience. Custom settings allow you to choose the minimum length of the word to be hyphenated, and how many characters are to be left on one line before starting a new line. Be aware that it is good typesetting practice to have few or no hyphenations in text set ranged right, ranged left or centered. When setting type this way, select the *H & J's* option, select *New* and uncheck the *Auto-hyphenation* control.

Ignore for now the *Lists, Dashes and Stripes* and *Print Styles* options.

In summary, many of the options in the *Edit* menu seldom need to be accessed with the exception of the *Undo* command, and the *Cut, Copy* and *Paste* commands.

The Edit Menu, v. 4.1.

Paul Berger, *Seattle Subtext,* Visual Studies Workshop Press, Rochester, N.Y., 1984.

THE PAGE MENU

The *Page* menu allows you to alter your document at the level of individual pages. Most of the operations can be better performed using the *Document Layout* palette. The *Insert, Delete* and *Move* commands are self explanatory and require no elaboration. However, use them with caution. The *Delete* and *Move* commands are capable of making irreparable or confusing changes. Save your work before using them.

The *Master Guides* option, however, is useful if after having set up your document you decide that the guides you chose when you created the document require modification. The option will only be active if the master page is on the screen.

The last option in the *Page* menu *Display* allows you to view your master page(s). If you select say master page *A–Master A* then it will display on the screen with all the guides and items you placed on it when you created the document. However, you can do this easier by double clicking on the master page icon in the *Document Layout* palette which will be discussed shortly. When you do this, as discussed above, the *Master Guides* option will become active rather than grayed out as is shown in the menu reproduced to the right. You can then alter the guides. You will not have to do this often.

If you wish to break your document into a number of *Sections,* then select this option. You will be able to re-start the page numbers to suit. It is unlikely you will be doing this if you are making a book as you will most likely already be using self-contained chapters as a device to pace the reader's progress through the work.

The remaining options help you navigate through the document. However, using the *Document Layout* palette to do this, is easier and faster.

The Page Menu, v. 4.1.

Joan Lyons, *Abby Rogers,* Visual Studies Workshop Press, Rochester, N.Y., 1976.

THE VIEW MENU

The *View* menu as its name suggests, allows you view your document in various ways, and more particularly at various sizes. It also allows you to access or view, certain palettes which perform specific functions as you work on your document.

The first group of six view options all alter the size of the document as it is displayed on your monitor. The first of these, *Fit in Window*, you will recognize from earlier in this chapter when it was suggested you memorize the keyboard shortcut Command Zero. This command is very useful. You will find as you work on your document that you will be toggling back and forth from magnified views of images and text to overall views of the page. This happens so frequently that using the Command Zero shortcut will become second nature. This shortcut also performs the same function in Photoshop so there is an extra incentive to remember it.

The next four commands select various levels of magnification. You can also change the magnification of your document in the box in the bottom left hand of your open document. You will see a percentage figure which lets you know what the current level of magnification is. Highlight this figure and then type in a new value. When you press the Return key your document will then be displayed at this new level of magnification.

Ignore the *Windows* option.

The next five options are extremely useful. All of them work on the principle that if they say *Hide* (then the option, for example *Guides*) then that option is currently displayed. If however, they say *Show* (then the option) then by selecting the nominated option the palette or feature referred to will be displayed. Thus, referring to the illustration above, the guides are visible, the baseline grid is hidden, the option of snap to guides is selected, the rulers are visible but the *Invisibles* (usually new paragraph symbols like "¶") are hidden.

The *Guides* are those guides created when you set up a new document. You will find it useful to toggle between having these guides visible and having them out of sight. Although the guides are extremely useful when you position images and text on the page, it is often helpful to hide them so you then see your elements displayed on a plain white background, much as they will look when printed. (The guides do not, of course, show when the document is printed.)

The View Menu, v. 4.1.

Bart Parker, *A Close Brush with Reality*, Visual Studies Workshop Press, Rochester, N.Y., 1981.

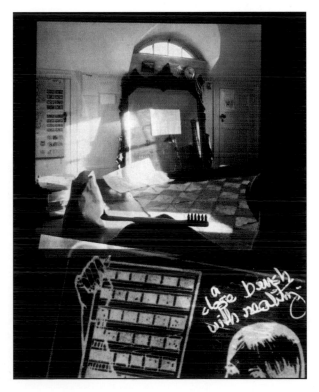

The *Baseline Grid* option is best appreciated by selecting this option on an open document. You will see that the baseline grid is a complex series of guides that can be useful to assist you when you wish to align text from page to page or fine tune the placement of your elements on the page. However, it does tend to clutter up your view of the page and you will find that you seldom need to use it.

The *Snap to Guides* option causes your guides to assume a kind of magnetic quality. If this option is selected you will see that as a picture or text box gets close to the guide the nearest edge of the box will "snap" into alignment with the guide.

The *Hide/Show Rulers* option makes the units of measurement either visible or invisible. The *Hide/Show Invisibles* option has already been discussed above.

The following options allow you to access the palettes available in the program. The *Hide/Show Tools* option either displays or hides the *Tool* palette, the functions of which were discussed early in this chapter, *pp. 82–84*. The same principle applies to the *Measurements* palette, the *Document Layout* palette and the *Colors* palette.

Although the *Measurements* palette and the *Document Layout* palette were discussed earlier, the *Colors* palette was not. This palette allows you to control the color of either your text or the box holding the text. Many of the operations can be better accessed in the *Style* menu for text, or the *Modify* option for the box. However, there is one thing that is best accessed through the *Colors* palette. This is the ability to create blends of color or shade as background for your box.

Referring to the illustration at the top of the page, when the third icon in the top box is selected then the background color(s) can be set either solid or to a choice of blend options. By placing the cursor over this box (which in this case shows the *Full Circular Blend*) a variety of blend options can be selected including rectangular and diamond shapes. You must assign two different colors and shades. You do this by selecting #1 and giving it a color and shade, and then repeat this step for #2.

The remaining options are best ignored at this stage.

Above:
The Colors Palette.
The third icon from the left, at the top of the palette, allows you select a blend which can be applied as the background color for either a text or picture box. You choose a blend type then select color #1 and color #2.

Rachel Siegel, *Faux-toes/Digit-eyes,*
Visual Studies Workshop Press,
Rochester, N.Y., 1999.

THE UTILITIES MENU

The *Utilities* menu contains various ancillary programs which can assist you to perform certain tasks. However, most of them you will not need to know until you have spent many hours becoming familiar with the program.

Of the options in this menu there are two that you will find useful immediately. For the others please refer to the manual that came with the program.

The *Check Spelling* option is a simple spell checking program that is useful if you have typed your text directly into QuarkXPress. However, if you have imported your text from a word processing document as advised in Chapter 2, *p. 19*, you should use the spell check in the word processing program where you prepared your text. The spell check in QuarkXPress is not as intuitive or as easy to use as the spell checks found in most word processing programs.

You can ignore the other options in this menu with the exception of the *Usage* option. This option lists the images and fonts you are using in your document. With respect to the pictures it indicates what their file type (i.e. TIFFS, PICTS, etc.) and whether they are OK to print. Similarly it will list the fonts used. This is extremely useful information. Your document will not print properly if picture files are missing, or the fonts you used are not installed in the computer from which you are printing. Most likely you will use this utility when you are using a computer at an institution and need to transfer the QuarkXPress file, the picture files and the fonts to a disk to take it elsewhere to be printed.

The Utilities Menu, v. 4.1.

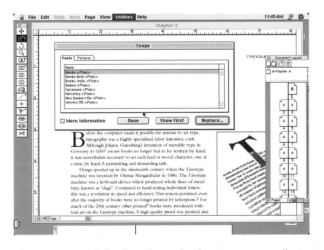

The *Usage, Font* dialog box shows the fonts you must collect when you take your document to be printed.

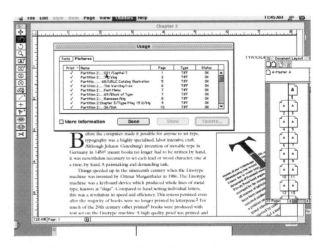

The *Usage, Picture* dialog box will indicate *(Status)* whether your images are *OK* to print, or whether they are *Missing*, or have been *Modified,* but not yet updated.

The Help Menu

Those of you familiar with the '90s television program, *Home Improvement,* will almost instinctively recognize the *Help* menu as being the close cousin of the Instruction Manual. As such it contains, as Tim Taylor would say, the "manufacturer's opinion" as to how to operate the program. Accordingly, the appropriate attitude to adopt is one of public scorn and private consultation. Use it to help you when you don't know what to do. Just make sure nobody is watching.

The Help Menu.
v. 4.1.

Conclusion

QuarkXPress is a powerful program. Its ability to combine text and images on the page, and alter their characteristics with great precision, makes it the perfect tool for bookmaking. As you gain practice and confidence you will appreciate more and more how the program can influence the appearance of your book. However, it is not necessary to use every single feature. Often the best books are characterized by simplicity and restraint, rather than flashy graphics and type. To be able to simply set type and place images on a page is in itself a wonderful thing. To be able to do this at home on your desk is almost miraculous. To produce a book of elegance and honesty you need only remember Jiminy Cricket's (paraphrased) advice: "always let your content be your guide."

You may wish to consider the opportunities presented by manually "tipping-in" images. In this case the artist has placed the image in the book in such a way as to cause it to fold against the gutter, imparting a three-dimensional quality to the double-page spread view.
Peter E. Charuk, *Men's Work III: Iron Hans.* Text by the Brothers Grimm, Sydney, 1998.

The Thin Man, Douglas Holleley, 1995. From the author's book, *Love Song.* Rockcorry, Woodford, New South Wales, 1995.

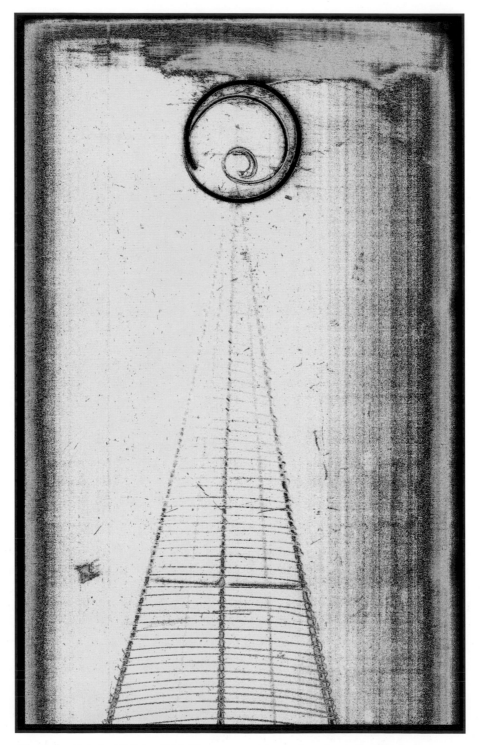

The Beacon, Douglas Holleley, 1996. Direct scanned image from the author's book, *Soft Landing in a Hard Place,* Rockcorry, Woodford, New South Wales, 1996.

Chapter 6

Scanning

I N this, and the following chapter, we will be using the program, Photoshop, to prepare images for your book. There are two main tasks. Firstly, to digitize, or scan images into the computer, so they can be imported into the page layout program. Secondly, to adjust these images so they print with the greatest possible quality. These tasks will be explained in detail, and you will need no prior knowledge of the program to be able to follow the instructions. Bear in mind however, that Photoshop is a complex program and can take many months, if not years, to master. This chapter, and the next, will tell you only what you need to know to scan and correct an image for the purposes of making a book. If you wish to know more, then you will have to either read the manual that comes with the program or consult one of the many books that specialize in this program. It is assumed that you are sufficiently computer literate to understand how to access a menu item and save a file.

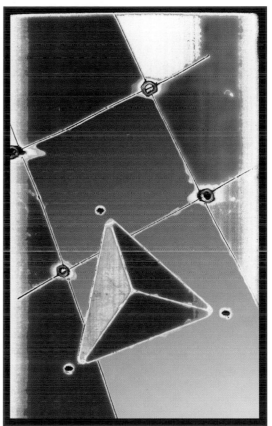

The Scanner

Images have to be digitized so they can be recognized by the computer. This process, termed *scanning*, is the first step where you exercise control over how your image, be it a print, negative or slide, will look when it is printed in your book.

Scanning is a process which "reads" an analog image and converts its information into digital code. The resulting *image file* can then be read by the computer and its image displayed on the monitor. This file consists of a grid, or *raster*, made up of small squares known as *pixels*. The appearance of your image is governed by how many of these pixels are used to approximate the continuous tone of your photograph. The more pixels you use, the finer the resolution of your image. The resolution of the scan is expressed in *pixels per inch*, (ppi).[1] The device that performs this operation is called a scanner. There are two main types.

The Memory of a Safer Place, Douglas Holleley. Scanned image from the book, *Soft Landing in a Hard Place.* Rockcorry, Woodford, New South Wales, 1996.

1. IMPORTANT NOTE: Although ppi is the correct terminology for image resolution, it has become common practice to use the measure dpi (dots per inch). This is both misleading and incorrect. However, in deference to popular usage, in this chapter we will use the term ppi/dpi to refer to image resolution.

The Flatbed Scanner

A flatbed scanner resembles a small photocopier. You
lift a lid to see a glass plate, usually US Letter size (8.5″
x 11″). Through the glass you can see a bar mounted
on a track. This bar moves beneath your image, reading
it a small portion at a time. In doing so the scanner
evaluates the image as a series of geometrically located
points, and assigns digital color and tone values to each
point, much like low-level aerial photographic
mapping. The result is re-assembled in order and
displayed on your screen. These scanners, for the most
part, do an excellent job of scanning flat artwork, such
as photographs, drawings, etchings or small paintings.
They work on the principle of reflected light, and your
flat artwork is simultaneously illuminated as it is read
by the electronic sensors.

   If you spend more money you can purchase a
flatbed scanner with a transparency adapter enabling
you to scan images with transmitted light. Thus you
can scan negatives and slides as well as prints. However,
unless you purchase a very expensive scanner of this
type, you will generally get poor results as a flatbed
scanner usually has low resolving power. It relies on the
sheer size of the original to gain its quality. This is an
important principle to understand. If your original is
large, say 8″ x 10″, then it can be scanned at relatively
low levels of resolution if it is to be reproduced at this size or smaller.
However, to enlarge a small negative or slide, you will need higher
levels of resolution to retain detail.

   The following example will make this more clear. To scan a 8″x 10″
photograph so it will be 150 dpi/ppi when printed at the same size, is
a simple matter with all flatbed scanners. However, to scan a 35mm
negative so that it will give you a 150 dpi/ppi image file when printed
at 8″x10″, you will have to scan the 1″x 1.5″ original at 1,000 dpi/ppi.
(See Table 6A, *p. 131*.) There are flatbed scanners which possess the
high levels of resolution necessary to permit this, but they are very
expensive.

   This is why the scale of your original artwork is critical. If you
have 4″x 5″ negatives to work from, then you need only have a scanner
which can scan at about 600 dpi/ppi to get an acceptable image when
printed at 8″x10″, a size suitable for most books. Originals smaller than
this however, are likely to be unsatisfactory when enlarged.

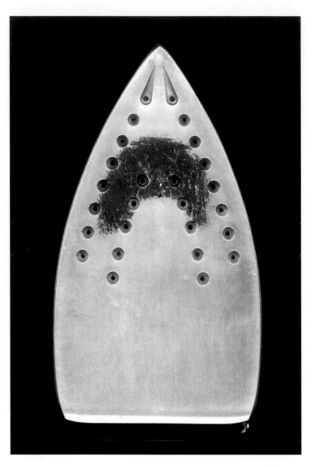

One of the great fascinations of flatbed
scanners is that you can use them to
image directly from objects. This
imaging technique is discussed in detail
in Chapter 8. Such scans can be left in
the "raw" state as in the example above
or they can form the basis for more
complex images which utilize the
many painting and transformative tools
of Photoshop to become colorful and
abstract compositions.
The Vaguely Familiar Object, Douglas
Holleley, 1995.

DEDICATED FILM SCANNERS

To overcome these problems you can use a dedicated film scanner. Such scanners are designed to work with the smaller scale of negatives and have a much higher resolving power. At the lower end of this category are scanners designed to scan only 35mm negatives. These scanners come in different levels of quality and usually cost more than low-end flatbed scanners. Even more sophisticated are scanners which will scan film of various formats, usually up to a maximum of 4″x 5″. Such scanners are expensive and generally out of the reach of most individuals. However, if you are a student, you will find that these days most colleges and universities have such a device that you can use.

The simplest film scanners use an array of light sensitive diodes which record the color and tone values of your negative. As you progress up the scale, both in technical sophistication and price, the scanning method changes. At the very high end, your negative is attached to a drum which revolves at high speed. As it revolves a laser reads the image in minute amounts. This process though highly accurate, is not speedy. High quality scans for large images can take up to an hour to complete. This combination of expensive equipment and slow operation can mean that such scans can be expensive if you commission an outside source to do it for you.

If you are interested in reading more about scanners, then you will need to refer to a more specialized book on digital imaging.[2]

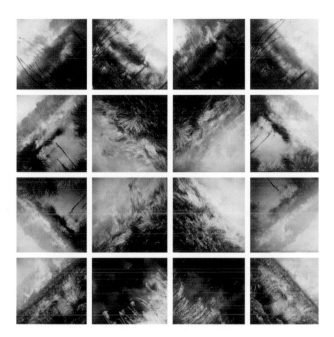

One of the great advantages of scanning pre-existing images is that you can either edition them, if they should be monoprints like the Polaroid SX–70 image shown above, or you can use the scan as a starting point to "re-visit" and transform images that otherwise may remained fixed in time.
Above: Fire on the Water, Georgia, Douglas Holleley, 1978.
Below: The Fiery Flood, Douglas Holleley, 1998. SX–70 multiple image, scanned and re-edited, 1998. From the author's book, *Adaminaby*, Rockcorry, Rochester, N.Y., 1998.

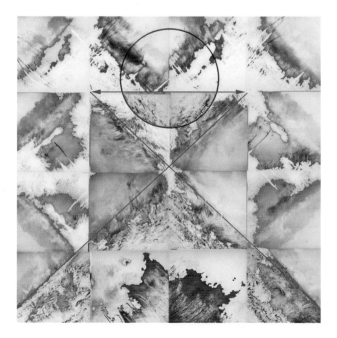

2. A useful text is the book,
Frank Cost, *Pocket Guide to Digital Printing,* Delmar Publishers, Albany, N.Y., 1997.

SCANNING YOUR IMAGES

For the purposes of this discussion we will assume you have a computer, attached to a scanner, that can be accessed through the program Photoshop. This is a reasonable assumption to make as these days scanner manufacturers have accepted the ubiquity of this program, and supply "plug-in" software that allows the image to be directly imported into Photoshop. All have a similar interface. As such, the following discussion will not discuss particular devices, but instead address the principles common to all scanners and their operation.

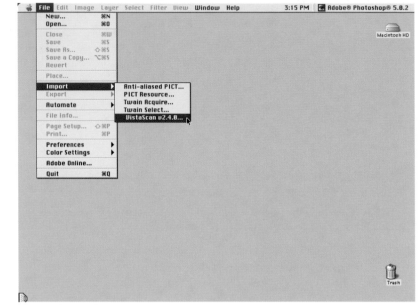

You will find the scanner software and user interface by going to the *File* menu and looking for the *Acquire* or *Import* option. (This will vary according to what version of Photoshop you have.) When you find this, slide across to the list of sub-options and identify which of them is connected to your scanner. Usually the brand name and model of the scanner is mentioned in the menu and this is the option you select. Thus if you have a Jade scanner, the option may well be labeled "Jade." (Some scanners do not directly mention the brand name of the hardware. For example, Umax scanners use software called VistaScan. Either try all the options until the interface appears or consult your scanner manual.)

Most scanners require that they are switched on before the computer is turned on. This way the computer "recognizes" the fact that a scanner is connected. If you forget to do this you may see a warning box which announces that the computer cannot find the scanner. If this occurs, first turn everything off. Then turn the scanner on, wait until it has finished making its start up noises and the ready light is on, then restart the computer.

If your scanner is correctly installed, and you have followed the correct start up procedure, a dialog box will appear on the screen when you select it from the *Acquire* or *Import* menu. Usually this box has a preview window where your image will appear when it is scanned. You will also see controls to adjust brightness, contrast and color. Other options can often extend well past this level of control and can be quite intimidating. Usually, it is best to trust the default settings.

This diagram shows the *File* menu of Photoshop open and the software for a flatbed scanner selected. In this case the choice is VistaScan. However, this will vary according to what brand of scanner and/or scanner software you have installed. After releasing the mouse on this choice the scanner window will open and you will see an interface that will mostly likely look something like the one on the opposite page.

Opposite:
As this image demonstrates, you are not restricted to scanning a single image. You can use the platen of the flatbed scanner to arrange a number of images so that the scanner digitizes a complete photo-collage.
The Kiss, Douglas Holleley, 1995. From the author's book, *Love Song,* Rockcorry, Woodford, New South Wales, 1995.

On the whole this is sensible advice as most modifications are usually best made in Photoshop, after the image has been imported. (There are exceptions of course to this rule which include unusually dark or unusually light "high key" images and images that exhibit other unusual tonal characteristics. Such images are usually in the minority.)

Place your print in the flatbed scanner, or your negative or slide in the film scanner. If using a flatbed, ensure that the print is square on the platen. This will avoid the need to waste time rotating your image in Photoshop if you scan it in crooked.

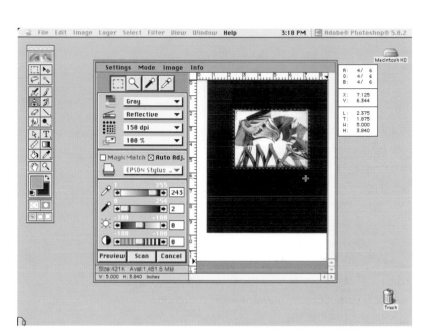

Similarly, follow the instructions when placing film in the film scanner. Again, make sure it is square and correctly oriented, with the emulsion facing the right way. There will be instructions to help you do this. Often the scanner will come with two film holders, one for strips of negatives, and one for mounted slides.

Now return to the scanner interface. As mentioned before, ignore the manual adjustments, especially the brightness and contrast controls. These are invariably crude. If you use them you run the risk of losing information on the scan. Nine times out of ten, the scanner's software will make exposure and contrast choices satisfactorily. The most critical control you can exercise at this point is the degree of resolution that your scan will have. This issue warrants detailed discussion.

This is the dialog box for a typical scanner. Because there are so many different brands, you will most likely find that yours will differ from this in layout. However, the principles are the same.

What you must do manually is set the *resolution*, the *mode* (i.e. grayscale, RGB color, etc.) and consider any *scaling*. The whole art of scanning is to consider resolution, the final printed size and the method by which the image will eventually be printed. Read this chapter in its entirety if this is the first time you are scanning an image.

As advised in the text, unless you have had considerable experience, trust the default settings when it comes to brightness and contrast. When in doubt leave (or set) them so the shadow is set at 0 and the highlight set at 255 as shown above. In this way you will maximize your chances of keeping the scan "in range" so that all of the detail and tonal information of the original image is retained in the scan.

RESOLUTION

Selecting resolution in digital photography is a contentious issue. Photographers, long accustomed to working with materials which (when used properly) reproduce the appearance of the world in continuous tone with amazing sharpness and resolution, are often perplexed by the digital medium. They find it difficult to understand that resolution is not like the given properties of a piece of film or paper, but is instead, a choice that one can make. To those accustomed to working with the beauty and detail of film and photo-paper this notion seems absurd. You

often hear the question: why choose a lower level of resolution when you can stipulate any level of resolution you so desire? And if you can so choose, why then a low level?

The fact is that the electronic file is not like a negative. A negative is a physical, self-contained, discreet and immutable object. It stays the same whether you are making a postcard sized print, or enlarge it to fill a gallery wall. All the information it contains is locked into its silver grains (or color dye molecules) and this information remains constant, irrespective of the final print size.

In comparison, an electronic image file is a rendition of this negative, and thus is much more like a print or duplicate negative, than the negative itself.[3] More importantly, it is prepared for a particular purpose. For example, the scan you would make of an image to appear on a web page is quite different from the scan you make if you were planning to reproduce the photograph at billboard size. To photographers, accustomed to working with an original matrix that is always of the highest possible optical quality, the thought that this negative when translated to a digital file can be of different sizes for different applications, can seem a wasted opportunity for achieving the highest possible quality when the image is printed. However, as we will see (overleaf), if there is too much information in your scan, it will simply be discarded when the file is sent to the printer.

If you look at the dialog box of the scanner interface you will see that to reproduce a 4″x 5″ image same size (100%) at 150 ppi/dpi you will have a file size of 421K. However, if you intend to print the image larger you will have to scan at much higher levels of resolution so that when the image is enlarged it will still be printing at 150 dpi/ppi. For example to print this image 33″x 42.5″ at 150 ppi/dpi, the scanning resolution was 1275 ppi/dpi and the file size was 30MB.

3. This of course is not true for images produced on a digital camera. In this case the "negative," or more correctly the original matrix, is an electronic file of fixed size.

RESOLUTION AND PRINTING CONSIDERATIONS

When scanning you must consider how the image will be printed. The assumption will be made that the book will be printed on either a desktop laser or inkjet printer. For these devices the images should be scanned so that they are 225 dpi/ppi at the finished print size. To all practical purposes, resolution above this level adds little or nothing to the appearance of the finished image. This is because desktop printers have relatively low levels of resolution, despite the fact that they can reproduce images with remarkable fidelity.

To understand this fully it is necessary to realize that printers cannot reproduce a continuous tone image without first translating it into a series of discrete dots. This process is called *screening*. A continuous tone image (for example, a photograph) when rendered as a series of dots is called a *halftone* image.

Visualize a printing screen as a transparent plastic sheet with opaque ruled lines drawn perpendicular to each other at regular intervals. To make a screened negative for an offset printing plate, the image is exposed onto film, through the screen. This process forms dots of different sizes, even though the holes of the screen remain constant. Larger ones are created where there is more light (in the shadows) and smaller ones where there is less (in the highlights). These can then be rendered in ink of a single color, in a single pass of the press, giving the illusion of continuous tone. (See *p. 188.*)

Careful consideration of resolution is essential to keep files manageable. After the image on the opposite page was colored and then converted to an RGB file the file size rose to 90MB. The print was made on an Iris printer which can produce beautiful prints at a resolution of 150 ppi/dpi. *San Pietro, Italy*, Douglas Holleley. Photographed 1989, digitally modified and printed 1999.

The closer the ruled lines of the screen are to each other, the finer the dot. The dot size is described by the term screen ruling which refers to the number of ruled lines per inch *(lpi)*. Screens with fewer than about 80 lines per inch (commonly found in newspapers) are considered coarse. Screen rulings of 100 to 150 lines per inch are considered medium to fine. Most good quality magazines are printed in this range. Screen rulings as fine as 200, even 300 lines per inch are possible, but are difficult to make and print. They are only found in (expensive) books of very high quality.

PostScript software replicates this process by mathematically translating the pixels of the image file into printable dots. This process is called raster image processing *(rip)*. Each dot is calculated from the information of about one and a half to two pixels. Any more than two pixels for each dot formed by the rip, is not counted and thus wasted—one pixel or less and the rip does not have enough data to calculate an accurate dot.

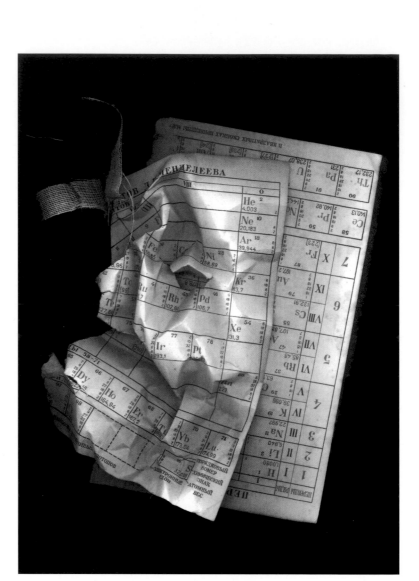

This information is then "drawn" on the paper by the printer, dot by dot. (The higher the resolution of the printer, the finer it can draw these halftone dots.) Do not mistake the resolution of the printer, expressed in dpi, with the size of the actual printed halftone dot, expressed in lpi. To understand the distinction it is helpful to use the word "spot" to describe the halftone dot the printer draws, rather than dot. Depending on the size of the line screen, the printer will have to use several of its fixed size dots to draw each spot convincingly. For example:

To draw a 60 lpi spot,
      the printer must have a resolution of 300 dpi.
To draw a 100 lpi spot,
      the printer must have a resolution of 1600 dpi.
To draw a 150 lpi spot,
      the printer must have a resolution of 2450 dpi.

If you are a novice it is quite normal to find the material in this chapter complex and somewhat unnerving. However, as you begin to print your book, the principles will become clearer as you test them in practice.

Most of these issues need only be considered in detail if you are sending your book out to be printed. If this is the case then talk with the printer before you begin to scan. However, if you are going to use a desktop printer you will obtain excellent results if you ensure that the image resolution is 150 ppi/dpi at the size it will be when printed.

The Table Fable, Douglas Holleley, 1994. From the author's book, *Love Song.* Rockcorry, Woodford, New South Wales, 1995.

As you can see, the relationship between dpi and lpi is not one-to-one. In fact, it is far from it. A 1400 dpi printer can only draw about 95 printable dots per inch.

It should also now be clear why image resolution in this chapter is expressed as dpi/ppi (dots per inch/pixels per inch). Strictly speaking, dpi refers only to printer resolution. The term ppi should be reserved for describing the resolution of the scanned image. The term dpi/ppi is used here to acknowledge common (if incorrect) usage. It is essential to understand the difference between these two measures. It can lead to the common error of assuming that if the resolution of the printer is 600 dpi, then you must scan your image at 600 dpi/ppi. This is quite incorrect. As mentioned above, to create a printable dot, the printer needs the information contained in about 2 pixels. (The exact amount is about 1.6 pixels.)

Thus a 600 dpi printer, with a screen ruling of about 80 lpi, needs a scan of only about 120 dpi at the size the image will be when reproduced.

The Implication

Thus when scanning you must consider, not the resolution of the printer expressed in dpi, but instead the size of the actual printed dot, as defined by the screen ruling. To do this you multiply the screen ruling by the amount of information the rip needs to calculate each printable dot. A 1400 dpi printer can only produce a printable dot of about 95 lpi. The image resolution for such a printer is thus 95 x 1.6 or 152 ppi. It thus follows, that theoretically, one need only scan at 150 dpi/ppi if you intend printing on an average–to–good desktop printer. However, in practice, it is a good idea to leave a margin for safety. It is for this reason the value of 225 dpi/ppi is recommended.

Although the issues discussed in this section pertain particularly to PostScript printing, random-dot inkjet printers exhibit a similar relationship between printer resolution and the printable halftone dot. Even though each method renders the image in different ways, much the same factors are at work when deciding image resolution.

The subject of screen ruling is also discussed in Chapter 9, *Printing the Book*. You will see in the collage above, scanned from a found (destroyed) LP album cover, evidence of the screen which creates the illusion of continuous tone in a printed image. The exaggeration of the halftone screen when material is scanned is a common phenomenon. It is best addressed by not engaging in this practice at all as usually it means you are using a photograph that is not yours. See Chapter 12.
Group Pressure, Douglas Holleley, 1993.

RESOLUTION AND IMAGE SIZE

Resolution also must consider the finished size of the image. Without knowing what the final size of the image will be when printed, decisions about resolution are meaningless.

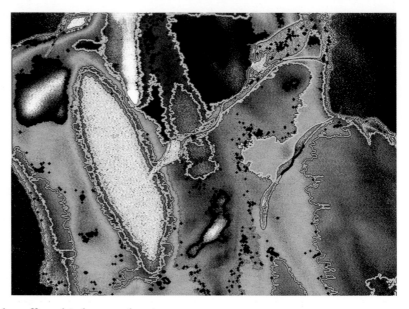

It is appreciated that this is not always practical. You may, as you lay out your book, change the size of an image to suit the content and your expressive concerns. However, there is one given which will assist you make this decision. This is the size of the book. The image cannot be bigger than the page (sometimes a double page) so there is no need to scan any larger than this. Do not be tempted to scan at the highest possible resolution and overlook the effect this has on the size of the image. You need only scan your image so it is the correct size for the page and the level of resolution you need for your device, and no more.

It is important to understand that the resolution varies as you change the size of your image. Equally true is the obverse. The size of your image will change as you change the level of resolution. It is important to understand this principle as different scanners use different methods to allocate resolution.

To apply this when scanning, you will have to look carefully at the interface of the scanner. Some scanners (particularly film scanners) have the ability to control the size of the scanned image by *scaling* as they scan. If there is a scaling choice it will be expressed in terms of a percentage value. Thus if you scan the image at 100% it will be scanned at the same size as the original.

To scale a print at 400% means to multiply its dimensions by four. Thus if you scale a 35mm negative, which has an image area of 1.5″ x 1″, at 400%, you multiply each dimension by 4, giving you a print size of 6″ x 4″. This is less of an issue with flatbed scanners where the size of the original is usually US Letter size, and thus big enough to fit your book. If anything you may have to reduce the size. (Scaling values less than 100% will permit this.) However, 35mm negatives or slides will almost always require some degree of enlargement.

Thus if there is a scaling option you can stipulate the *finished*, printed level of resolution in the resolution field, and then adjust the

When using certain equipment sometimes decisions are made for you. This image is "grabbed" from a video source. As such the file size is pre-determined by the nature of the equipment. There is quite simply a limit to how large it can be printed. Do not always search for the "ideal" solution. Instead view the resources available to you as a source of participation, if not inspiration, rather than a limitation.
An Escapist's Response to a Buffalo Blizzard, Douglas Holleley, 1997.

Size of original negative	Nominated resolution when scanning	Scaled using the scanner interface	Actual resolution when scanning	Print size	Actual resolution at print size	File size
35mm (1″ x 1.5″)	150 dpi/ppi	100%	150 dpi/ppi	1.5″ x 1.0″	150 dpi/ppi	33K
35mm (1″ x 1.5″)	150 dpi/ppi	400%	600 dpi/ppi	6″ x 4″	150 dpi/ppi	528K
35mm (1″ x 1.5″)	150 dpi/ppi	600%	900 dpi/ppi	9″ x 6″	150 dpi/ppi	1.16MB
35mm (1″ x 1.5″)	225 dpi/ppi	100%	225 dpi/ppi	1.5″ x 1.0″	225 dpi/ppi	75K
35mm (1″ x 1.5″)	225 dpi/ppi	400%	900 dpi/ppi	6″ x 4″	225 dpi/ppi	1.16MB
35mm (1″ x 1.5″)	225 dpi/ppi	600%	1350 dpi/ppi	9″ x 6″	225 dpi/ppi	2.61MB
35mm (1″ x 1.5″)	300 dpi/ppi	100%	300 dpi/ppi	1.5″ x 1.0″	300 dpi/ppi	132K
35mm (1″ x 1.5″)	300 dpi/ppi	400%	1200 dpi/ppi	6″ x 4″	300 dpi/ppi	2.06MB
35mm (1″ x 1.5″)	300 dpi/ppi	600%	1800 dpi/ppi	9″ x 6″	300 dpi/ppi	4.64MB

TABLE 6A

INTER-RELATIONSHIP BETWEEN SCALING, RESOLUTION AND FILE SIZE FOR 35MM FORMAT

The File size indicated is for a grayscale image. To estimate the File Size for RGB Files multiply it by three.

Note: File sizes are measured by how many bits of information they contain. A bit is a single "yes or no" instruction. Eight such instruction sets form a byte. One thousand and twenty four bytes (2^{10} bits) to are called a kilobyte (K). A megabyte (MB), is 1024^2 or 1,048,576 bytes.

scaling so this level of resolution will apply, not to the current size of the print or negative being scanned, but to the size it will be when printed. The table above shows the role of scaling in the scanning process.

Thus if you want to scan a 35mm image to be 225 dpi/ppi at 9″ x 6″, you can select a resolution of 225 dpi/ppi, if you scale the image to 600%. However, some scanners do not have a scaling option. In this case you will have to alter the resolution while you scan to reflect the change in effective resolution when the print is re-sized to fit your page. Table 6A is also useful for this purpose. Thus, using the same example you can ignore the scaling, and instead scan the original image at 100% using a resolution of 1,350 dpi/ppi.

Take the time to examine this table and be sure you understand thoroughly the principles that lie behind it. Nothing wastes more time as questions about resolution without an accompanying description of the final printed size. At the risk of repetition, the correct resolution is the best compromise between the size of your original artwork, its finished size in the book, and the type of printer being used.

RESOLUTION: PROCESSING AND STORAGE CONSIDERATIONS

In addition to the previous considerations, you must also consider the practical necessity of processing and storing all your image and page layout files. Photoshop requires about five times the amount of processing memory (RAM) as the file size to process an image efficiently. Thus to use an example from Table 6A, a grayscale 9″x 6″ image with resolution of 150 dpi/ppi will have a file size of 1.16MB and thus will require about 6MB of RAM to process. In comparison a grayscale 9″x 6″ image with resolution of 300 dpi/ppi will have a file size of 4.64MB and require about 23MB of RAM to process. If the images are in color, you will have to multiply all the above figures by a factor of three.

Additionally, you must consider the storage of your files. A book of twenty images, if each file is 12MB, will require a disk, or series of disks, with a capacity of 240MB. To this you must also add space for the fonts, and the QuarkXPress file itself, which can get quite large as your document grows. You can scan your work at high resolution, but at the end of the day you will need a place to store these files.

If you have access to a CD burner which can store up to 650MB of data, then storage is less of a problem. However, if you are relying on disks of around 100MB it is necessary to carefully consider the size (scale), resolution and subsequent file size of your scans. The simple message is that all of the variables involved in the production of your book will affect your decision about resolution and file size.

SCANNING MODE

The next decision is in which mode to scan. This is a relatively easy decision. If the image is monochrome then you will scan in gray scale, if it is color, then scan in color.

However, most scanners offer a range of options within these broad categories. Often film scanners have settings for specific brands and emulsions in addition to generic descriptions such as color negative, color slide, black and white negative, etc. If the scanner has an option that is specifically related to your film type then choose this.

Also, depending on the scanner, there will be an option called line art, black and white or bitmap. All refer to the same thing. In this mode the scanner will read the image and simply decide whether the portion of the image it is reading is either under or over middle gray.

Sometimes all the calculations in the world are overtaken by sheer practical necessity. The above image was digitally "hand-colored" in Photoshop when the author had a very low-powered computer. In order to be able to complete the image in less than a week it was necessary to have a very small file size.

Despite the fact that one can enlarge images to an extent by interpolation, in this case when I attempted to do this, both the hand-applied gradients and fills, and the remaining photographic information, became so blurred that the believability of the image was threatened. Consequently this image cannot be printed much larger than 2″x3″.

Painted Towers, Luna Park, Sydney, Douglas Holleley, 1995. From the author's Ph.D. thesis, *Luna Park, the Image of a Funfair.* University of Sydney, 1997.

If under, it will record it as pure black, if over, it will record it as pure white. Because the decisions are simple (each pixel is either on or off, black or white) you can scan at extremely high levels of resolution and still have a very small file. This option is used if fine line artwork is to be scanned. It may seem paradoxical, but simple line art requires considerably more definition than a photographic image. The hardest thing a computer can do is represent a line in a pixel based (or raster) image, particularly an angled line or a curve. The pixels have to be extremely small to permit the line to be represented without jagged edges.

In Summary…

- Resolution is a relative, not absolute, quality. A scan is a rendition of the original image, prepared for a specific task.

- Most desktop printers have relatively low levels of resolution. Their effective screen ruling is about 100 lpi. However, manufacturers usually express the printer's resolution in dots/inch. (This sounds much better!) Often values as high as 1440 dpi are claimed. Do not confuse this measure with either the screen ruling (lpi) or the image resolution (ppi).

- A simple rule of thumb to determine scanning resolution is to double the screen ruling of the printer.

- The size of the finished, printed image must be considered when scanning.

- Practical issues of processing and storage also require consideration.

- When in doubt, excellent results from all *desktop* printers can be obtained by scanning at 225 dpi/ppi *at the size the image will appear when printed.*

The Seemingly Safe Haven, Douglas Holleley, 1995. From the author's book, *Soft Landing in a Hard Place*, Rockcorry, Woodford, 1996.

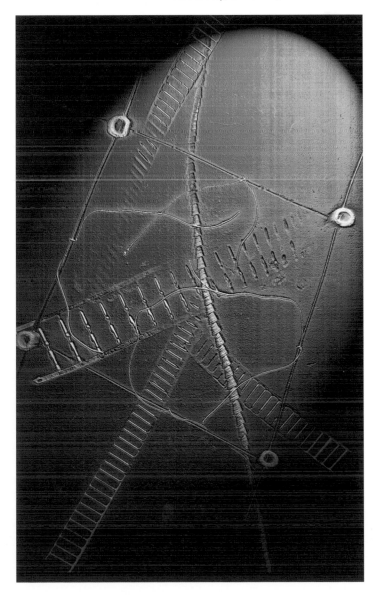

Making the Scan

Usually there will be a button labeled *Pre-scan* (or *Preview)*, and another labeled *Scan*. Click on the *Pre-scan* button. The scanner will now make a preliminary scan of the image. Usually a preview of the image will appear, either in the scanner window or on the desk top.

When this preview displays you will most likely find that there are little crop lines, much like the picture boxes in QuarkXPress. Move these lines adjacent to the image so there is no white (or black) border showing, and only the image area is defined for scanning. As the scanner will evaluate the image for color and density before commencing its final scan you do not wish it to factor into its calculations non-image areas such as borders, either black or white, that may be present.[4]

Some scanners at the pre-scan stage offer a histogram of the image. If this is the case it can be used to check that all of the image is falling within the range of the digital tone scale without losing either shadow or highlight detail. Histograms will be discussed shortly. (See *Checking the Range of the Scan, pp. 136–137.)*

Having defined your scanning area, make your scan by clicking on the *Scan* button. When the scan is complete it will appear as an "untitled" image on your desktop and will be in Photoshop, ready to be checked and then subsequently titled, saved, adjusted and corrected.

4. Allowing borders into the scan can be a useful method of control. If an image persistently fails to retain highlight detail, leaving a white border around the image can often "trick" the scanner into thinking there are more highlights than there actually are, and thus make a scan which favors retention of detail in these areas.

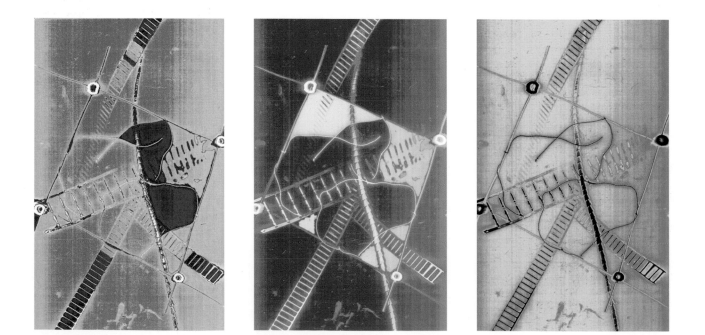

CHECKING THE SIZE AND RESOLUTION OF THE IMAGE

In Photoshop, go to the *Image* menu and select *Image Size*. A dialog box like the one below will open. It will display the following data about your image.

The top third of the box displays the *Pixel Dimensions* of the image. In this case it is 2250 x 1775 pixels and the file size is a manageable 3.81MB. Proceeding to the next box we can see the *Print Size* of the image expressed in inches and the *Resolution* at this size. In this case the image is about 10"x 8" and the resolution is 225 dpi/ppi. Thus we know that the image comfortably satisfies the resolution requirements of a desktop inkjet printer, as long as it stays this size or less. Having verified the settings in this way we must now perform one final check to make sure the image will ultimately print satisfactorily

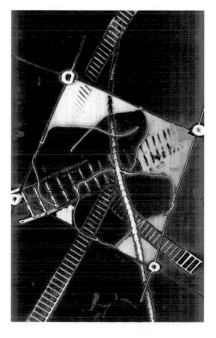

The four images to the left, and *The Seemingly Safe Haven* reproduced on the previous page, are all variations derived from a single direct scan. Originally it was made from a number of small pieces of scrap metal suspended over a flatbed scanner from a contraption made of coat hanger wire and bamboo. The variations show how a scan, once made, becomes a matrix of potential that has the possibility of being realized in many different ways.
Various Variations, Douglas Holleley, 1996.

After scanning check the resolution and size of your scan in the *Image Size* window found in the *Image* menu of Photoshop. Here you can ascertain whether the scan will suit the scale of your book at the level of resolution you have decided is appropriate, having considered all the variables discussed in the chapter so far.

CHECKING THE RANGE OF THE SCAN

You will recall that earlier a reference was made to the histogram. The histogram is a diagrammatic representation of the dispersal of color and tonal values of your image on the digital tonal scale. Go to the *Image* menu. Under *Adjust* you will see the choice *Levels.*

There is much valuable information presented in this dialog box. The horizontal axis of the graph represents all the possible tones of gray that the computer is capable of rendering. The left-hand side represents the deepest black and the right-hand side, pure white. Within these two

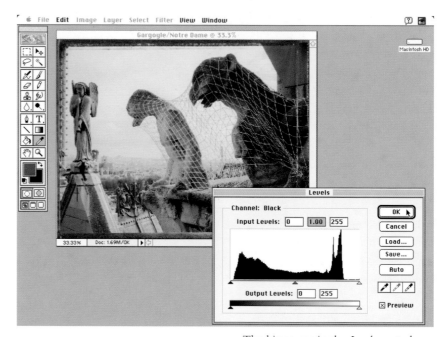

poles are 256 shades of grey. Value 0 is counted which is why the scale stops at 255. The varying height of the histogram shows how many pixels, or how much of the image, is assigned to each of these points on the tone scale. Readers familiar with the zone system may find it useful to think of the far left as zone 1 and the far right, paper base or zone 9. However, in the digital scale, between these two extremes are not nine zones, but 256 shades of gray.

It is helpful to relate the histogram's distribution of pixels to areas of tone within the image. For example, the large cluster of pixels at the right-hand side, or highlight section of the scale, corresponds to the area of sky. You will observe that there are relatively few middle grays represented on the histogram. These areas correspond to the small area occupied by the rooftops and the gray areas of the left gargoyle. There is another hump on the left-hand side, or shadow section of the scale, which corresponds to the large amount of shadow on the right-hand side of the image.

However, the most important thing to check is that the histogram falls totally within the 256 gray scale range. The area to the left of the shadows has no pixels at all. Similarly at the right-hand of the histogram all of the highlights fall well within range. This means that the image has been scanned in such a way that all the highlight and shadow detail has been successfully retained.[5]

A histogram of a bad scan, looks quite different. It will show instead that the image has been cut off or "clipped" at either the shadow or highlight end.

The histogram in the *Levels* control will indicate whether the highlights and shadows of the scan fall within the range of the digital tone scale. If the histogram is "clipped" at either the highlight or shadow end, detail has been irretrievably lost. If this occurs you must rescan the image until all the information is registered on the scale.

5. This is the histogram of a grayscale image. If we were looking at a color image the histogram would be a composite graph of the red, green and blue channels combined. By going to the Channel selector at the top of the dialog box you could select and view each of the separate channels for the Red, Green and Blue information, which when added together (as light) give you the full color image.

The example below shows a histogram where the highlight detail has failed to register. Sometimes it seems Photoshop can do anything you can imagine. However, it cannot create information where none exists. Thus if the histogram looks like the illustration below, highlight detail has been lost forever. If this occurs there is no choice but to re-scan the image, perhaps reducing the brightness (or including some white border as discussed in *Footnote 4, Page 134)*, to ensure that all of the data in the original image is rendered within the 256 step gray scale.

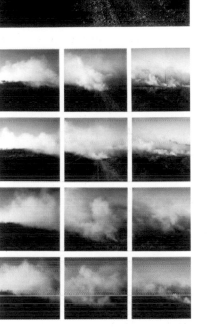

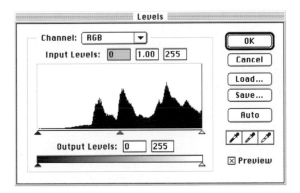

Left:
An example of a histogram showing an image with no highlight detail.

For the photographers reading this, think of this particular histogram as a diagrammatic representation of a print made from an overexposed and overdeveloped negative. In such a case, all highlight detail is "blocked up" and impenetrably dense in the negative, resulting in blank highlights in the print.

To carry the photographic analogy further, think of the histogram as a kind of photograph of your photograph. Just as you try, by altering the exposure and development of your film, to get a negative which best "fits" the tonal range of your subject, so do you need a scan, which similarly best "fits" the tonal range of your negative, slide or print.

Some scanner interfaces have a histogram built into the scanner software. This is useful as it enables you to check the histogram at the pre-scan stage, before you make the final scan. This saves a lot of time.

Having satisfied yourself of the values of the scan, continue scanning, checking each image in this way as you proceed, until you have collected all the images you require for the book. It is good practice to save them as you scan to both conserve memory and ensure that if something happens (like a power failure or system freeze) you do not lose all your work.

Above and Below:
When making a book you may need to scan and present your work differently to the way it was originally conceived. This image was spread over two pages when published, but when exhibited was arranged as above. *Burning Kikuyu Grass.* From the book: Douglas Holleley, *Visions of Australia,* Angus and Robertson, Sydney, 1979.

SAVING YOUR SCAN

If you look at the *Save As* dialog box in
Photoshop you will see the following
options under the box labeled *Format.*

You will notice that there a large
number of choices available. As a general
rule of thumb, select TIFF for page layout
programs and PICT for audio-visual
purposes. Of course there are many
subtleties and variations to this somewhat
simple advice, and other formats will work
in QuarkXPress, notably JPEG, EPS, and
to a lesser (and slower) extent even PICT.
However, if you always choose the TIFF
file option you can be sure your document
will print easily, and with fewer errors,
than any other file format.

Scanners usually scan the images in
RGB mode. Save the image in this mode.
(See Chapter 9, *Printing the Book, pp. 186–187.*)

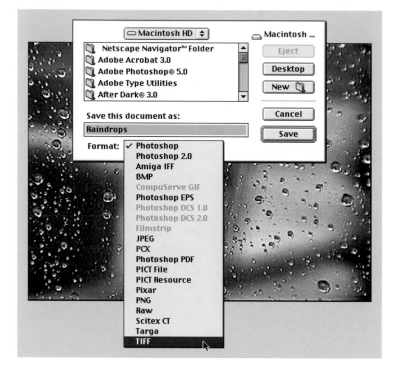

THE PHOTO CD AND
CUSTOM SCANNING

You do not have to own a scanner to digitize your images. A particularly useful service is that offered by Kodak, who at the time of
processing your film, can also make scans directly from your negatives
and record them on a compact disk. These are relatively inexpensive
and are of excellent quality. The scans are made directly from the film
negative and come in five levels of resolution so there is a file size
suitable for most purposes. This method is highly recommended, even
if you have a flatbed scanner. As they come directly from the negative,
and are color corrected in much the same way as the prints, you are
starting with a scan that is of reasonable quality both in range and
color correction.

An additional benefit is that unlike the prints, the scans are not
cropped. The whole image area is represented on the file. If you
compare most commercially prepared prints with the actual negative,
you will find that you are losing as much as 25% of your photograph.
This is because most photo labs have film carriers that obscure the
edge of the negative.

Above:
You can see that there are a variety of
formats from which you can choose to
save your scan. Of them, TIFF works
with the fewest problems when
working with a page layout program
such as QuarkXPress, Pagemaker or
InDesign.

Why they do this is difficult to understand. It may be as simple as compensating for the fact that the average snap shooter stands too far away from the subject. However, I would hope any reader of this book would be more careful with his or her composition than that. Such intrusions on the frame are not made for aesthetic reasons, but are simply mechanistic crops for their own sake. Thus using machine-made prints as raw material for scanning, is not recommended. Even qualitative judgements as simple as whether to use, or not use, an image, based on these prints, must be exercised with caution.

This CD writing service is best suited (and most affordable) for the 35mm format. Film larger than this requires more sophisticated equipment and it is correspondingly more expensive as these formats are less common, and economies of automation and demand do not factor in moderating the price as they do with the more ubiquitous 35mm format.

OPENING THE PHOTO CD

The Minor Monument, Douglas Holleley, 1992.

You will notice when you put your CD in the CD ROM drive that its icon appears on the desktop. If you double click on the icon you will see that you have the option to view your images as a slide show. If you double click on the slide show icon you will see all of the images displayed on your screen, one after the other, as if you were watching a conventional slide show. If you are seeing your images for the first time this is a good way to preview the contents of the entire CD. You will notice as the slide show progresses that the file number of the image is displayed in the corner. You may wish to watch the slide show a few times before choosing your images. Note the file number(s) of any images you may wish to use in your book.

After watching the slide show you will see there is a folder entitled "Photos." This folder contains the scans of each of your photographs. Each image has been scanned at five different levels of resolution each for a different purpose.

The sizes are indicated by the pixel dimensions. The smallest is 192 x 128 pixels and the largest 3072 x 2048 pixels. The smallest size, when opened, gives you an image suitable for an image on a web page. (The file size is 72K and the physical dimensions are 2.7″ x 1.8″ at a screen resolution of 72 dpi/ppi. This is obviously unsuitable for use in a book unless the image was to be used as a very small element of a layout.) More useful are the two largest folders. The folder 1536 x 1034 for example, will give you an image 7″ x 5″ at about 225 dpi/ppi.

The following table will help you decide which file size is suitable for your needs.

Pixel Dimensions	Size in inches @ 150 dpi/ppi	Size in inches @ 225 dpi/ppi	Size in inches @ 300 dpi/ppi	File Size
192 x 128	1.3 x 1.8	0.85 x 0.57	0.64 x 0.43	72K
384 x 256	2.5 x 1.7	1.7 x 1.14	1.3 x 0.85	288K
768 x 512	5.1 x 3.4	3.4 x 2.3	2.5 x 1.7	1.3MB
1536 x 1034	10 x 6.8	6.6 x 4.6	5.0 x 3.4	4.5MB
3072 x 2048	20.5 x 13.6	13.7 x 9.0	10 x 6.8	18MB

TABLE 6B
OPENING THE PHOTO CD

Use this table to choose the most appropriate folder when opening from the Photo CD. For book work, the most frequently accessed folder is 1536 x 1034.

There is no absolutely correct choice. You must select a size that is appropriate to the size of your book, the printer you intend to employ and the amount of computer speed, RAM and storage you possess to be able to process and store the files without waiting all day, or having to spend large amounts of money on storage media. For most purposes the highlighted folder 1536 x 1034, will give you a reasonable compromise between quality and ease of operation. Surprisingly, images from this folder are seemingly sharper, even when enlarged through interpolation, than the images in the 3072 x 2048 folder. Thus if you prefer working with higher levels of resolution, and/or need to print an image larger than 7″ x 5″, this folder is still the best choice. You will, however, need to interpolate the image to maintain a resolution of 225 ppi/dpi. (See *pp. 163–164.*)

When you open a folder you will see that the images are arranged in order and are viewed as a series of thumbnails, or miniature representations of the image. You will find that if you double click on them, they will not open in Photoshop. Instead a box will appear that asks you whether you would like to open them (if using a Macintosh computer) in the program, *Simple Text*. This of course will not allow you to correct your images as you could in Photoshop.

Instead, launch Photoshop and then go to the *File* menu and select *Open*. Click *Desktop* and the Photo CD will appear as one of the choices. Click on this. Then select the folder labeled *Photos* and then select the folder that holds the images in the size you wish to employ. (For example, the folder labeled 1536 x 1034.) The images will then appear in a list, and a preview image will appear in the dialog box as you scroll through the list.

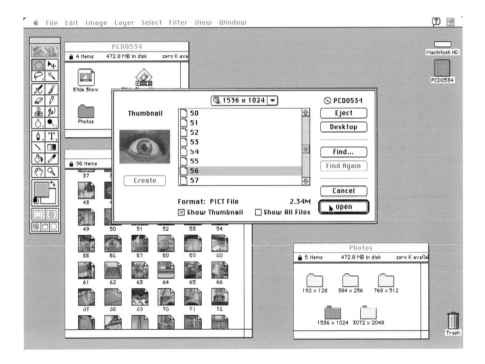

Here you can see an image being selected from a Photo CD prior to being opened. For most book work, the folder labeled 1536 x 1034 (pixels) is the most satisfactory choice. Surprisingly, the images scanned at 3072 x 2048 (pixels) seem less sharp. If unconvinced, try a few tests before settling on a system of your own.

Having done this, select the *Save As* option from the *File* menu and save this image as a TIFF file. Title and save it in a suitable location so that you will be able to both recognize and find it when you need to. All scanned images will require some correction in order to print with maximum quality. In the following chapter this process is explained in detail.

Another variation of the scanned image reproduced on *p. 123* of this chapter. This image is from the author's book, *Adaminaby*, Rockcorry, Rochester, N.Y., 1999.

These images were photographed on 35mm film and scanned by Photo CD. They have been first corrected and then modified considerably. In some cases areas of the image have been replaced with solid "fills" of color. From the author's Ph.D. thesis, *Luna Park, the Image of a Funfair,* University of Sydney, 1997.

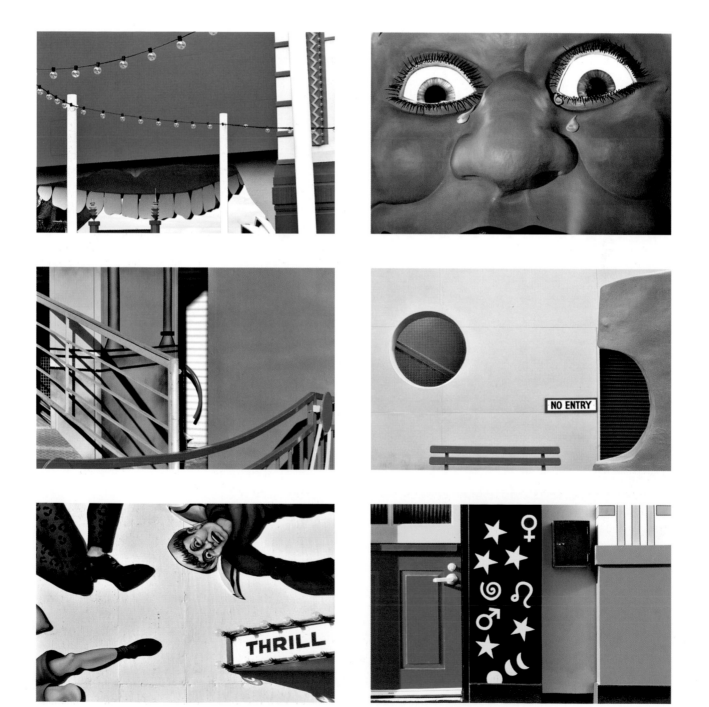

CHAPTER 7

CORRECTING IMAGES

THIS chapter examines how to use Photoshop to fine tune your scanned images to ensure the highest level of print quality. Initially the discussion will concentrate on using the *Levels* and *Curves* controls to ensure that the image fully utilizes the entire digital tone and color scale. For clarity, we will work with the same image, and apply a variety of adjustments to illustrate the basic principles behind image correction. Later in the chapter localized control and retouching will also be addressed. For all operations ensure the *Preview* command is checked in the relevant dialog box.

USING THE LEVELS COMMAND

In the previous chapter we discussed how important it was that the image scan should "fit" within the 256 step digital gray scale. We did this by checking the histogram, the diagrammatic representation of the dispersal of the pixels of the scanned image, to ensure that all of the pixels fell within the range of the digital tone scale. Now we must ensure that these pixels are fully spread over the entire tone scale so that all of the possible tones (and colors) can be reproduced by the printer. In this way when the image is printed it will display deep rich blacks and crisp clean highlights. This is done by adjusting the spread of the pixels so the shadows and highlights intersect or "clip" either end of the tone scale.

To do this we can use either the *Levels* option or the *Curves* option to make the appropriate corrections. All these adjustments are found in the *Image* menu. The screen image to the right shows the *Image, Adjust* menu open. You will see that *Levels* and *Curves* are at the top of the choices.

The first operation we will perform is to examine the histogram of a sample image in *Levels* to check its range, and then make adjustments. Select *Levels* from the *Image, Adjust* menu (Command L). *Remember, all keyboard commands are for Macintosh computers.*

The basic principle of image correction is to ensure that the entire dynamic range of the digital tone scale is fully utilized.
Lighting Tower, Luna Park, Sydney, Douglas Holleley, 1991. From the author's Ph.D. thesis, *Luna Park, the Image of a Funfair,* University of Sydney, 1997.

Below is a view of the open *Image, Adjust* menu. It is here you exercise control over the appearance of the scan. Although you can see a control labeled *Brightness/Contrast,* avoid its use in image correction.

You can see that although the image is "correctly" scanned in the sense that all of the information is contained within the gray scale, there are areas that are quite underutilized. If we were to print it in its present form it would look "weak" and flat. If you look at the section of the histogram labeled (a) you can see that the darkest part is not at the point of maximum density (value zero), but instead starts well into the gray portions of the tonal scale. As a result the deepest shadows will not print black but rather a chalky dark gray tone. Similarly, and even more pronounced, is the

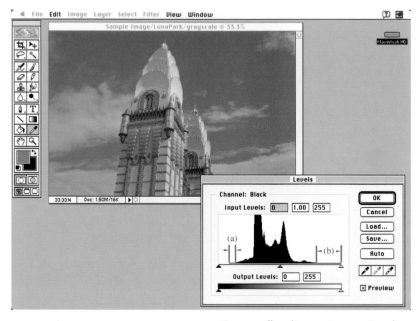

unused portion of the tone scale represented by the area marked (b). Here the highlights stop well short of the point of their maximum brightness and will print with a "muddy" quality. To correct this we can modify the histogram so that the image occupies the entire scale.

In the first instance we will it correct manually. To adjust the shadows, so that their deepest tone prints pure black, start by grabbing the left hand black triangle and move it to the right so that it just intersects that part where the pixels begin to register. To adjust the highlights, perform a similar operation with the white triangle. Move it to the left so that it intersects the point where there are no more pixels registered above the base line.

When you do this the histogram will at first look like the diagram at right.

Notice how the image looks much better. The flat appearance has been eliminated and it exhibits a full range of tones. If you look at the dialog box you will see that it displays, in numerical form, the place on the tone scale where you have now decided to place the darkest and lightest part of the image. In the case of the shadow area this point was 44, in the case of the highlights the value was 201.

To manually adjust an image using the *Levels* control first make sure that your image falls within the range of the 256 step gray scale. Then move the highlight and shadow triangular indicators in towards the histogram in such a way as to intersect the point where information begins (at the shadow end) and ceases (at the highlight end).
Above: See the histogram before adjustment.
Below: See how these *Clip* points have been identified and adjusted.

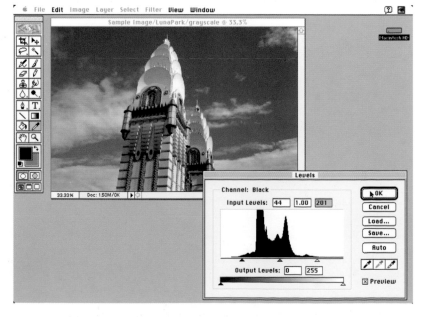

Thus in its uncorrected state the image used out of a possible 256 shades of gray, only 157 shades (201 minus 44). In other words over a third of the potential gray scale was quite simply underutilized, unprintable and wasted.

Press *OK*. The *Levels* box will disappear and the correction will be applied to the image. Now reopen the *Levels* dialog box and examine what effect this adjustment has had on the histogram.

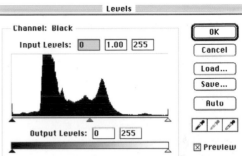

You can see how the image is now occupying the full range of the 256 possible shades of gray. The gray triangle in the middle of the histogram adjusts the mid point of the image. After the shadow and highlight cut-off or clip points have been established, you can control (if you wish) where middle gray is best located. Moving the triangle to the right will allocate more of the pixels under middle gray. The result is that the image gets darker. Moving it to the left will lighten it.

This method of control offers many insights into conventional photographic processes. For those of you who may have struggled to understand the zone system, you should already be beginning to understand its principles with a new clarity. The essence of the zone system is to match the range of your subject to the range of your film and paper. A good negative is one that takes the brightness range of the subject and by exposure and development controls, best "fits" this to the negative. A good negative has barely perceptible detail in the shadows and retains detail in the highlights until eventually only the very brightest parts of the image register on the print with no detail at all. In doing so the full potential of the negative is realized. There are no overly thin shadows with little detail registered and no excessively dense, blocked up highlights. In other words the entire range of the film is utilized.

This is the very process we have just performed digitally. However, in this case the raw scan was the subject, and the corrected (in this case, extended) histogram, the digital equivalent of a well processed negative. The corrected image now fully occupies the digital tone scale.

You can also use the *Auto* button to correct the histogram. The auto command makes its correction by cutting off the bottom 0.5% of your image, and allocating it the value of 0, or complete black. Similarly, to the right of the histogram, the program will cut off the top 0.5% of highlight detail. This means the very lightest highlights will be completely white. If you decide to use the *Auto* command it is often useful to alter the highlight cut-off point (or *Clip*) to around 0.25% so you lose less detail in the bright areas of the image. You change these cut-off points by holding down the Option key. The *Auto* button will now be labeled *Options*. Click on this button. A box will appear that allows you to change these settings. Make your changes and click OK. Now press the *Auto* button on the main window.

After making the adjustments described on the opposite page, the *Levels* control is again accessed in the *Image, Adjust* menu. You can see how now the histogram, the diagrammatic representation of the distribution of the pixels that make up the image, occupies all 256 shades of gray.

USING THE CURVES COMMAND

Similar control can be exercised using the *Curves* command. Like *Levels,* it corrects the scan so that the entire range of the digital scale is used. It can also affect the distribution of the midtone values, like the gray triangle does. However, the *Curves* offers extra control as it presents the opportunity to change the midtone values differentially.

From the *Image, Adjust* menu, select *Curves* (Command M). You will see underneath the graph, a small two headed arrow. Click on this arrow to change the direction of the gray scale so that the shadows are on the left, and the highlights on the right.[1] The straight line now depicts the tonal response of the image, with the shadows in the bottom left hand corner, and the highlights in the top right hand corner.

You set the cut-off points manually in *Curves* by using the black eye dropper to set the shadows, and the white eye dropper to set the highlights. (Ignore the middle one.) It is, however, acceptable practice to use the auto control. To maximize highlight detail, hold down the option key. The *Auto* button will change and will now be called *Options*. Click on this box and change the "white clip" setting to 0.25%. Close the box and you will return to the standard window. Now press the *Auto* button.

You can see how the curve has contracted both in the shadows and the highlights in a way that echoes how the *Levels* histogram changed when we moved the black and white points to meet the baseline.

1. This is the reverse of normal photographic practice when plotting the tonal response of prints. Usually characteristic curves use the y-axis for density and the x-axis for exposure. Thus conventionally the bottom left hand corner is the "toe" (highlights) and the top right hand corner the "shoulder" (shadows).

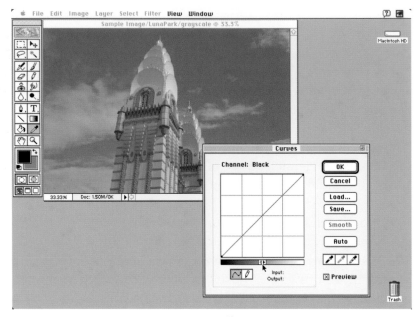

Above:
Clicking on the arrows where the cursor is pointing will allow you to put the shadows either to the left or the right of the gray scale. It is good practice to have the shadows to the left as indicated here.

Below:
This diagram shows how, after selecting *Auto,* the curve contracts to show how much of the tone scale was formerly underutilized. It echoes the way the histogram changed in *Levels.*

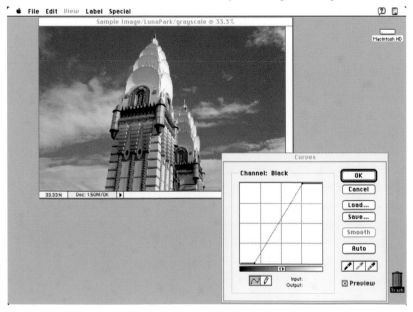

The improvement to the overall tonal response of the image itself is also very similar. What differs is the ability to alter the tonal response within these parameters.

You adjust the curve by clicking on it to create an anchor point. You can create up to 17 such points. To increase contrast (as shown in the image to the right) place the mouse on the lower part of the curve and drag the curve down slightly. This darkens the shadows. However, the highlights will also darken slightly. To offset this effect, place another point on the curve, this time towards the highlights, and drag the curve up. As you do this you create a "steeper" characteristic curve.[2] If you do not like the result, drag the anchor point(s) off the graph. Alternatively, hold down the Option key on your keyboard and the *Cancel* button will change to *Reset*. Click this and you will be back to the original straight line.

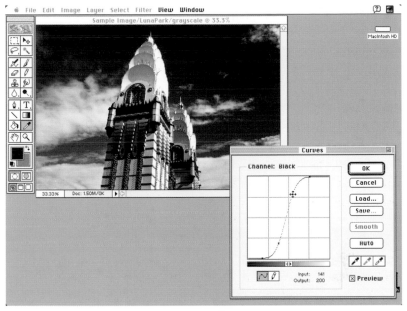

Above:
A high(er) contrast *Curves* adjustment.

2. Those of you familiar with the Zone System will gain much insight by opening an image and replicating characteristic curves by changing the slope and shape of the digital curve. See Phil Davis, *Photography*. Wm. C. Brown Publishers, Dubuque, Iowa, 1990. See *Exposure and Development Controls*.

Adjustments are not just limited to controlling contrast. The best way to understand this is to experiment with various curve shapes to see their effect. You will soon gain a grasp of the principles. Test yourself by imagining what a negative curve would look like, and what a solarized (or Sabattier effect) image curve would look like.

As you may have anticipated, the slope for a negative curve will be a complete reversal of the normal progression from black to white. Thus a negative curve would look like the diagram, at right.

Here the shadow areas of the print are placed where the highlights usually are and vice versa. You can modify this curve to alter its contrast by applying the same principles as before. However, as the values are reversed, this time you will have to modify it by dragging the line in opposite directions to the example above.

Below:
A negative rendition of the image.

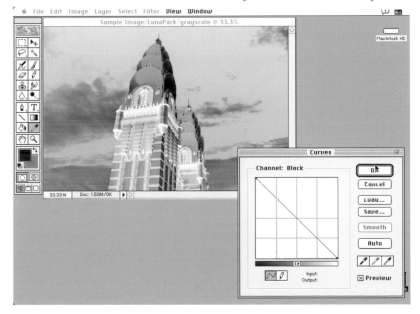

To the second hypothetical question, "what would the curve of a solarized print look like?" Before looking at the next illustration, think what happens when a print is solarized. You allow it to develop so that the shadows become visible. The developing solution, in these areas, becomes exhausted from converting the latent image to a visible image. You then briefly turn on a light and give the print more exposure. The developer remains active where there were once highlights, and it begins to develop up the newly exposed latent image in these otherwise unexposed areas. The highlights begin to go dark. The print becomes solarized. What would such a curve look like?

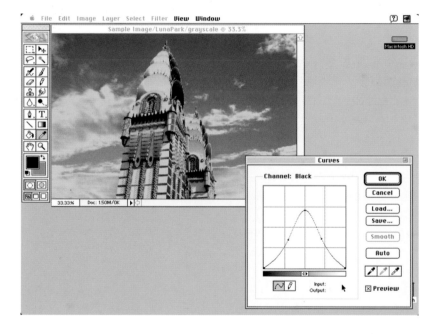

Although the *Curves* control is usually used to "fit" the scan to the digital tone scale, and to alter contrast, it is capable of many other effects, most of which have counterparts in the analog photography vocabulary. In this instance the curve has been adjusted to give the impression of a solarized (Sabattier effect) photographic print.

The curve starts in the shadow area (at the bottom left hand side of the graph) and proceeds normally. However, around the midpoint, the direction changes. Instead of continuing to the top of the scale, the curve reverses direction and dips down to the baseline. What was once white, is now black. In this example the curve has also been modified by making each of the two sides steeper, increasing the contrast of the image.

These examples will help you understand how much the *Curves* option can control the distribution of tones. Do not be tempted to resort to the more familiarly named *Brightness/Contrast* control to adjust your images. This is a crude instrument. Using the maximum range of the 256 grayscale should be your aim in image correction. Your printer can accurately reproduce the complete digital tone scale, but only if it is present. Using either the *Levels* or *Curves* command as discussed above, will ensure that this occurs.

USING LEVELS AND CURVES TO CORRECT COLOR IMAGES

The principles for correcting color images are much the same as for monochrome. Like grayscale images, color photographs need also to be adjusted so they occupy all 256 tones. The only difference being that in a color image, there is a channel for each of the additive primary colors of Red, Green and Blue.

You can do this manually or use the auto control using either *Levels* or *Curves*. When you select the cut-off points manually you retain the existing relationships between the individual curves of each channel. Thus the color cast of the image remains the same. When you choose the auto setting, each of the three primary additive colors of Red, Green and Blue are adjusted to occupy the full range of tones within each channel. This can change the shape of the histograms of each of the channels in relation to each other. In doing so often the color of the image will change considerably. Usually this results in an improvement to the appearance. However, on other occasions it may change the image in a less desirable way, especially if there is a strong cast to the image which you may wish to retain. The message is to be aware of these two methods in both *Levels* and *Curves*. Try each in turn.

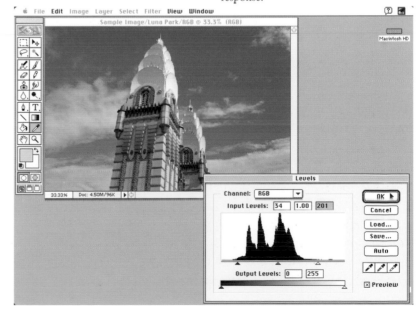

This image shows what a typical color scan might look like before adjustment and correction. Although "in range" it is nevertheless flat and uninteresting. *The Towers of the Luna Park Entrance, Luna Park, Sydney*, Douglas Holleley, 1991.

THE LEVELS CONTROL WITH COLOR IMAGES

We will compare the effect of the *Levels* control when used manually and then with the auto setting. You will see both methods produce similar results. Either enables you to "fit" your image to the tone scale.

Here the image has been manually adjusted by moving each of the arrows to intersect the point where the pixels start and stop registering on the histogram. You can see that the tonal response of the image has improved. The "flat" quality has disappeared but the color of the image retains the same magenta cast. In this case this is not desirable, but there will be occasions when you may wish to retain the original color cast. If so, use this method.

A simple first step to correcting such a scan is to manually apply the *Levels* control in much the same way as you would do with a black and white (grayscale) image. Such a strategy preserves the original color balance of the image while improving the tonal response.

We will now look at the effect this adjustment has on the histogram of each of the individual color channels. As you can see (to the right) after manual adjustment, each of the separate color channels retain their individual configurations. (Compare this to the *Auto Levels* example on the opposite page, where each channel has been normalized.) In this example you can see that highlights of the Green and Blue channels stop well short of the end of the histogram. Similarly the Red channel has few pixels in the shadow area. Retaining the original shape of each of the individual histograms (and their relative position) maintains the original color balance.

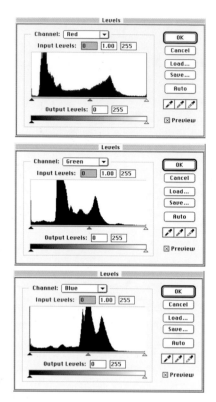

It is useful to see the effect of manual adjustment on each of the individual channels that make up the full color image. Although the composite RGB curve is "normalized," or adjusted to fit the full tonal scale, each individual color channel is not necessarily occupying the full tone scale. As you can see, each channel retains its individual configuration and relative position to each other. This is why the color balance does not change.

Compare these histograms with those of an *Auto Adjust* on the opposite page.

In comparison look below at the image after it has been corrected with the *Auto Levels* control.

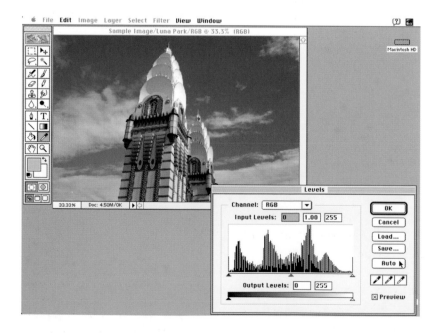

The histogram for an image that has been auto adjusted looks quite different to a manual adjust. The shape of composite histogram shown here foreshadows the corrected shapes of the individual channels. With an auto adjust, all channels are corrected so as to individually occupy the full 256 step scale.

Here the image is not only corrected for range, but also (to an extent) for color. This occurs because each of the individual color channels, not just the composite channel, have been adjusted to fit the 256 tone grayscale. The default *Clip* points of 0.5% for both the highlights and shadows were used. In the diagram at right you can see the effect obtained by going to *Levels* and using the *Channel* selector to view how each color histogram has been altered.

There is a third way to correct your image using the *Levels*. In this case you are required to ascertain the brightest and darkest point of your image and set these points manually by using the *Eye Dropper* tools located in the *Levels* dialog box. This requires some skill as these points are often difficult to ascertain. Remember that the darkest points are usually a deep shadow area, rather than something you know to be black. In photography, and in Photoshop, black is not a color but instead the absence of light. Try this method by all means; however, you will most likely find you can get better results by using the *Auto* command. (At least at first.) Use the black eye dropper to the left to set the shadows, and the white eye dropper to the right, to set the highlights.

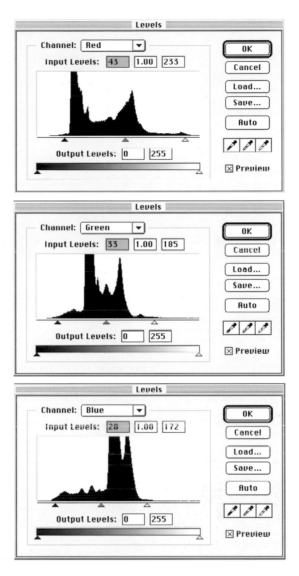

Observe how the individual channels all occupy the entire range of the channel. In this way new color relationships occur, usually for the better. However, sometimes you may wish to retain the original cast of your image. If so, adjust your color image using the manual method.

You can use also the *Levels* control to refine the color balance of your image. This requires some skill, so if you are new to Photoshop you may wish to use the more familiar controls found in *Color Balance*. (The use of this control will be discussed later.) However, adjusting the color of your image using the levels is an excellent way to further understand how your image is rendered by Photoshop. Use the *Auto* adjust option to give you a starting point.[3] Then toggle through the individual color channels and try moving the *Clip* points, and the midpoint triangle around, observing as you do, the effect on the color.

3. Remember you can access the box to change these *Clip* points by holding down the Option key when the *Levels* box is open. The *Auto* button will change to *Options*. Click on this button and experiment with changes in the *Clip* values (*Black Clip and White Clip*). 0.5% is usually good for the shadows but lesser values for the highlights will retain detail that might otherwise be lost. Try 0.25% as a start.

THE CURVES CONTROL WITH COLOR IMAGES

We will now correct the image, applying the same principles, but using the *Curves* control. To use the *Curves* control manually you find the brightest and darkest point of your image and set these points using the eye dropper tools in the *Curves* dialog box. As explained before use the black eye dropper to set the shadows, and the white eye dropper to set the highlights. This method requires some skill, but for some reason (that would appear to have no basis in theory) it seems to be easier to do this using the *Curves* controls than the *Levels*. The points selected for this image are indicated on the illustration above. You can see the highlight eye dropper on the image near the indicated white point.

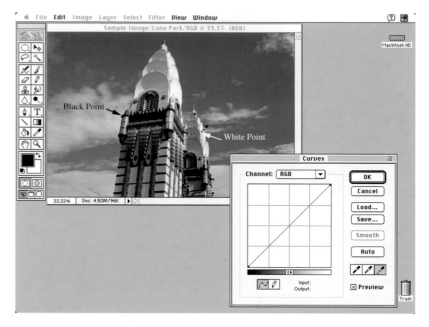

As you can see the image is greatly improved, exhibiting very little color cast. You will find that selecting different areas will have a marked affect on the appearance of the image. The highlight selection is particularly critical. Detail will disappear above the value of the point you choose so you must select the last (brightest) discernible highlight. Selecting too low a value of white will mean your image will look "raw." Selecting a specular highlight reflection (where there is no detail at all) will make the image "muddy." You will also find that varying the selection point can dramatically alter the color cast of the image. It is worthwhile spending an hour or so with these tools. At first they seem somewhat counter-intuitive but perseverance will pay off when you realize how much control you have over both density and color by the careful selection of clip points.

If you find this method difficult then you may simply wish to employ the *Auto* control to adjust the curves. Again, experiment with different cut-off points or "clips."

Above:
To adjust the *Curves* manually it is necessary to use the eye dropper tools to set the black point and the white point. This illustration shows two suitable sample points to make such an adjustment.

Below:
Here you can see the result obtained by simply using the *Auto* adjust option in the *Curves* window.

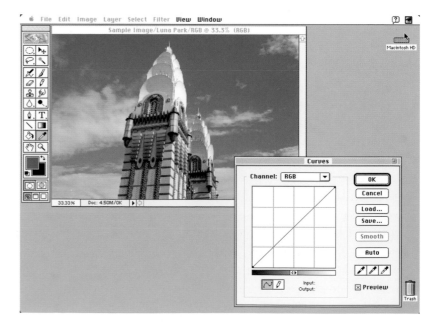

The bottom image on the facing page has been corrected using the auto setting using the default settings of 0.5% *Black Clip* and *White Clip*.

The image is very close to correct. It is slightly "cool" in color and will require correction for this color cast. However, the clarity is excellent. As a cross check, return to the *Levels* control and see what effect auto adjusting the curves has on the appearance of the histograms.

As the diagram to the right shows, each of the individual channels have "spread out" or "normalized" to occupy the full tone scale. If you compare these histograms with those obtained by selecting the *Auto Levels* control you will see there is not much difference between the two methods.

It is often a useful strategy to use the *Auto Curves* in the first instance, and then select the shadow eye dropper and experiment by assigning differing (shadow) parts of the image the value black. Select the shadow eye dropper and click on what you consider to be the deepest shadow in the image. If you do not like the result hold down the Option key and *Reset* the *Curves*. Try this procedure on a number of different shadow points. Often selecting barely differing shadow areas can produce dramatically different consequences for the density and color balance. This hybrid method can be quite miraculous and it is highly recommended you persevere with it and try it on a variety of images. It ensures you are making the absolute most of the information in the file. The only danger is choosing too high a shadow value and assigning it the value of pure black. If you do this you may lose too much shadow detail. The color balance may also shift dramatically. However, if this happens it will be immediately apparent on the screen. If this occurs simply reset the *Curves*, by holding down the Option key and the *Cancel* button will change to *Reset*. Click this button and start again.

You can also adjust the individual channels in the *Curves* control to correct color balance. Here you can make adjustments to the curve of each of the channels by selecting them in turn from the *Channel* box at the top of the *Curves* window. For example, if the image looks too green, select *Channel, Green* and pull the curve down slightly.

This method requires some skill and judgement (and lots of practice). You are best to try setting the black point *(Clip)* manually after using the *Auto* command as described in the previous paragraph. More often than not this will adjust the image for color as well as density if you select the right area to be designated black. However, if you are new to Photoshop you may be more comfortable using the *Color Balance* controls explained overleaf, *pp. 155–156.*

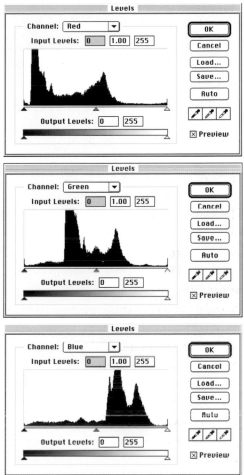

In a manner not to dissimilar to that of *Auto Levels*, the *Auto Curves* option adjusts each individual channel so that each of the primary colors occupies all of the available digital tone scale.

However, before proceeding to color balance correction let us recapitulate the main points.

- Ascertain that your scan is "in range," i.e. all the values of the image fit the tone scale with no cut-off of either the shadows, or more importantly, the highlights.

- Use the *Levels* or *Curves* controls to spread your image values over the histogram so that the shadows of your image start at value 0, and your highlights stop at value 255.

- Make a decision whether to adjust your image manually or by using the *Auto* setting. Try each and observe the effect on your image before you decide.

- If using the *Auto* adjustment, experiment with the *Clip* points of the histogram in *Levels* or the *Clip* points of the *Curves* to retain highlight detail. Try a value of 0.25% for the highlight clip in both cases.

- Try the combination of *Auto Adjust Curves* and then manually setting the black point with the shadow eye dropper.

- Do not adjust color balance until you have first corrected your image so that it fits the full range of values.

The Whirler, Luna Park, Sydney, Douglas Holleley, 1995. From the author's Ph.D. thesis, *Luna Park, the Image of a Funfair,* University of Sydney, 1997.

CORRECTING COLOR BALANCE

The *Variations* option is helpful if you are new to color correction. (*Select Image, Adjust* from the menu bar. The last menu item will be *Variations*.) When this option is selected you will see that the screen displays a variety of alternatives surrounding the *Current Pick* (your screen image).

The *Variations* option quickly indicates which direction to shift the color to correct the image. In this case the blue, cyan and green choices are clearly wrong. Adjustment is required in the direction of red or magenta. You will notice that you can preview the changes so they effect the *Midtones, Shadows* or *Highlights*. Using the *Midtone* setting is usually sufficient to identify the shift. You can also vary the degree of adjustment from *Fine* to *Coarse*. However, do not make your corrections using this control because the image is too small to judge accurately. Simply note the main direction to follow, in this case red/magenta, cancel the box, and from the *Image, Adjust* menu, select *Color Balance.*

Display your image at a reasonable size on the screen. Command Zero will make it fit the screen. You can also use Command plus (+) to enlarge it or Command minus (–) to make it smaller. (You can provide a neutral background by selecting the center box from the three little boxes at the bottom of the *Tool* palette. The keyboard shortcut is F. Selecting F again will place your image on a black background. Selecting it a third time will restore the full desktop view.)

Try both the Magenta and Red choices, by sliding the arrow along the little bar towards each of these in turn.

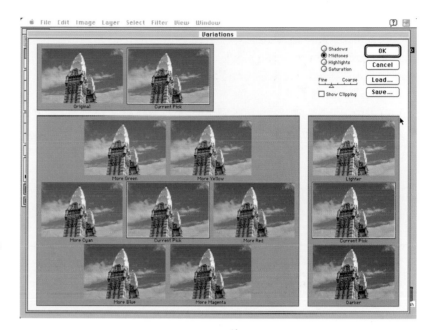

Above:
To adjust color balance, select from the *Image, Adjust* menu, the *Variations* control. This will give you a general "feel" for the shift.

Below:
After establishing the general direction of the color shift, perform the actual adjustment by using the *Color Balance* controls in the *Image, Adjust* menu.

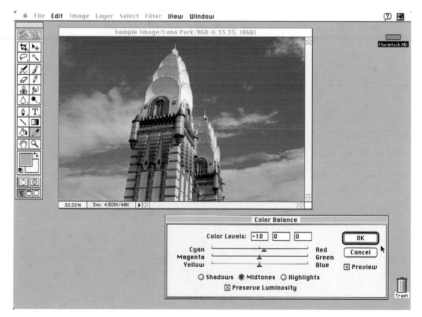

In this example it appears that a slight shift towards red is the most appropriate choice. When correcting color try to find an area that you wish to be neutral and observe the effect in this area. In this image, the clouds are the best indicator. When magenta correction was applied the clouds went quite pink. This did not occur when red was applied. In this case only a small correction of 10 units is required.

Adjust the *Midtones* first. After getting them correct, then click on the *Highlights* button and adjust the brighter areas of the image. Usually a small amount of the same shift helps, but the operative word is small. In this case the highlights were corrected 5 units towards red. You can then proceed to adjust the *Shadows* in the same manner. When you are happy with the result select *OK*. Then undo and redo the correction a number of times by going to the *Edit* menu and selecting *Undo/Redo Color Balance*, or by using the keyboard shortcut Command Z, to be sure you are happy with the result.

Be sure to save the image as a TIFF file and name it clearly so you will recognize it again. If you are very organized you can also give the image file a number, corresponding either to the page it will be printed on, or its order in the document.

These corrections are usually enough to render an image suitable for reproduction. However, often you will need, or desire, to make further refinements. Most commonly these involve retouching the image to remove spots or other problems and/or you may wish to enhance the image with some judicious sharpening.

To illustrate the ability of the *Rubber Stamp* tool to function as an image re-touching device we will use this image which has a few minor flaws, much as most images do when first scanned. We will use this tool to correct a blemish in the eye, and also hide flaws in the actual paintwork of the attraction that are deemed to be distracting, at least for these purposes.

Detail of decorative panels originally employed on the Cinema 180, Luna Park, Sydney, Douglas Holleley, 1982. From the author's Ph.D. thesis, *Luna Park, the Image of a Funfair*, Sydney University, 1997.

RETOUCHING YOUR IMAGE

Photoshop permits you to eliminate small imperfections such as dust spots and/or scratches quickly and easily using either the painting tools (which replicate the action of Spotone or other retouching inks and dyes) or the *Rubber Stamp*, also known as the cloning tool. The *Rubber Stamp* is particularly useful as it "paints" over the offending area with the color and the texture of a sampled area of the image. Photographers will appreciate all these tools as they work equally well over either black or white imperfections.

Double click on the *Rubber Stamp* icon in the Tool palette. A smaller palette will appear. Make sure that the *Aligned* option is selected. You will also see that you can vary the *Opacity* of the tool, but in most cases setting it at 100% will give you the best results. (You may wish to close the *Rubber Stamp* palette at this point to keep your screen uncluttered.)

The *Rubber Stamp* tool, like the painting tools, requires that you set a brush size. From the *Window* menu select *Show Brushes*.

You can see that there are a variety of brushes from which to choose. Not only is there a choice of size, but you can also choose whether the brush has a hard or soft edge. For most retouching work, the soft edge works best.

In this image there is a small black spot in the white area of the pupil. Additionally on the right hand edge there is an area of peeling paint, revealing the old blue color underneath. Although some might argue that this area contributes to the interest of the picture, for the

The *Rubber Stamp* dialog box is accessed by double clicking on its icon in the *Tool* palette. For most purposes ensure the *Aligned* box is checked and the *Opacity* is set to 100%.

The *Brushes* palette is found in the *Windows* menu. For retouching purposes, the softer edged brushes are usually used. Consult your manual for instructions on how to create new brush sizes and shapes.

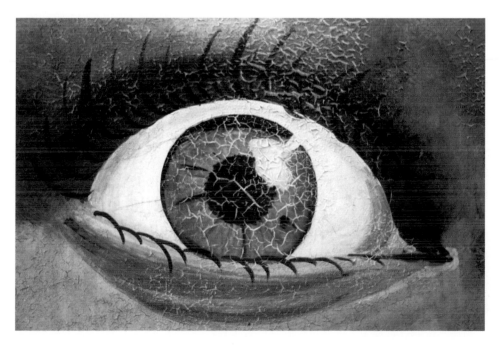

The same image after retouching.
Detail of decorative panels originally employed on the Cinema 180, Luna Park, Sydney, Douglas Holleley, 1982. From the author's Ph.D. thesis, *Luna Park, the Image of a Funfair,* Sydney University, 1997.

purposes of demonstration we are going to eliminate it by using the rubber stamp to "clone" from nearby areas, and use these sampled colors and/or tones to cover over this blemish.

To define a sample point, select the *Rubber Stamp* tool and hold down the Option key. Choose an area of the image you think will match the area you wish to retouch, click the mouse once and release the button. Then move the *Rubber Stamp* over the area to be retouched, press the mouse button and begin to paint with the color and texture of the sampled point. Best results are obtained if you paint only a small part of the blemish. Then select another sample point and slowly build up the new color and texture over the flaw. Experiment with various brush sizes and shapes to observe the differing effects. Be sure to save your image before you commence as it is easy to go too far. If you have the latest version of Photoshop you will have the luxury of multiple undos, found in the *History* palette. Otherwise, *Save* when you are happy with your progress and then you will not have to start all over again if you make "a dog's breakfast" of the image. You need only select *Revert to Saved* from the *File* menu.

Above:
This is a "straight print" scanned directly from the negative.

Below:
In its final exhibition form the image has been modified with the *Gradient* tool, as discussed in this chapter, and printed on an Iris printer at 29″x 36″. *The Winch, Lago Maggiore, Italy,* Douglas Holleley. Photographed 1989, Iris printed 1999.

USING SELECTIONS TO CORRECT YOUR IMAGE

There are many tools in Photoshop to alter the appearance of your image. You will notice some are reminiscent of conventional photography practice, such as the *Burn* and *Dodge* tools. However, unless the area you wish to darken or lighten is relatively small, this is not recommended. A far more useful approach is to select part of your image and then use the levels or curves to alter the values in these areas.

A common modification is darkening the sky of an image. The following example shows a way of achieving this effect. We will then proceed to further modify this area in a way impossible with conventional photography. If you consult your manual you will see that there are many ways to make such a selection. You can use the *Marquee* tools to select a rounded or rectangular shape. You can also use the *Lasso* tool to select odd shaped areas with great precision. You should also be aware that you can *Feather* the edges of these selections to blend into the rest of the image so the adjustments are barely observable.[4]

4. You can choose from the *Select* menu a whole variety of options that will permit you to modify your selection. Please refer to the Photoshop manual for further details.

The following steps show how you can use a selection to restrict corrections to a particular area of your image.

You can see how little detail there is in the sky. We will use the *Magic Wand* tool (which selects areas of similar value) to select the sky which is reasonably well defined by the border of the image, the columns and the mountains. In this case we assigned the *Magic Wand* a tolerance of 32 pixels. This means the wand selects areas 16 pixels above, and 16 pixels below a sampled area in the image. Initially it was applied to the clouds. Having done this it was apparent that the wand failed to select the darker areas of sky at the top of the image. By holding down the Shift key, you can retain the current selection and add to it by selecting another area. A little plus sign next to the cursor will let you know you are doing this successfully. This procedure resulted in the total sky are being selected.

The "crawling ants" indicate the boundary of the selection. In this case because the edges of the selection are bound by definite boundaries there is no need to soften the edges of the selection by using the *Feather* option in the *Select* menu. To check the selection you use the *Quick Mask* tool. The *Quick Mask* is obtained by clicking on its icon as indicated below. As you can see the selection is then displayed as if it were painted. If you double click on the icon you will be able to choose whether the *Quick Mask* displays the selected area or the unselected area. By toggling between these two options you can use the painting tools to alter either the selection or the unselected areas, to fine tune your selection.

To return to the "crawling ants" view, click on the button to the left of the *Quick Mask* button.

NOTE: Be aware that you can retain the selection, but hide the visually

Above:
Here you can see the selection made by the *Magic Wand* in "crawling ants" view. The selection was made by assigning the *Magic Wand* a *Tolerance* of 32 pixels and clicking firstly on the clouds.

Below:
The view obtained by selecting the *Quick Mask* option. In this view you can use the painting tools to precisely modify the selection.

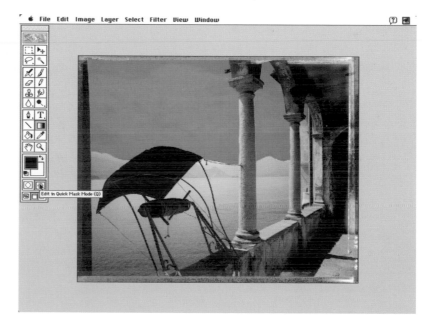

distracting crawling ants. Either go to the *Select* menu and choose *Hide Edges*, or simply use the keyboard shortcut, Command H. It is also good practice to save your selection when working in this manner. If the selection is saved you can reuse it at any time in the future if you find you need to make further modifications. In the *Select* menu you will see the command *Save Selection*. You will also notice that under this is the command *Load Selection*. You use the latter to retrieve your selection when and if you need it.

To obtain more detail in the sky go to the *Image, Adjust* menu and select *Curves*. Drag the curve down as shown in the diagram. In most cases this is all you will need to do.

For purposes of demonstration we will make one more change to this image. In a similar way to the practice of early collodion photographers who had difficulty getting detail in the skies of their images because of the hyper sensitivity of the emulsion to blue light, we can make more sophisticated alterations. We can either paste in a sky from another image, or use the *Gradient* tool to simply create a sky.

In this case we are going to replace the sky with a graded blend of tones. To do this select the *Gradient* tool from the *Tool* palette. Double clicking on the icon brings up the *Gradient* dialog box. There are a variety of gradients available, some circular, others straight. In the diagram we can see that a *Linear Blend* is selected. The range of tones (or colors in an RGB image) that will appear in the blend is also displayed. These values are set in the *Background-color/Foreground-color* box in the *Tool* palette. In this case the two values were sampled from the image. The *Gradient* will only operate within the selection, leaving the other areas of the image intact. If you apply it without a selection, the entire image will turn into a blend.

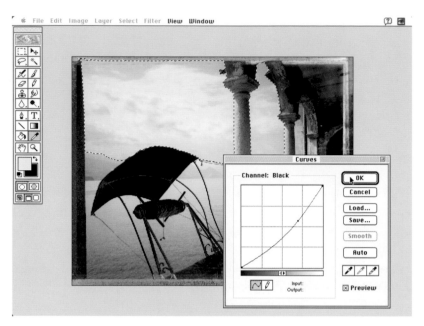

Above:
You can use the *Curves* as shown here (or *Levels,* by moving the mid-point control), to darken the area bounded by the selection to create a "burned-in" effect to the sky.

Below:
Once a selection has been made you may wish to try other ways of altering the tonal balance of the image. In this case the selection has been filled with a linear blend.

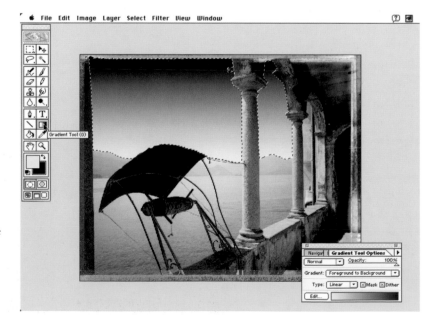

This form of image modification is more the exception rather than the rule and is explained briefly by way of example. However, it is included to give the reader some idea of the range of options available when working with selections. Selections are most commonly used to help refine an image by lightening or darkening selected areas.

As this example shows selections can be used for more extreme effects and can allow you to introduce areas of tone and color as well as gradients. Many of the illustrations in this chapter use this technique. You can create hybrid photo-paintings that would be difficult to achieve using conventional materials. Traditionalists may shudder at this apparent lack of regard for the photograph's quality of verisimilitude. Certainly it would not be good practice to use such techniques when documentary integrity was either appropriate or essential. However, using such tools emphasizes the very real fact that when making a photograph, you are also making a picture.

SHARPENING YOUR IMAGE

The final step after adjusting the range, correcting the color, and removing blemishes is to *Sharpen* your image. Although nothing can make a badly blurred photograph sharp, this tool can help restore sharpness to an image that has been enlarged or reduced in the process of scanning and re-sizing, and to an extent can make a borderline image useable. However, it best used to give a well corrected image a final boost, much like a coat of varnish enhances the color of a finished painting.

A combination of image correction techniques have been applied to this image. After checking and correcting the tonal range, the image was colorized by applying a duotone curve to create a warm overall base color. Further color was then applied to individual areas of the print using the *Paintbrush* tool.

The Duomo, Orvietto, Italy, Douglas Holleley. Photographed 1989, digitally colored and Iris printed 1999.

Sharpening, like varnish, should be applied only when the image is finished.

You will find the sharpening options in the *Filter* menu under *Sharpen*. There are a number of choices. The most useful one is the *Unsharp Mask*.

The *Unsharp Mask* filter does not, as its name might suggest, make your image soft or blurred. It is named after an analog photographic process where a "soft" transparency can be sandwiched with a high contrast contact positive to increase the apparent sharpness of the subsequent print or duplicate slide. This filter can be adjusted to make a variety of enhancements to your image. You will see the above right dialog box when you select this option.

The dialog box has three variables you can alter. You will find in practice that you need only alter the *Amount* and the *Radius*.[5] Leave the *Threshold* set at 0. The default setting is an *Amount* of 50% and a *Radius* of 1.0 pixel. This works well for most images. However, in this case the *Amount* has been set to 76% and the *Radius* to 1.6 pixels. This extra sharpening suits the graphic nature of this image. You can preview the sharpening effect on the screen by placing the cursor over an area of the image and watch how the image changes in response in the preview window in the dialog box. Eventually, if the *Preview* box is checked, the entire image will sharpen on the screen. However, to be sure of your choice of values, select *OK* and wait for the filter to perform its task. Then go to the *Edit* menu and use the *Undo* command (Command Z) to toggle back and forth between the sharpened and unsharpened version of the image. You will find that the effect is often more apparent when your image is printed than it is on the screen. If in doubt it is best to use too little, rather than too much.

Because sharpening increases contrast it is unwise to apply it to an image that you think you may be resizing in the future. The "edginess" that the filter gives can look good while the image is at its current size, but if enlarged, can cause unpleasant "artifacts," i.e. visual defects that can happen during digital processing. It is good practice to keep your corrected file in unsharpened form and sharpen a copy of it when you are ready to print, after you have sized it for a particular purpose.

The *Unsharp Mask* window.

5. The *Amount* refers to the intensity of the effect of the *Unsharp Mask* filter. Although not precise, think of 50% as moderate and over 100% as significant. The *Radius* refers to the "spread," or number of pixels, that will be affected by the filter. Using too much will produce a "halo" effect. This is the appearance of light areas around objects of different tone to the background. The default values of *Amount* 50% and *Radius* 1 generally produce excellent results. The *Threshold* determines how many samples in an image will be sharpened. A setting of 0 will affect every sample. It is best left at 0 for most images. As with most things, a series of tests will provide you with data suitable to your taste and your images.

CHANGING THE SIZE
OF YOUR IMAGE

Best results when printing from a
page layout program are obtained
when the image is sized so that it is
located in the page layout program at
100%. In other words the Photoshop
file is exactly the size of the box
drawn for it in a program like
QuarkXPress. In Chapter 5,
p. 92, the reader was cautioned
against enlarging an image in a page
layout program. Although not as
detrimental to quality, it is also a
good idea to not have to reduce it
either. Reasons are many, the

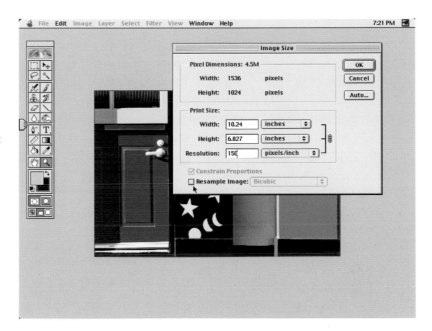

simplest being that the document will print faster and easier if the size
of the image does not have to be re-calculated as it prints.

You change the size of an image in Photoshop by going to the
Image menu and selecting *Image Size.* The dialog box illustrated above
will appear. As you can see the image is displayed in both *Pixel
Dimensions* and the *Print Size* and the resolution these will render at
when printed at 100%. In this case the resolution is 150 dpi.

You will observe that the last box at the bottom of the window is
labeled *Resample Image.* With this box *unchecked* the physical dimensions
of the image will change when the resolution is altered. Alternatively, if
the physical dimensions are changed, then the resolution will change
accordingly. Essentially the amount of information in the image file
will produce a larger print at lower levels of resolution, or smaller print
with higher amounts of resolution. Thus in this example, with the box
unchecked, when the resolution of the image is changed to 300
dpi/ppi then the physical dimension of the print will reduce to
5.12″ x 3.413″.

This is always the best way to change the image size as no
information is either being created or discarded. The integrity of the
original scan is maintained.

However, there will be occasions when you wish to enlarge or
reduce an image's physical size, and also change the resolution of the
image. You may for example wish to print the example above at 300
dpi but retain the same print size. To do this you will have to create
more pixels. This process is called *interpolation.* In doing so be aware
that some loss of image quality will inevitably occur.

In the *Image Size* dialog box you will
observe that the very last box at the
bottom of the window is labeled
Resample Image. With this box
unchecked the image will retain the
same file size while the dimensions
and/or the resolution are altered. You
should only check it if you really must
enlarge the image while retaining the
same resolution. Be aware that some
quality loss may occur if you do this.

Photoshop will perform this operation by sampling each pixel, and the values of its neighbors and make an informed "guess" (calculation) as to what the new pixel value should be when it adds new information to the image. It can calculate these values in a variety of ways. The best results are obtained by selecting the *Bicubic* form of interpolation from the small box at the bottom of the *Image Size* window. As mentioned before, if you must do this, do it to an un-sharpened image file and then apply the sharpening filter when the image is re-sized.

The diagram shows how the file size grows in response to this interpolation. It will give you some idea of how much new information is being calculated in this operation.

You can see the file size has more than trebled. This means around two thirds of the information in the new re-sized image has been "created." It is surprising how well this works but it is unwise to make a habit of this process. The possible exception is when enlarging direct scans as discussed in the following chapter. However, if you have no choice it is there as an option.

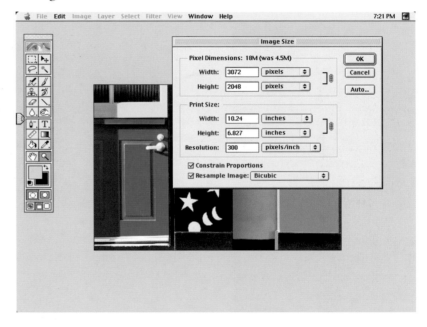

STORAGE OF IMAGES

As you process your images you will find you need a place to keep them. This will especially be the case if you are using a computer at an educational institution which must be left free of personal files so the computer can be used at anytime. However, the problem of storage can also extend to working at home on your own computer. Image files can be very large. Once you begin to assemble your book you will also find that you need extra room to hold your page layout files.

There are a number of proprietary brands of storage. If you are using a computer belonging to a school or a friend, you have little choice but to buy removable media to suit the brand they are using. If you are considering doing a lot of bookmaking or digital imaging you may find it better to buy a CD writer. They are relatively inexpensive and the disks store 650MB of data. If you intend to do any serious amount of digital work, the purchase of such a device is highly recommended.

Photoshop allows you to re-size your image should you wish to enlarge it while at the same time maintaining the existing level of resolution. It does this through a process known as inter-polation. This process creates new information, based on the pixel values of the existing image. The program effectively inserts extra data as the scale of the image is increased. It is good practice to select the *Bicubic* form of interpolation as shown in the box above. Notice how the file size of this image has increased dramatically as a result of this practice. Enlarging an image in this way can cause the quality to deteriorate. However, it is quite astonishing how well it does work with the majority of photographs. It is far less successful with images containing many fine straight lines.

Whatever you choose, use it only for storage of your files. Do not put the disk in the drive and begin to work. Often they will fail if used in this way. If this occurs you will lose all of your work. It is good practice to copy the image (and page layout) files you need to the hard disk of the computer and work on them there. In this way you will not put excessive demands on the drive of the portable disk, and you will minimize any potential disk errors. When you have finished working transfer the new files back to the removable storage.

Luna En-trance, Luna Park, Sydney, Australia, Douglas Holleley, May 30, 1995. From the author's Ph.D. thesis, *Luna Park, the Image of a Funfair,* University of Sydney, 1997.

This image was scanned from a piece of perforated paper photocopied
from a nineteenth century book (now lost). It tells the story of how a
Native American war party executed a raid on a rival tribe. The book
purported the original drawing to be an accurate representation of Native
American pictographic language. More likely it reveals more about
nineteenth century Western anthropological methodology and attitudes
than it does any indigenous culture.
The Dream Map, Douglas Holleley, 1994. From the author's book,
Paper, Scissors & Stone, Rockcorry, Woodford, 1995.

CHAPTER 8

ALTERNATIVE METHODS OF ACQUIRING IMAGES

IN addition to scanning preexisting prints, negatives, and transparencies, there are other ways of gathering digital images. What is interesting in using any or all of these methods is that one can approach the computer without any conventional photographic paraphernalia. There is no negative, no print and no darkroom work. These methods approach a state where the computer is the primary means of image generation. As such they may assist the discovery of a digital aesthetic, in the same way we have a photographic aesthetic or a painting aesthetic.

There are three main ways of doing this, each with their own characteristics, advantages and drawbacks. They are:

The Conversation
A direct scan of the recto and verso of a page made of stone. The "page" was made by cracking two river rocks against each other. This fragment, along with three more from the same rock, formed a "found book" in the sense that the fractured stone cleaved so perfectly that it was capable of being re-assembled and then opened and read, one page at a time, just like any book of paper. In the image you can see the fossilized impression of long dead sea creatures, their form permanently imaged by the direct impression of their shells in the mud of some ancient sea bed. This direct connection of an object to its trace is a naturally occurring imaging method analogous to the highly indexical process that is direct scanning. The stones were scanned in grayscale mode and then selectively colored.
The Conversation, Douglas Holleley, 1996. From the author's book, *Soft Landing in a Hard Place,* Rockcorry, Woodford, New South Wales, 1996.

- Direct scanning to make images from "life."
- Frame grabbing from an analog or digital video source.
- Using a still digital camera.

But why should new means of making images be so crucial to this issue? This is partly because the computer is an unusual development in the history of picture making. For the first time in history we have a new imaging process, but no new finished product to accompany that process. The image on your computer screen can find its final form as a photographic print, an image printed with ink on paper, an offset publication, even a movie or video tape. There is no finished object that can be readily identified as "a computer image."

Compare this with the invention of photography, itself as big a revolution in the nineteenth century, as digital imaging is today. Then as now, a whole series of inventions and processes (hardware and software if you like) had to be created in order for the process to work as a whole. It was necessary to invent the camera and be able to expose, develop and stabilize the image. But most importantly, at the end of the day these processes combined to produce a photograph. A tangible, physical, hitherto unknown artifact. In France, Louis Jacques Mandé Daguerre invented the Daguerreotype, while in England, William

Henry Fox Talbot pioneered the calotype, creating two quite different imaging systems. Yet both are recognizable as products of this new set of inventions and processes, and there is no difficulty (or confusion) in calling the final product of either of them, a photograph.

In comparison ask yourself, "What is a computer image?" Just like the invention of photography we have a whole new imaging system that enables us to make "computer images." But what does a computer image look like? What makes a computer image different from a photograph, or any other graphic arts medium? Is a photograph that has been scanned, imported into the computer and then modified, a photograph or a computer image? Is a photograph made with a digital camera different to a scanned photograph? Is there a digital aesthetic?

It may well be that such questions are inappropriate to ask of this new medium. They embody the modernist assumption that each medium of expression has its own aesthetic, which can be revealed through a self-reflexive investigation of its characteristics, especially the qualities of the artifacts each medium produces. Thus, in the case of photography John Szarkowski argues,

The Chimera, Douglas Holleley, 1996. From the author's book, *Soft Landing in a Hard Place,* Rockcorry, Woodford, New South Wales, 1996.

The pictures reproduced in this book *(The Photographer's Eye)* were made over almost a century and a quarter. They were made for various reasons, by men (sic) of different concerns, and varying talent. They have little in common except their success, and a shared vocabulary: these pictures are unmistakably photographs. The vision they share belongs to no school or aesthetic theory, but to photography itself.[1]

1. Szarkowski cited in Douglas Crimp's article, "The Museum's Old/The Library's New Subject" in Richard Bolton (ed.) *The Contest of Meaning,* MIT Press, Cambridge, Mass., 1993.

Such a claim is difficult to make for images created on the computer. A computer may best be described as a chameleon, or even more appropriately, a chimera. The screen, which seems so tangible, and basks in the descriptive metaphor of "the desktop," is a blown glass tube with a thin phosphorescent coating on the inside excited by electrons emitted from a kind of "gun." But its most salient quality is the fact that it contains nothing but a vacuum. The central processing unit itself is similarly abstract. After lifting the lid one looks down at a miniature version of a modern city, with roads or pathways, points of intersection, and one can only imagine the invisible traffic of the electrical pulses which industriously shuttle back and forth as directed.

Thus an approach which asks this highly abstracted device for the processing and display of electrical signals to somehow "reveal itself" or "demonstrate its character" is probably doomed. Unlike the characteristic trace of light patterns registered on the sensitive surface of the photographic negative, or the deeply ingrained imposition of ink pressed into paper by the pressure of the etching press, the computer deals only with a series of electronic codes which have no structure or quality of their own other than to describe either a simple "yes" or "no" to represent, in the complexity of their accumulation, a command the operator has requested.

Below and Left:
The Thief and the Loot, Douglas Holleley, 1993.
Below and Right:
The Comfort, Douglas Holleley, 1993. From the author's book, *Paper, Scissors and Stone,* Rockcorry, Woodford, New South Wales, 1994.

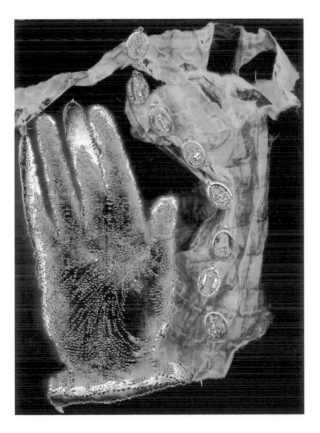 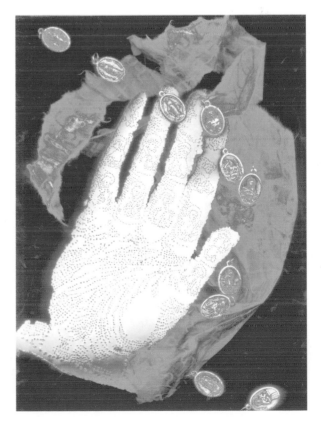

If you ask the computer to reveal itself and its characteristics, it answers such questions with another question. Seemingly having no fixed identity of its own, it asks instead that the operator reveal him or her self. Like Narcissus' reflective pool it is inscrutably passive, revealing only that which it is asked to reflect, or reflect only that which it is asked to reveal.

Thus if a "digital aesthetic" does exist, it will most likely appear as a function of process rather than outcome. This is not to claim that the following techniques, employing as they do, purely digital forms of image creation, will solve the dilemma. However, they do present a point of entry into the medium that represents a direct interface between the world and its digital image, and consequently may facilitate, if only by accident, insights that might otherwise remain hidden from conventional lines of investigation.

This scan was made from an image that preceded the digital era, but in some ways anticipated the cross-media possibilities that have arisen by the ability of digital code to describe all data, music, images, words, etc., into one single computer language. In its original form this image was generated by using an early version of a fax machine. By using a Xerox Telecopier it was possible to send an image over a telephone line. In doing so the image was converted to a sound signal. While this transmission was occurring, a tape recording of the sound of a Humpback whale, the subject of the image, was also transmitted along with the coded visual information. The net result is shown partly here. The "field" the whale is swimming through is created by the impression of the sound as decoded by the telecopier. The word "partly" is used, as the original image was 120 feet long.
Whale Song #1, Douglas Holleley, 1978/2000.

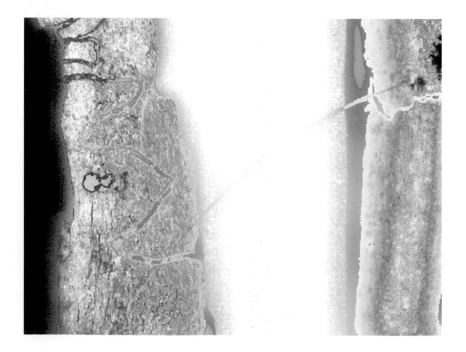

Left:
Where Waters Meet, Douglas Holleley, 1996

DIRECT SCANNING

Customarily the flatbed scanner is used to digitize a photograph into a series of digital instructions that may be displayed on the screen. However, this device has many other interesting characteristics. It can also be used as a camera.

It has several qualities which distinguish it from conventional cameras. Perhaps the most obvious is its size. It approximates an 8″x 10″ large format camera. In photography, when it comes to negative size, bigger is almost always better, and this is most certainly the case with digital imaging. Many problems occur when you need to "scale up" a 35mm or even 4″x 5″ negative. When enlarging from a small scale negative, high levels of resolution and subsequent large file sizes are necessary to produce enough "bits" of information to keep the pixels small so the photograph retains its veracity. Many of the problems in digital photography vanish when a large scaled image is introduced into the computer as a first generation matrix.

Additionally the size of the scanner has a certain symmetry within a digital imaging system. Its image collection area is approximately the same as a 17″ screen so there is a natural accord between what is placed on the scanner and what appears on the screen. This similarity of scale also extends to the common desktop printer. What is captured (or imaged) appears more or less in scale on the screen, usually only seconds after the scanner has made its pass(es). This screen image can then be subsequently printed, again at about the same size. Making images in this manner can provide significant insights into the nature of digital imaging.

The first insight is that if one asks the scanner to make the original matrix, rather than simply reproduce a two dimensional photograph, then the image that appears on the screen is a direct transcription of reality encoded completely in digital terms. The file that is created and saved in the computer is a first generation image. It is not a recoding or a reproduction. It has the same status and validity as any negative a photographer may make. It is an original digital file. It is one example of how the computer can render (a) reality.

Two variations of a direct scanned image.
Top: The Strange Attractor, Douglas Holleley, 1995.
Bottom: The Troubles Within, Douglas Holleley, 1995.

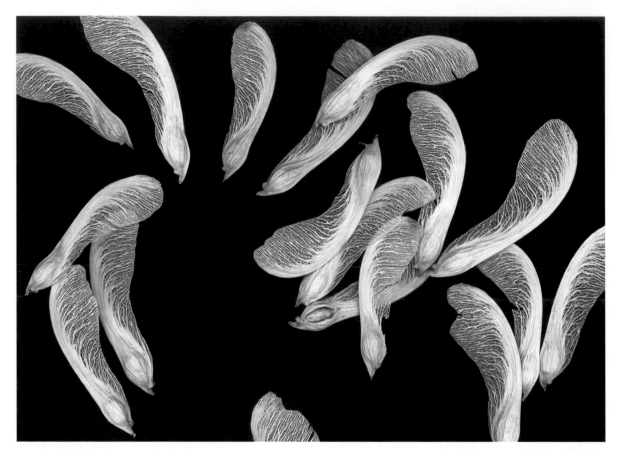

Seed pods from a maple tree placed directly on a scanner formed the basis of this image. Direct scanning is a useful way of exploring the digital aesthetic, relying as it does on the syntax and vocabulary of an intrinsically digital device. *Things that Fall from the Sky,* Douglas Holleley, Rochester, N.Y., 1999.

When you scan a photograph, you are not scanning the skies, fields, trees, rocks or people in the photograph, you are in fact scanning the very sub-structure of the image. Essentially you are asking the computer to reproduce an image created in another language. The language of photography is for the most part a function of its image structure, based typically on small particles of silver, clumped together to form what photographers call "grain." All images have a sub-structure. For example with oil paint it is pigment suspended in a medium. With digital images it is a regular grid of square "bits" of information in the form of pixels.

Where difficulties occur is when these two forms of sub-structure collide and interfere with each other. If one is to reproduce a photograph, a tension is immediately set up. The problem exists of how to translate an organic sub-structure of grains into a regular grid of pixels. In order to retain the clarity of definition and detail that one unconsciously expects from a photograph, it is necessary to make the digital transcription invisible. In other words it is necessary to make the digital sub-structure so small and so fine as to lose itself behind the grains. The paradox is that this may even be necessary when often a very coarse grain structure is the object of this process. It seems bizarre that the eye is able to forgive and accept an extremely grainy print, but in order to reproduce this print it is necessary to still maintain a high level of resolution to reproduce what is essentially a very crude transcription of reality. Paradoxically, large grains need the same level of resolution as do fine grains if it is the grain that we want to see, or more correctly not notice, rather than the pixels.

The second insight is that being a direct transcription of an object, there is an instantaneous jump in the quality of the image. The problems caused by pixels attempting to reproduce the grain structure of the photograph evaporate. There is simply no grain at all. The conflict of image sub-structure ceases to be an issue. The scanner image is entirely composed of pixels. They are not defining any other sub-structure but instead, the object itself. As such the eye forgives their presence in much the same way that it forgives grain in a conventional photograph.

The third insight is the realization that there is an optimum level of resolution to achieve the illusion of believability. Because of the large size of the flatbed scanner relative to a conventional photographic negative, it is not necessary to have high levels of resolution. It appears that the eye will accept a resolution of 150 dpi/ppi at the size of the finished print and effectively see no image sub-structure. That is to say it appears to have no grain, or pixels, of any kind.

Additionally, this image can be enlarged, almost infinitely, through interpolation and if anything, gain quality rather than lose it. This is possible again because of the intrinsic properties of the digital image.

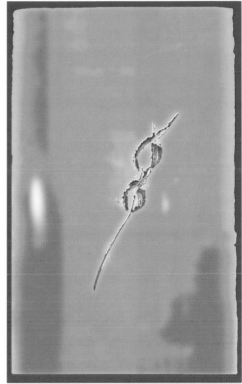

The Secret, Douglas Holleley, 1995. An "out-take" from the author's book, *Soft Landing in a Hard Place,* Rockcorry, Woodford, New South Wales, 1996.

Left:
This image was made in a similar manner to *The Dream Map* (reproduced at the beginning of this chapter). The shape came from that of a shadow found in a photograph made in the Italian city of Verona in 1989. *The Repentant Devil,* Douglas Holleley, 1993. From the author's book, *Paper, Scissors & Stone.* Rockcorry, Woodford, New South Wales, 1995.

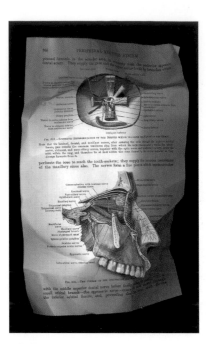

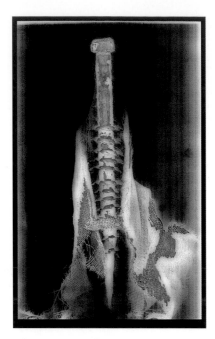

The Tear.   *The Dangerous Object.*   *The Agitated Spirit.*

In comparison with photography, enlargement in digital imaging is a function of more, not bigger. When one enlarges a photograph, one enlarges each of the individual grains that make up the image. In other words, the bigger the print, the bigger the grains. When one enlarges a digital image one instead creates more pixels of the same or similar values clustering around each original pixel. Thus a large print does not consist of a whole collection of great big pixels, but a larger number of same size pixels that share the information of the original image. This process is termed interpolation. Thus it is possible from direct scans of this nature to produce large images (24″ x 30″ or bigger) from initial file sizes of only 3 megabytes in full color. Black and white image files created this way are even smaller. Because the interpolation is occurring to the rendition of the object itself, not to the photographic grain, the occurrence of distracting artifacts caused by the interference of these two image sub-structures, is minimized.

The disadvantage of this form of image capture is that the size of the objects you can image is limited by the size of the bed of the scanner. Most scanners have a surface area about 8.5″ x 11″ but increasingly tabloid scanners are becoming available enabling you to work with an 11″ x 17″ area. However, these scanners are relatively expensive, especially if they are designed to perform the double duty of also being able to scan from small scale transparencies and negatives. However, cheaper models with lower levels of resolution will give you quite stunning results if you employ the whole area of the platen.

All six images across this page are from the author's book *Soft Landing in a Hard Place.* Many of the images were created from small, rather sharp pieces of metal. By the time this work was finished, so was my scanner. Should the reader desire to work with similarly destructive raw materials, be sure to place a protective sheet of plastic over the glass platen, especially if the scanner is not yours.

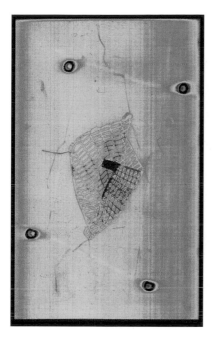

Escape Seemed the Safest Option.

The Flight.

Equally Valid Choices Presented Themselves.

The basic practical rule of scanning objects is that the object is modeled by its distance from the glass. In order to get a white scan using a white piece of paper, place the paper flat on the glass. Lifting the paper an inch or so off the glass will produce a middle gray. Removing the paper entirely, with the scanner lid left open in a darkened room will result in a black scan. Thus the tonal range of the image will reflect the three dimensional qualities of the original object as if illuminated from the front. Those parts of the object closest to the glass will be rendered lighter than those farther away.

All six images across this page are from the author's book *Soft Landing in a Hard Place,* Rockcorry, Woodford, New South Wales, 1996.

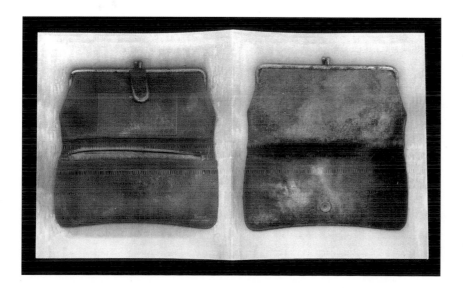

Joan Lyons' purse disappeared for some twenty five years. In 1998 it was returned to her and she found within it pay slips, receipts and other personal items dating from the time of her life when the purse was lost.

The unexpected discovery of this personal time capsule prompted the creation of this book. Using direct scans she combined images of the purse and its contents with personal reflections and comments which evoke the poignancy of the passing of time. Joan Lyons, *Twenty Five Years Ago,* Visual Studies Workshop Press, Rochester, N.Y., 1998.

FRAME GRABBING FROM VIDEO

Like the flatbed scanner, frame grabbing from your video camera, is another way of directly using the pixel structure of the computer to render reality without reference to a preexisting photographic matrix. However, the difference in quality between this and the flatbed scanner is profound. Quality is directly related to the scale of the sensor in your video camera. These chips are tiny, often less than one quarter the size of the already diminutive 35mm negative. As such the descriptive power of the large scale flatbed scanner is denied

Tijuana, Mexico, Douglas Holleley, 1996. From the author's book, *Past and Future Tense*, Rockcorry, Rochester, N.Y., 1998.

you. However, you may still find there are many advantages to using such a device. If you use a video camera (digital video in particular) your image will have only the structure of the pixel as its basic picture element for defining the world. Thus, any lack of sharpness will not be a function of interference between pixel and grain, but simply a lack of resolution when describing the appearance of the subject itself.

What is particularly useful about this method of imaging, is the ability to take advantage of the often quite extraordinary optical properties of the video camera. Mitchell[2] argues that digital imaging is still in the "horseless carriage" stage. In much the same way that the first automobiles resembled the carriages that used to be drawn by horses, so digital imaging represents, not a new way of seeing, but a replication of photographic conventions, practices and particularly equipment, that have evolved for quite different reasons.

On this note it is interesting, but somewhat depressing, to consider how much digital cameras replicate the specifications of their analog counterparts. A digital still camera tends to look like a 35mm camera. It usually has a lens of fixed focal length, or at best a relatively short zoom range, and stores about the same number of pictures as a roll of film. None of these things have to be. They are conventions which have been established over a long period of time in response to the characteristics of 35mm film and its associated optical and mechanical requirements. However, it means we have the incongruous situation of

2. W. J. Mitchell in an address to the conference, *Still Photography*, Melbourne, Australia, 1994.

a new medium imitating the qualities of the old, even to the point where the same limitations are imposed for reasons of nostalgia and habit, not because this new medium requires them.

Video digital cameras and even the video Hi8 format, for the same reasons, replicate the qualities we are accustomed to expecting in movie cameras. Because of the smaller negative size of movie film, zoom lenses are cheaper to make and more compact, and are thus usually provided. Long recording times are also expected. Yet all of these (helpful) qualities could be easily incorporated into still digital camera design, but for reasons of habit and convention, they are not.

The point is that the still digital camera, and the moving digital camera use, not two different sizes of film with two different properties, but in fact often use the identical light sensitive chip to record the image. The original reason for different camera designs no longer exists. The image quality of both camera types is the same.[3]

Consider what opportunities occur as a consequence. If you use a video camera to make (still) images for your book, you instantly gain

3. This is less true now than it was only a couple of years ago. The new generation of still digital cameras are using larger, "megapixel" chips which are bigger than their video counterpart. These chips may well yet find themselves in video cameras so the reader is encouraged to make careful enquires when considering the purchase of digital equipment.

Above and below:
These two images were originally captured on videotape (Hi8) and then "frame grabbed." All images on this page were made in Tijuana, Mexico, in 1996 and are from the author's book, *Past and Future Tense*, Rockcorry, Rochester, N.Y., 1998.

two quite extraordinary advantages over using a still digital camera. Firstly, in all but the cheapest video camera you get a zoom lens of often 20:1 range. The equivalent in 35mm photography would be a 35 to 700 mm focal length range. Secondly you get a tape which can record not 24, 36 or even 72 images but 90 minutes worth of images from which you may select when it comes time to download these images into your computer. In comparison, the still digital camera usually stores 20 to 40 images and usually has simple optics which pale in comparison to those of most video cameras.

You will find if you try this method of imaging, that you cannot simply make movies and grab still frames from them. More often than not the images will be blurred and of poor quality. Movies work by relying on the eye's ability to smooth out the transitions from frame to frame. Each individual frame can be quite soft. When these frames are isolated it sometimes seems there is no time when anything is actually sharp. Thus if you are using a video camera to capture images for the computer, you will have to adapt your method of photographing to suit. Frame carefully and hold the camera as still as you would if shooting with a slow shutter speed with a conventional camera. Fortunately, video cameras often come with a device that senses the movement of the camera relative to the subject, and makes incremental adjustments so as to maximize sharpness. This is very useful when using a 20:1 zoom lens.

Images made in this way are ideal for books. Usually the pixel dimensions of the raw image are 480 x 640 but some video capture cards enable you to grab the single frames at resolutions of 600 x 800. This is sufficient size for most books. Images of great beauty can be made with these cameras because of their sophisticated optics, such as the remarkable zoom characteristics which facilitate precise framing and extreme macro focussing qualities. (These qualities have a direct bearing on image quality.) With a zoom it is possible to frame so precisely that cropping need never occur.

In the Chapel of Cornell University, Douglas Holleley, Ithaca, N.Y., 1999. From the author's book, *The Frock*, Rockcorry, Ithaca, N.Y., 1999.

This maintains the largest file size possible for any given image.) Additionally, experimenting with unusual framings, and photographing incidental, even serendipitous, events is both possible, and encouraged, because of the freedom to make hundreds of images on the one large capacity tape. This extended image storage capacity promotes creative risk taking and can facilitate the growth of your visual vocabulary.

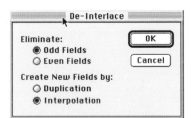

Detail of the Chicago Public Library, Douglas Holleley, Chicago, Ill., 1998. From the author's book, *The Frock,* Rockcorry, Ithaca, N.Y., 1999.

To import and process the images it is necessary to ascertain, based on what type of camera and computer you have, what method you will employ to "frame grab" the individual images.[4] It is a case of reading the instruction book that came with your equipment. Irrespective of the method you choose, there are one or two basic principles that remain the same for all occasions. The most important of these is to be aware that the video image is made up of two "fields" which overlay each other to construct each frame. If these fields are not completely in synchronization, usually because of slight camera movement, then your picture will appear unsharp and may have jagged edges. In the Photoshop *Filter* menu there is in the sub-category *Video*, a filter called *DeInterlace*. This filter eliminates either the *Odd* or *Even* field and creates a new one either by interpolation or by duplication. A useful setting is to eliminate the *Odd* fields and create new fields by interpolation. (See the box at right.) Try experimenting with other combinations to see if you get a result more appropriate to your equipment.

You will find that as the image is captured from video the resolution of the image will be 72 ppi/dpi at about 8″ x 10″. You may wish to resize you image immediately to 150 ppi/dpi retaining the same physical dimension by using the bicubic interpolation, found in the *Image Size* menu in Photoshop. If you do this immediately, any corrections will be applied at the new, larger size and be less subject to amplification and artifacts than if you resize it at a later stage. Your file will still be a manageable size.

4. I have had success with a Hi8 video camera by plugging the camera into the video-in jacks using the Apple video player software to grab the frames. Newer Macs with Fire Wire technology can directly import digital video and still images.

If grabbing from video try using the *De-Interlace* filter (from the *Filter* menu) to see if it helps the quality of your frame grabs. It is important to use this filter before making any corrections, adjustments or modifications to your image.

STILL DIGITAL CAMERAS

There are two main classes of still digital cameras. The first of these is the relatively inexpensive, single chip camera. The second is the digital scanning back for larger format cameras such as medium format studio cameras and still larger backs for 4″ x 5″ cameras.

The single chip camera relies on a light sensitive chip not unlike that in a video camera. This chip is quite small, although manufacturers are increasing the size and sensitivity with every new generation. The cameras work like conventional still cameras, and as discussed, mimic most of their advantages and disadvantages. At the lower end of the market the cameras resemble the simple point and shoot 35mm camera. They usually have a rangefinder view finder and a lens of fixed focal length, the better models having a modest zoom range.

There are also very high end single chip cameras which are usually based on existing good quality 35mm reflex cameras. These models have a larger light sensitive chip and usually have a small hard drive attached to the camera so more images can be stored without having to stop and download them onto a computer. Storage is one of the biggest limitations of still digital cameras. If you are considering purchasing one, find out how many images you can make and whether you can add or change memory modules on location. Also get some estimate of the battery life and the speed of downloading. Increasingly there are many excellent digital cameras that are quite inexpensive. However, some may have drawbacks not immediately apparent.

The best of the smaller cameras are capable of making images that when imported into the computer can give you a photo-quality image at 11″ x 14″. This is a level of quality that is quite suitable for a book of average (US letter) page size. The technology is improving so quickly, that still digital cameras will very soon prove to be a viable alternative to conventional film.

Above:
All the images on this double-page spread were made with a 3.34 mega-pixel digital camera. In comparison with the video stills on the previous page, they exhibit the levels of resolution associated with conventional silver photography.
Venus of Mumford, N.Y. Douglas Holleley, 2000.

The second type of still digital camera is not really a camera at all, but instead a removable back designed to suit studio cameras which customarily have film sizes of 120 mm or larger. These backs are attached to the camera where usually there would be a film back. They work in much the same way as a flatbed scanner. A moving bar "reads" the image projected onto the back by the lens.

These backs are very expensive and suitable only for subjects which do not move as the exposure can take several minutes. Additionally, for the very same reason, the light source must be continuous throughout the exposure, making the use of strobe lighting impossible. These camera backs can produce images of very high quality and they are much in demand for high end catalog production, food and product photography and other applications where the subject is essentially inert.

Most likely you will not have such a camera. However, if it is your good fortune to have access to one you will find it a great advantage to be able to import your files directly into the computer. The same applies for the more modest single chip cameras discussed earlier.

The methods for getting these images into the computer will vary from manufacturer to manufacturer. There may be software specific to the brand of camera you are using and again you should read the directions. If you are going to use the images in your book then they should be saved as TIFF files in Photoshop and named and stored so you can retrieve them as required.

Above:
The Road Sign, Douglas Holleley, 2000.

Below:
Give us our Daily Message,
Douglas Holleley, 2000.

Interactive Reading, Douglas Holleley, direct scanned image, 1993. From the author's book, *Paper, Scissors & Stone*, Rockcorry, Woodford, New South Wales, 1995.

CHAPTER 9

PRINTING THE BOOK

MODERN desktop printers are capable of producing prints of remarkable quality. A well-corrected inkjet print can exhibit a full range of tones from the deepest and most saturated black to the most delicate and articulated highlights. Using one of the oldest and most traditional forms of imaging, ink on paper, this modern technology allows you to publish your work in a way unimaginable in the past. However, having the latest and fastest computer, and the latest and most highly-specified printer does not automatically guarantee a good result.

Printing is an art as well as a science. Computers may exhibit the qualities of precision, but they are still only tools that can be used well and intelligently, or thoughtlessly and insensitively. They do not replace the need for knowledge, practice, and a rigorous program of testing.

Above:
A page from the *Gutenberg Bible.* This book, printed in 1450–1455, was the first in the Western world to use moveable type. *Courtesy of the Cary Graphic Arts Collection, Rochester Institute of Technology, Rochester, N.Y.*

CALIBRATING THE SYSTEM

It is possible to calibrate your system to a very high degree. However, the more specific you make the settings for both the program and the monitor, the greater the chance of creating a system that will work well for you but not if you should choose (or need) to take your files to be printed elsewhere.

Accordingly, the best strategy is to use the global controls in your system and rely on the proprietary software created by the computer manufacturer, to provide a base level of calibration that will not deviate too much from any norm (or any other system you may encounter).

Different printers, even different programs, can interpret the same file in various ways. Variations can also occur when using the same printer. Different papers, different inks, different settings, and different combinations of these variables can all combine to create quite radical variations of the same image. Such variations, occurring even within a well-calibrated system, emphasize the need for a thorough knowledge and understanding of all of the characteristics (even idiosyncrasies) of your particular printer/software combinations.

The first calibration is to ensure your computer knows to what type of monitor it is connected. In the Apple software there is a system of color management called *ColorSync*. Go to the *Control Panels* in the *Apple* menu and select the *ColorSync* option. A dialog box will appear with a variety of monitors from which to choose. Be sure that the monitor connected to the computer is the monitor selected. If the monitor does not appear in the list of choices, then, depending on the size of your monitor, select the *13″ or 16″ RGB Standard* option.

Your computer must know to which type of monitor it is connected. From the *Control Panels* select *ColorSync* and select your monitor from the list of choices.

The image processing program you are using will also need to be synchronized with your computer/monitor combination. If you are using Photoshop go to the *File* menu and select *Monitor Setup*, which (depending on the version of the program) will either be in *Preferences* or in *Color Settings.*

In the *Monitor* menu there will be a list of monitor types from which to choose. Again, select the monitor type you are using. The *Gamma,* or contrast value is a default 1.80. This is suitable for most printing purposes and is best left as is. The *White Point* value defaults at 6500° K. This should also be left alone.

The *Phosphors* menu describes your monitor type. If it is not in the menu look in the instruction book that accompanied your monitor to find the "chromacity coordinates" and enter them in the field that opens when you select the *Custom* option.

Further calibration must be made within the image processing program itself. Find the *Monitor Setup* and again select the type of monitor you are using. You will also be able to make other adjustments as described in the text to ensure your system displays your images as accurately as possible.

The final adjustment is to the *Ambient Light* levels. This adjusts the monitor brightness to suit the light of the room where you are working. For the most part the default setting of *Medium* is suitable but if your computer is consistently in either a very bright or very dark space then this selection may be altered to suit.

After ensuring that the computer and the monitor are correctly synchronized, the next task is to get the best possible match between the density of your print and the appearance of the image on the screen. This is easy to do and will assist in obtaining good prints consistently. Select a well-printed black and white photograph with a level of brightness and contrast you consider to be correct. Scan and correct it as discussed in Chapter 7. Print this image using photo quality (matte) coated inkjet paper, setting the printer to the highest quality settings for this paper. Then use the contrast and brightness controls on the monitor to alter the screen image so that in terms of brightness and contrast, the screen matches the print. Although you use a grayscale image for this calibration you will find that benefits will also accrue to your color images. (With the monitor controls set in this way, color changes due to variations in print density are minimized.)

These elementary calibration procedures will give good results for most kinds of desktop printers. The files produced will not be so specific or skewed from "normal" to cause any serious problems. Ultra fine calibration is for experienced printing press operators, familiar with the characteristics of their own printing devices. If in the future, you take your files to such a printer for output, the basic calibration steps outlined in this chapter will provide a good baseline standard. If you also enclose a good quality proof print made from your own printer, you should get excellent results.

THEORETICAL PRINTING ISSUES

COLOR SPACE: FROM MONITOR TO PAPER

Digital printing requires you to understand that the way the image is displayed on the monitor is completely different from the way it is imaged on paper. The monitor display works by mixing together the additive primary colors of red, green and blue. The principle of additive color was demonstrated by James Clerk Maxwell on May 17, 1861.[1] Maxwell showed that all the colors of the spectrum could be reproduced using only three additive primaries: red, green and blue. Maxwell photographed the same event, from the same viewpoint, three times through each of these colored filters in turn. He then processed each piece of film so it would be a positive transparency. Each piece of film was then sandwiched to glass tinted the same color as the original filter. In this way the transparency photographed through the red filter was colored red, the blue filtered transparency, blue and the green transparency, green. He then set up three projectors and projected the three images over each other so they were in registration. The image on the screen was thus in full color.[2]

The screen of the computer monitor utilizes the same principle. Within the video tube, there are three phosphor "guns" which project three beams of colored light, each red, green and blue, onto the coating of the screen where they combine to create the illusion of full color. Digital files which store data to produce color in this way are said to be in RGB mode. (See the diagram at right.)

Right: This diagram shows how red, blue and green *light* combine to make white light. You will observe that where two primary colors overlap, the colors yellow, magenta and cyan are formed. These colors are the subtractive primary colors which when combined as *pigment,* enable the image to be printed on paper using ink or toner.

1. Brian Coe, *Colour Photography, The First Hundred Years 1840–1940,* Ash and Grant, London, 1978.

2. You can test this by setting up three slide projectors, one with a red gel, another with a green and the third with a blue and project them onto a wall. Where the colors overlap, white light is produced. In contrast, if you were to combine the red, green and blue primary colors using ink or paint (pigments) on paper, then the result would be black.

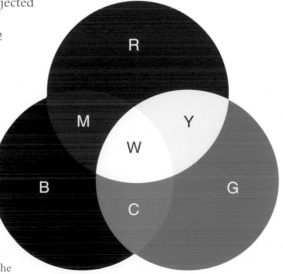

However, the printer cannot mix light together; it must instead use pigments (inks, dyes, toner, etc.) applied to paper. It works by creating the separate red, green and blue components of the image by using their complementary colors: cyan, magenta and yellow. Thus to reproduce a red in your image, yellow and magenta pigment are laid on the paper. White is created, not by adding red, green and blue light together, but instead by with-holding pigment, allowing the white paper base to show.

In theory, to produce black you mix these three colors together, but in practice you usually get a dark muddy brown called process black. To ensure rich shadows when using these pigments, a separate layer of black ink is also deposited on the paper. This ink is given the designation "K" to distinguish it from "B" for blue.

This mode of color is called subtractive color because colors are formed by subtracting or absorbing energy from white light (which contains all the wavelengths of the visible light spectrum.) Colors that are not absorbed are reflected back into your eyes. Thus if an object is yellow, the yellow pigment absorbs all of the blue component (the pigment equivalents being cyan and magenta) and reflects back to your eye only the yellow. Just like mixing paints, the more the colors are mixed together, the darker the color appears because more of the white light is absorbed. Digital files which store the data in this form are said to be in CMYK mode.

Because these two systems render color in different ways, it is inevitable that there will be some degree of variance as the same image is displayed firstly on the monitor screen, then subsequently rendered on paper.[3] This raises the question: which is the most appropriate mode in which to save the files?

In almost all cases (when printing at home in particular) the RGB mode is best. Desktop printer software contains its own color mode conversion tables and assume an image calibrated in RGB. These printer color tables produce excellent results and it is best to use them.

Working with CMYK images is more complex as *you* are responsible for the reallocation of the RGB data to the CMYK profiles. In doing so you must clearly understand all of the variables involved in the system that will eventually print your image. This includes knowing the color characteristics of the ink or toner that will be used, the characteristics of the paper you intend to print on and any system biases that the printer may possess.

Subtractive color is the system used by your desktop printer. By mixing the three subtractive primaries together most of the colors displayed on the screen of the computer can be reproduced on paper. Unlike RGB colors, white is produced not by adding colored light together, but by withholding pigment, allowing the white paper base to show through. The more pigment applied to the paper, the darker the image.

3. Some colors displayed by the monitor have no equivalents when printed in ink. Such colors are said to be out of gamut. There is a *Gamut* indicator in Photoshop under the *View* menu. You can use the *Sponge* tool to de-saturate the questionable areas if you desire, but it is not recommended you do this until you have printed the image and then decided whether or not the result justifies modification of the file. Unless the image prints poorly, leave things alone.

The only time you will need to use CMYK is if you are taking your images to be printed by a commercial printer. You may be asked to submit your files in this form. Be very cautious if this is happens. The translation from the color space of an RGB image to a CMYK image is a critical step and to expect you to assume this responsibility is expecting too much. To do this properly you have to know all the characteristics of the target printing device (and the paper stock) and be given the appropriate information. This will then need to be entered in Photoshop to make the color separations accurately. If these values (and precise instructions) are given to you, then you have found a good printer and you may proceed with confidence. If not, ask for clear advice, do a series of tests, or find another printer.

Put simply, you will find you will obtain consistently good results saving your images in RGB format. The files will be smaller and you will be able to save more images on each disk. On your desktop printer they will of necessity, be converted to CMYK when you print, and for the most part the color tables in your printer's software will do an excellent job.

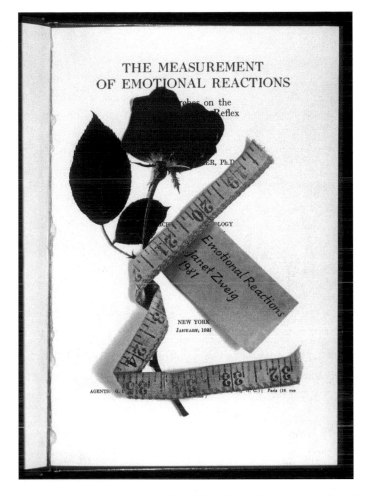

Above: The highly dimensional quality of this printed page is due to the fact that Janet Zweig made the color separations "in camera." Three 4″ x 5″ negatives were exposed through filters of each of the additive primary colors. Offset plates were then created from enlarged film renditions of these exposures.
Emotional Reactions, self-published, Toronto, Ontario, 1981.

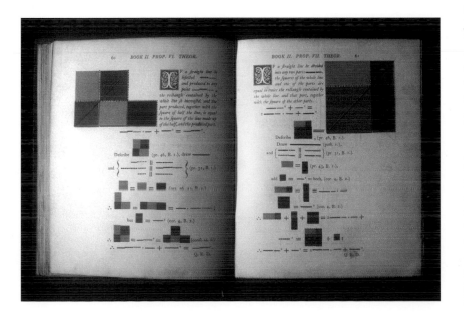

Left: This idiosyncratic book attempted to use colored geometric shapes to facilitate an understanding of Euclidean Geometry. Not surprisingly it confounded most readers and quickly went out of print.
Oliver Byrne, *The First Six Books of the Elements of Euclid, in which colored diagrams and symbols are used instead of letters for the greater ease of learners,* London, William Pickering, 1847.

FROM PIXELS TO DOTS

Desktop printers, like commercial offset presses, cannot reproduce a photograph in continuous tone. Instead the printer lays down a series of closely spaced dots of ink (or toner) which when viewed by the naked eye, blend together to form the illusion of continuous tone. The image file must be processed in such a way that the pixel values can be translated into a series of dots of either yellow, magenta, cyan or black ink. It is important to understand that the individual pixels of the image file do not directly translate to these dots of ink. The pixel information must be processed. There are two ways that this occurs. For the most part inkjet printers use a random dot process and laser printers use PostScript software.

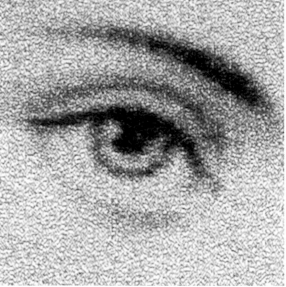

The illustrations show how the same image is rendered by the two screening processes. In the example above you can see the organic nature of the stochastic (random dot) screen, variations of which are used by most inkjet printers. Compare this half-toning to the regularly spaced, but different sized dots of PostScript image processing as shown below. This screening is found on Laser printers.

Inkjet printers usually employ a form of image rendering known as stochastic screening. In this process, the image data is converted to a series of irregularly placed dots, all of the same size, which correspond to the tone and color values of small groups of pixels. Changes in image density depend on how many of these equally sized dots are clustered in a particular area. This method produces (in raster images) an organic visual impression, exhibiting quite remarkable properties of tactility and smoothness.

Laser printers and offset presses on the other hand create the illusion of continuous tone by creating large or small regularly spaced dots, arranged in a grid. The software/hardware combination which creates these dots is called PostScript. This process emulates the traditional printing screen. (Refer to Chapter 6, *Resolution and Printing Considerations, pp. 127–129.*) PostScript is seldom found in inkjet printers. However, occasionally, some employ a software package which emulates its effect.

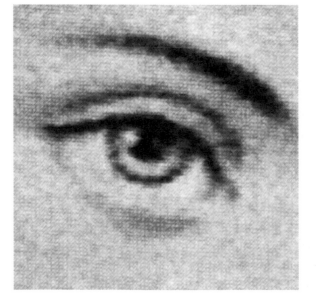

PRINTING WITH INKJET PRINTERS

Inkjet printers have a print head which deposits minute droplets of ink on the paper. Manufacturers employ various ways to break the ink up into these fine droplets. Some, like Epson, employ a tiny vibrating quartz crystal. Canon uses a small heating element inside the print head to cause the ink to form a bubble which bursts onto the paper.

The finer these droplets, the greater the resolution and apparent sharpness of the finished print. However, the size of the droplets is only half the equation when considering how to maximize the sharpness of the print. The final printed resolution of the image is dependent not only on the size of the ink droplet but also on the characteristics of the paper that receives it. The role of paper is so critical that it is addressed in the following chapter.

Other than paper selection, obtaining maximum quality (assuming your image files have been carefully scanned and corrected) depends on how well you use the various controls in the computer. It is assumed that you are using the best printer you can afford. Obviously the more expensive the printer, the more likely it is that it will print well. Some modern inkjet printers print at resolutions as fine as 1400 dpi (approximately 100 lpi). However, excellent results can be obtained with the most basic of printers with resolutions as low as 300 dpi. Certainly the images may have a "grainy" quality in comparison with a printer of higher resolution. However, if these qualities are used sensitively and appropriately, they can enhance, rather than detract, from the finished print.

The main form of control is the dialog box. This controls the software and permits many levels of adjustment to the image. Some of them are useful. Some of them are unhelpful and in some cases actually harmful to image quality. Printer software is termed *driver* software.

The first thing to do is to fully explore the controls. The following diagrams show the choices available in the Epson driver software. Other printers will have similar choices to those illustrated here. It is essential to thoroughly investigate the choices available to you in your particular driver. You will find choices in both the *Page Setup* box and the *Print* box. There are often boxes within boxes. Check them all out. You will need to know what they all do, even if you do not use them everyday. Although the advice given here is based on many years of practice, there is still no substitute for practicing with your printer, using your own images and paper. Just as photographic prints improve with practice and experience, so too will digital prints.

In the first instance we will look at the global controls that govern print quality. After this we will proceed to a discussion of the various options that are specific to QuarkXPress.

Inkjet printers can produce books with qualities unobtainable with conventional methods of printing. The two books above are printed and bound using the French fold set-up. With photo-quality matte paper, the image fidelity is very high and the pages are thick and very tactile as a consequence of them being folded in half.
Vertical Book:
Douglas Holleley, *Love Song,* Rockcorry, New South Wales, 1995.
Horizontal Book:
Douglas Holleley, *Paper, Scissors & Stone,* Rockcorry, New South Wales, 1995.

The diagram at right shows the main dialog box for the Epson 1520 when the *Print* command is selected. It may be that your dialog box will look different from this.

However, all drivers share much the same logic. The only differences are in the number of options available to you and the way these are displayed. They may look complex at first, but if you patiently examine them, ideally making prints (and notes) as you proceed, you will gain understanding and control.

The first two choices are self-explanatory. The *Copies* box allows you to nominate how many copies you would like printed and the *Pages* option allows you to specify which page(s) you would like to print.

Also it is here you have control over print quality. This particular driver software offers two main choices, *Automatic* and *Advanced*. If you select *Automatic*, the printer will print at high speed and will produce acceptable quality for proofing purposes. However, it is likely you will wish to maximize your print quality to take advantage of the quite remarkable quality of modern inkjet printers. To do this you will have to select the *Advanced* option. When you do this the *More Settings* button will become active, rather than grayed out. When this is done you will see you have a host of choices available to you.

The first choice is *Print Quality*. In this case *Fine–720 dpi* is selected. This setting is suitable for most high quality work. It provides a reasonable compromise between speed and print quality. There is a higher level which is labeled *Superfine–1440 dpi*. This setting provides the highest possible quality. It does this for two reasons. Firstly, the printer "draws" a finer and more precise dot. The second reason is that the speed of the printer is reduced dramatically. This reduction in speed greatly improves quality. Because the paper moves more slowly through the printer, banding (the presence of thin, white, un-printed lines on the horizontal axis) is almost completely eliminated.

Above:
A view of the first window you will encounter when you select *Print* with an Epson printer. It is essential to become familiar with all of the controls of your printer. Within the print dialog box of each machine are a variety of options that will help you to obtain maximum print quality. They will not all look like the example above. However, make the effort to become familiar with the controls in *your* printer. Conduct a series of tests to determine the settings that work best for your images, on your choice of paper, for your book. Click on *Advanced,* then *More Settings,* to see the window below.

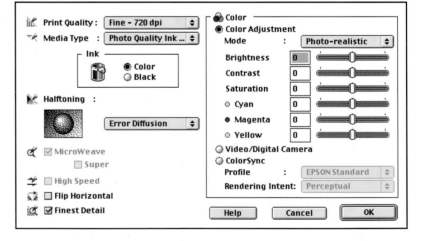

When your select *More Settings*, control increases dramatically. Do not adjust the individual *Contrast, Brightness* and *Color* controls. Instead, try each of the choices in the *Color Adjustment* and *ColorSync* boxes.

This is especially helpful to remember when using some of the fine art papers described in the following chapter. These papers are particularly prone to banding and it is essential to reduce the speed of printing as much as possible to obtain optimum results. However, there is a price. Your document will take *very* much longer to print. However, with most proprietary inkjet papers, the Fine–720 dpi setting will provide an excellent compromise between quality and printing speed.

The selection of the type of paper, or media, you intend to print on allows considerable control. This choice controls how much ink is deposited on the paper. *Transparencies* require large amounts of ink, *Coated* paper requires less, and *Plain* paper, because of the amount of bleed, needs even less. Knowing this you should print an image on each of these settings when you are testing a new paper, particularly one not intended for use in an inkjet printer, such as high quality drawing papers or other speciality stocks. Note which settings are employed for each test print and then compare the results. Ignore the fact that the driver gives them specific names. Simply test and make the decision on which setting to use on the basis of how the image looks on a particular paper. You will also find that the colors of the image will shift as you try different settings. Again this is all useful information and should be written immediately on the test print(s).

You will find that sometimes you will have little choice. For example, the Epson printer will not permit you to select plain paper with some of the high resolution/slow speed settings. You will thus have to nominate a photo-quality stock even if you are using a plain uncoated art paper and then experiment with the different color controls (discussed overleaf) to get your file to print successfully. You will find that the colors will vary when you nominate different papers. You will also find that different brands of paper will have different color characteristics, even though they are nominally the same product, and share the same setting. Practice and experimentation is the only solution.

In the *Halftoning* box you can choose the method of screening the image. Most inkjet printers offer the choice between using a slower more elegant stochastic screening option, or a faster but less satisfying regular screen pattern which mimics (crudely) the appearance of PostScript. Any image will be best printed using the random dot screening option. In Epson printers this is called the *Error Diffusion* setting.

Below:
Just as you select different photographic papers for different print techniques, so to you can choose different papers to suit your book. Some of these papers will require that you experiment freely with the settings, ignoring their nominated function, and simply working through the options to find a setting that suits your purposes. The image below was hand-colored on matte photographic paper. When reprinting the image with an inkjet printer, it was appropriate to select a matte paper stock with similar visual and tactile properties to the original. Using a glossy stock would have been quite unsuitable.
Coney Island, Luna Park, Sydney, Douglas Holleley, 1991.

If you have the choice (sometimes there is no option) ensure that the *MicroWeave* setting is selected. This will help minimize banding of the image. *Flip Horizontal* means what it says. For fine work select the *Finest Detail* option. Remember however, that every extra feature will have an adverse effect on printing time.

If you have an Epson printer, you will see there is a box which permits a variety of choices over color adjustment. The three main choices are *Color Adjustment, Video/Digital Camera* and *ColorSync*. If you are making a book, most likely you will not be using the *Video/Digital Camera* setting so we will ignore it for the purposes of this discussion. Instead we will concentrate on the options of *Color Adjustment* and *ColorSync*. In my experience using the *Color Adjustment* control provides the best results.

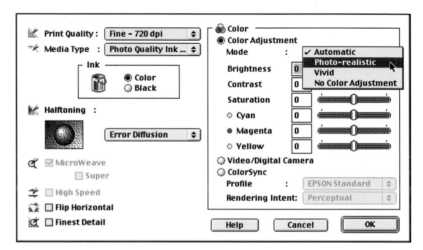

You will notice that there is a box at the top of this control that has several options. These are *Automatic, Photo-realistic, Vivid* and *No Color Adjustment*. Selecting *Photo-realistic* usually will give excellent results. Further down you will notice that there are controls for *Brightness* and *Contrast*. Do not use these controls. If you have to alter the brightness and contrast at the printing stage then the image is not properly corrected. You should go back to the original Photoshop file and make the adjustments there using either *Levels* or *Curves*.

Similarly, when using paper made by the same company who made your printer, avoid using any controls that affect color balance (*Saturation, Cyan, Magenta* and *Yellow*). If you have a well-corrected image, and have performed the calibration steps outlined in the beginning of this chapter, there is no reason why the file should not print accurately.

Above:
The *Color Adjustment* control gives you a choice of four settings. Try each in turn making sure you note on your print the setting you chose. Similarly, experiment with the *ColorSync* settings at the bottom of the dialog box where you will find a further three choices. It is far better to apply these global controls to your file than it is to make adjustments to density and color by using the individual slider controls in *Color Adjustment*. If you have corrected your image as discussed previously, there should be no need to change the color and density at the printing stage.

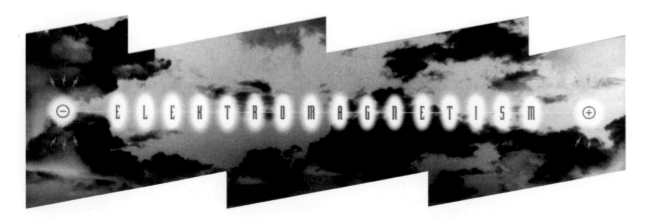

When you use the *ColorSync* option, you can select profiles that attempt to match your monitor display to the printed page. If you have followed the instructions for basic calibration at the beginning of this chapter, you may wish to see how the *ColorSync* renders your file. Theoretically this is the most exact method of ensuring the best match. If using an Epson printer, set the *Profile* to *Epson Standard*. In the *Rendering Intent* box you will see there are three choices. *Perceptual*, best for printing photographs, *Saturation*, best for graphics and *Colorimetric* which theoretically provides the closest match to your screen image. It is essential to try all three methods and then compare the results to the *Color Adjustment* option discussed previously. Usually *Perceptual* works best if you try this method.

You will find when you do this that the same image file will print quite differently on each of the settings. I find it useful to stick with the basic *Color Adjustment, Photo-realistic* setting as a base level and then use these other choices when printing on different papers. As you change papers, and especially if you use products not intended for inkjet printing, the color balance can gyrate wildly. Do not be put off by this but instead try to "fool" your printer into correcting for the different paper by selecting each of these options in turn.

In saying this I am mindful of the fact that this discussion is based around a specific brand of printer. However, almost all printers will have similar controls and all are capable of excellent results. The names may vary slightly but essentially they will be the same. The basic principle is to get to know your printer by doing a series of tests and keeping careful notes for each test print.

At the risk of contradicting the above advice, there is one occasion when you may find it useful to use the Color Adjustment settings. You will find that if you wish to print on the *SuperFine* setting (1440 dpi), with Fine Art papers, that the driver will not permit you to select Plain paper. This will result in a print that is greenish. In this case it is acceptable practice to increase the magenta by 4 points. This works

Below and Opposite:
This book is printed on an Iris inkjet printer. These printers are a larger, more sophisticated (and expensive) version of the printer that is most likely sitting on your desk at home. You do not need such a device for most books. However, if as in this case, your book is very wide (14′ when unfolded) you may need to take a deep breath and find the money to pay for such prints. Iris machines print beautifully on heavyweight, acid free papers, producing books with superb tactile qualities.
Philip Zimmermann, *Electromagnetism,* Space Heater Editions, Rhinecliff, N.Y., 1995.

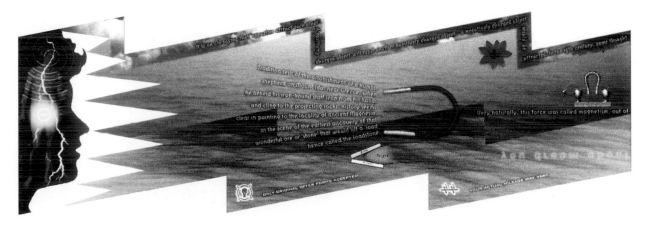

quite well. However, this advice is specific to Epson printers, for a specific circumstance. More important is to understand that such decisions are best made after a series of rigorous tests.

As mentioned before, printing is an art as well as a science. Only practice and experience will produce good results. The printer is literally your desktop darkroom. No one expects to get a good print on the first try in the darkroom, so be prepared to make similar efforts when you begin to print digitally.

Finally, there will be a control to help you maintain the printer in good working order. In the Epson driver this is called *Utility*. Here you will find tools that check the alignment of your printer's print head, clean the jets or nozzles of the head, and sometimes even tell you how much ink is left in the tanks. (See the diagram above right.)

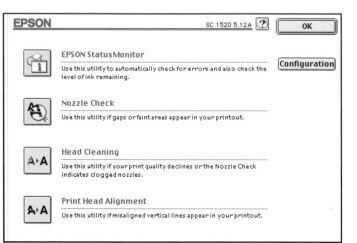

All printers will have a *Utility* dialog box similar to the one shown above. It is here you can clean and align the print heads to ensure optimum quality.

Below: Clifton Meador, *Long Slow March.* Produced and printed at the Center for Editions, Purchase College, SUNY, Purchase, N.Y., 1996.

In conclusion, it is appropriate to recapitulate the basic principles…

- The calibration controls may have a name referring to a specific function and/or product but essentially they are controls you can use to fine tune your print quality.
- Test each setting rigorously, making notes as you proceed.
- Do not use the individual *Brightness* and *Contrast* controls to adjust your print at the printing stage. Instead, try to find a "global" setting (in the *Color Adjustment* or *ColorSync* controls) that makes the adjustment for your image/paper combination in a consistent and predictable manner.
- Remember that when you change papers, your settings will also most likely need adjustment, especially when printing with non-standard inkjet products.
- Enjoy the fact that printing is an art as well as a science. Embrace the freedom and expressive possibilities rather than search for the "wonder setting" that works for all occasions, all images and all papers. There is no panacea.

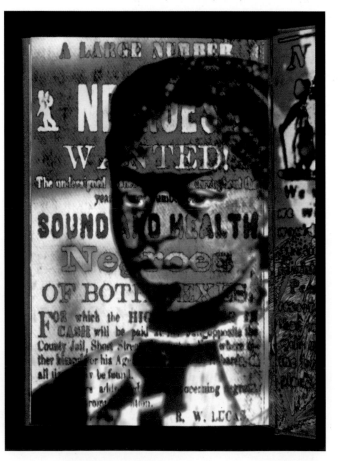

PRINTING FROM QUARKXPRESS

When you print from QuarkXPress your driver will show more choices. Most of these are common to both inkjet and laser printing as they control the general behavior of the program. For this discussion we are going to use the *Page Setup* and *Print* dialog boxes of an inkjet printer. Choices not available to (non-PostScript) inkjet printers will be grayed out. Following this discussion the PostScript driver will be discussed.

Below:
The QuarkXPress *Page Setup* box. When you are printing from QuarkXPress the dialog boxes alter to suit the more specific requirements of this program. As with all aspects of printing it is essential to become familiar with all of the options available.

PAGE SETUP/INKJET PRINTER

Go to the *File* menu and select *Page Setup*. This box (right), or one like it, allows you to select the *Paper Size* and *Orientation* of the page. Note that you can also change the scale at which the page will print. You can reduce the page size by altering the scaling to less than 100%. You can enter a value between 25% and 400%. However, values over 100% will usually print poorly. Finally, make sure the *Color Printing* option is selected.

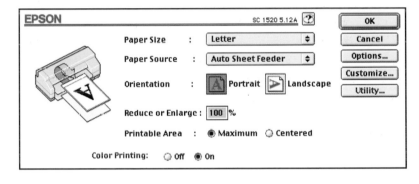

INKJET PRINTING OPTIONS

Go to the *File* menu and select *Print*. The dialog box will look like the diagram at right. The first few choices such as the number of *Copies*, the *Pages* to be printed, the *Print Quality, Mode, Paper Type* and *Ink* (Color or Black) are common to all programs. However, the remainder of the choices are specific to QuarkXPress. Note: This is the *Print* dialog box for Version 3 of QuarkXPress. I have used it for illustration as all the information is on one level. Version 4 has the same information (and more) but it is arranged as a series of tabs within boxes, much more like the PostScript dialogue boxes to be discussed later in this chapter, *pp. 198–203*. If your box looks different to this, don't worry. The same information will be there but may require to be accessed in a different way. Be patient and work methodically through the choices. It will work.

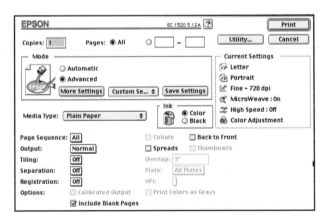

Above:
The QuarkXPress *Print* box for an Epson printer.

The *Page Sequence* allows you to choose whether to print *All* pages, the *Even* numbered pages or the *Odd* numbered pages. You use this if you are printing on both sides of the paper. If you print only the odd numbers first you can then put the paper back in the printer (testing for the correct orientation) and by selecting *Even*, print on the back of these sheets. You can combine this setting with the *Pages* option so, for example, you could print the odd pages between 3 and 11. (When printing from Quark you must enter the page numbers exactly as they are written, i.e. with any prefixes, or if in Roman numerals, then these must be used. You can avoid this by typing "+" before the absolute page number. In this way QuarkXPress will print Page 3 for example, whether it is designated Page 1:3, Page iii, or any other variation you may have selected.)

Output allows you override the printer's own quality control and you can print a draft copy of your document.

Tiling permits you to use your small desktop printer to print an oversize document by breaking up the document into smaller pieces called tiles. If, for example, you size an image at 30″ x 40″ (and create a QuarkXPress document the same size, or larger) the tiling option will print the document in a series of letter size prints that when recombined will enable you to see the image at this size, much like how a large billboard is made up of a number of smaller sheets. There are three tiling options. *Off,* *Manual* and *Auto.* If you choose *Off,* no tiling occurs. If you use *Auto,* the program will decide where the document is segmented. If you choose *Manual,* you can choose where the breaks occur by repositioning the ruler origin in your document. You can also determine the amount of tile overlap by entering values between 0 and 6 inches in the *Overlap* field to the right of the Tiling box (0.5″ is usually OK).

Separation is seldom used at home. This option is usually selected by a commercial printer when making offset plates for full-color reproduction.

The *Print* dialog box as you might find when printing with an Apple/Canon brand printer. You will observe that the choices specific to QuarkXPress remain the same from manufacturer to manufacturer.

Detail from a medieval manuscript on alchemy. *Courtesy of the Cary Graphic Arts Collection, Rochester Institute of Technology, Rochester, N.Y.*

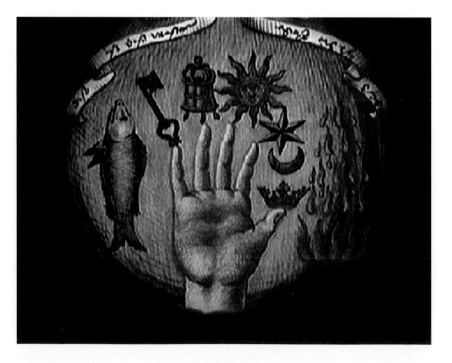

Selecting *Registration* will cause QuarkXPress to print trim marks around your document to show where to cut it down to create the finished size of the page. When used correctly, it accurately positions your artwork on the page. It is used by commercial printers who often place more than one page at a time on a large sheet and then trim to suit. This option is seldom used at home as usually you are working with standard size paper and want to use the whole page. If you have a letter size printer, and are printing a letter size document, selecting this option will force some of the print area off the paper because of the space required for the registration marks. It is only useful if you are printing a small document or have a large printer. (To see how it works create a small page, say 6″ x 4″, and select *Registration*. You will see that the 6″ x 4″ page will appear on the letter size paper with trim marks indicating the boundary of the page.)

While engaged in this process it is worthwhile to spare a moment to be grateful for the gift of vision. The image above is a photograph of a double-page spread of braille text. Imagine how different this way of exploring the contents of a book is compared to absorbing images and text through the medium of sight. To be able to read through one's fingertips, communicating with the book only through the sense of touch, is a very different way of receiving content. For a moment try to conceive of such a world and the very different set of spatial and textual cues with which you would have to engage.

If you are using an inkjet printer, the options unavailable to you will be grayed-out. This is the case in the two color options on this driver.

The *Include Blank Pages* option is usually left checked. If there is a blank page, it is usually part of your layout and you will want it included.

Collate is selected when you want to keep pages in sequence when you print multiple copies of a document. If *Collate* is left unchecked, the program prints the requested number of copies of one page, and then all copies of the next page and so on until the job is finished. Leaving the box unchecked speeds up printing time with laser printers.

Selecting *Back to Front* will instruct the program to print from the last page first. Thus the document will be in order when the printing is done.

Selecting *Spreads* will allow pages adjacent to each other in the *Document Layout* palette to be printed next to each other on one sheet of paper. This is useful if you intend to saddle stitch your book.

This concludes the printing options available to an inkjet printer. Next we will look at the dialog box for a PostScript printer, such as you would find on a laser printer, to see what controls are offered.

PRINTING A QUARKXPRESS DOCUMENT WITH A POSTSCRIPT PRINTER

Many of the controls are the same as those available to inkjet printers. However, PostScript drivers offer more choices. Some you will access frequently, others seldom if at all. Do not be overwhelmed by the apparent complexity. It is simply a matter of going through the options in a systematic way. In all there are a total of eleven dialog boxes, three for *Page Setup*, and eight for *Print*.

PAGE SETUP WITH A POSTSCRIPT PRINTER

You can see that you can set the *Format, Paper size, Orientation* and *Scaling* of the document. You will observe that the box at the top left hand side of the dialog box is labeled *Page Attributes*. There is also an arrow in the box indicating that more choices are available.

Select this arrow and move on to the next level. You will now see there are choices particular to the program from which you are printing. In this case we are printing from QuarkXPress. The display will now look like the second box at the bottom of this page.

Select your *Printer Type*. The *Resolution* of the printer will be displayed and will usually be governed by the characteristics of the printer you have selected. If the printer has a higher resolution than 300 dpi, it should say so in this box.

The *Paper Size*, if you are using standard size paper choices determined in the previous *(Page Attributes)* box, will be grayed out.

Data Format refers to how you want the data to be coded. There are two choices, ASCII or Binary. Binary uses less code and prints faster, so select this option.

The *Halftone Screen* will depend on the level of resolution of the printer. As discussed in Chapter 6, *p. 128*, printers of 300 dpi can usually only print at 60 lpi. The higher the level of resolution of the printer, the finer this value can be set. You can select a higher value to reduce the screen's visibility, but if you do so there will be a trade off. The gray scale will not be rendered as smoothly and the image may look posterized as the tones "jump" from one level of gray to the next.

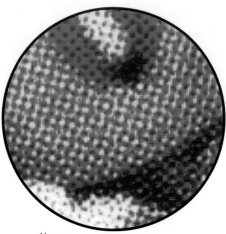

Above:
Reproduced at full size is a detail from the book cover on the opposite page. This halftone dot pattern is typical of PostScript offset printing.
Philip Zimmermann, *Long Story Short, Home is Where the Heart Is,* 1997–99.

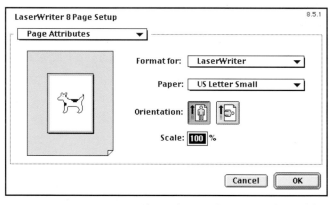

Above: The initial *Page Setup* box of the PostScript driver.

Below: The second box (found in *Page Attributes*) displays the options specific to QuarkXPress.

You can experiment with this to see if it suits your document. Screen rulings of 100 lpi can often work well if you have a 600 dpi printer.

Paper Offset, Paper Width and *Page Gap* are for use with professional imagesetters and will only require setting if you are having your book printed commercially. Similarly, ignore the *PDF Screen Values* setting. If this box is not grayed-out, selecting it will tell QuarkXPress to use the Screen Set Values defined in the MF file for the selected printer. If it is grayed-out, the program will use its own default values.

The final Page Setup box is labeled *PostScript Options.* There are two classes of options.

The *Visual Effects (Flip Horizontal, Flip Vertical* and *Invert Image)* are self-explanatory.

In the *Image and Text* category if you select *Substitute Fonts,* the printer will substitute a suitable PostScript font for any bitmap fonts in your document. Thus, for example, the font "New Century Schoolbook" will replace "New York." Leaving it unchecked will mean the printer will print the non-PostScript font. If you select *Smooth Text,* these fonts will look better when they print. Similarly you can check *Smooth Graphics* to improve the quality of any bit map images in your document. In this example the default settings are displayed. They are usually sufficient

Below:
You will seldom need to access the final *Page Setup* box in the PostScript driver. The default settings work well enough for most jobs. However, be aware that these choices exist.

Top Image, Opposite Page and Right: Zimmermann is an experienced and talented offset printer. In this book he deliberately references and exploits the halftoning pattern of a PostScript rip. The screen, normally either invisible or barely noticed, forms an important graphic signifier. It suggests that the sometimes obscure images are simply part of an everyday, even ubiquitous, currency of printed visual information.
Philip Zimmermann, *Long Story Short, Home is Where the Heart Is.* Co-published by Nexus Press, Atlanta, Ga. and Space Heater Editions/Zimmermann Multiples, Rhinecliff, N.Y., 1997–99.

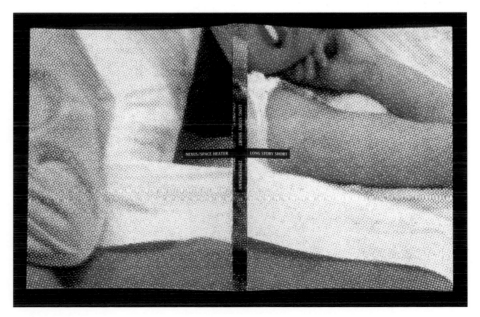

POSTSCRIPT PRINTING OPTIONS

Again, a single box will appear but there are eight further levels of choice. Most of these you can safely ignore but we will look at each. The first box is labeled *General*.

The choices here are much as those for the inkjet driver discussed earlier in this chapter. You can nominate the number of *Copies*, whether they are to be *Collated* or not and which *Pages* of the document you wish to print.

You will however, observe a couple of significant differences. Firstly, you can select whether the printer will accept paper from the paper tray *(Cassette)* or via *Manual Feed*. You can also choose to print the first page from one and the others from a different source if you are using two kinds of paper or substrate.

Finally you can decide whether to print your document as a paper copy by selecting the *Destination* as *Printer* or whether to save it as a PostScript file by choosing the destination *File*. This is useful particularly if you wish to either send the file to be printed elsewhere, or prepare it to be distilled and published on a CD ROM. (See Chapter 10, *Printing Your Book Electronically, pp. 216–217.)*

The second level of choice, as with the *Page Setup*, is specific to QuarkXPress. Again, this box is very similar to the options available to the inkjet printer as discussed earlier. (See *Inkjet Printing Options, pp. 195–197.*) However, the PostScript driver allows more choices.

Options available here, but not available to non-PostScript inkjet printers, include the following.

The *Thumbnails* option allows you to print a thumbnail view of your document. This produces a miniature version of your entire book and is useful for ensuring that all images are in the correct place and for checking the overall "feel" without using very much paper or toner.

The first level of the PostScript *Print* dialog box. Here basic paper and document handling tasks can be controlled.

The driver also contains instructions specific to QuarkXPress. Refer to the text for an explanation of these choices.

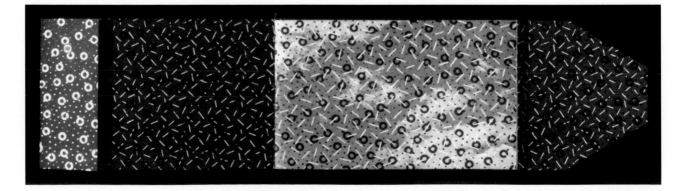

The *Option: Calibrated Output* should be selected. Also useful is *Print Colors as Grays*. If you are using a black and white laser printer this will convert any color images in your document to gray scale with maximum fidelity.

The *OPI* (Open Prepress Interface) selection allows you to print your document without the pictures should you just wish to proof read the text. (Including all of the images means the document takes longer to print.)

This double-page spread illustrates the beauty of offset printing when used by an artist with an enhanced sensibility of print quality.
Carl Sesto, *Ordinary Events,* School of the Museum of Fine Arts (SMFA) Press, Boston, 1994.

Left Opposite and Right:
The patterning evident in *Long Story Short* was anticipated almost 15 years earlier in *Civil Defense.* At first glance the repeated circular motif on the cover appears to be an enlarged halftone screen. However, closer inspection reveals that the small circles forming the pattern are in fact defined by an even smaller halftone screen. The persistence of this aesthetic, and the intimate relationship it shares with the medium of offset printing, suggests Zimmermann regards the (sub)structure of the printed image to be an integral part of the communicated content.
Philip Zimmermann, *Civil Defense,* Space Heater Multiples, Barrytown, N.Y., 1983-84.

The next box controls *Background Printing.* Here you choose *Foreground* to print your document immediately. Choose *Background* to spool it so you can work on your computer while the document prints or, if you wish, set the *Print Time* (and date) to print it later if the printer is currently being used by others or you have a large job and do not want to inconvenience colleagues.

Above: The *Background Printing* dialog box.

The next dialog box allows you to create a *Cover Page* before or after your document. The cover page includes the document name, and the date and time printed.

The next box allows control over the *Color Matching* method. The default setting is *Print Color* set to *Color/Grayscale.* If this is selected the *Intent* and *Printer Profile* choices will be grayed out. This is correct for most purposes unless you have a color printer which uses the ColorSync matching method. If this is the case, select the *ColorSync Color Matching* option in *Print Color,* leave *Intent* set to *Auto* selection and then select the printer/paper combination from the *Printer Profile* list of choices.

Above: The *Cover Page* dialog box.

The *Layout* box is shown below. This dialog box gives you the choice to print more than one page per sheet. You will seldom require this feature unless the book is significantly smaller than a standard paper size.

Below:
The *Layout* dialog box.

Above: The *Color Matching* dialog box.

The box to the right, *Error Handling,* controls how printing errors are reported. If you wish to use this, usually it is sufficient to select *Summarize on screen.*

Right: The *Error Handling* dialog box.

The final *Save as File* dialog box is used if you are saving your document as a PostScript file. At the moment it is selected for compatibility and correctability over file size. Choosing *Level 1 Compatible*, and saving it as an *ASCII* file means the document will work on most systems and can (to an extent) be edited if there are any errors. Selecting *Level 2 and 3,* and *Binary* will give you a much smaller file but this file cannot be edited.

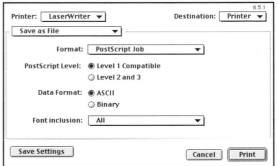

Above: The *Save As File* dialog box.

 Font Inclusion is best set to *All*. Usually you will only use this option if requested to do so by a commercial press operator. If this occurs you will receive full instructions on how he or she prefers such files to be prepared. Follow their directions.

 This concludes the discussion of the PostScript printing options. Although there are many choices, in reality most are seldom used. However, if you intend to use a laser printer frequently you need to know they exist.

CONCLUSION

This discussion focuses on the theoretical and practical aspects of achieving maximum print quality within the computer system. It has often been said that image editing programs like Photoshop are a "digital darkroom." However, never forget that the real purpose of a darkroom is to make prints. Sometimes it seems after performing all the corrections to the images that printing the image is a simple and straightforward extension of this work. It is not. The fact is, digital printing requires as much practice and skill as conventional darkroom work. The most important aspect of printing is knowing your machine. This involves becoming familiar with all of the controls in the software and which combinations to use to gain the print quality most appropriate to your images and your desired intention. The only way to do this is to conduct a rigorous testing procedure and above all practice, practice, practice.

 Even so, gaining knowledge of the characteristics of your printer is only half the equation. The other significant variable is the choice of output substrate. This term is usually a long winded way of referring to "paper" but its use does acknowledge there are materials other than paper that can be used to print your book (including electronic media such as CD ROMs). The following chapter addresses the role these materials play in inkjet and laser printing.

Janet Zweig, *Emotional Reactions,*
Self-published, Toronto, Ontario, 1981.

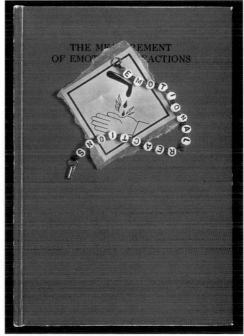

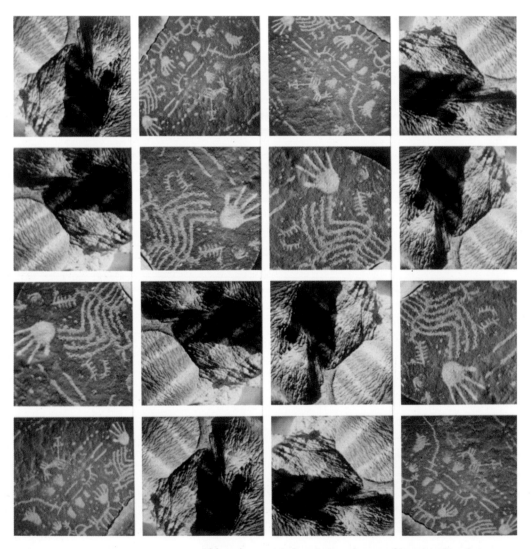

Although not strictly printing, the act of imaging directly on stone, as shown in this Polaroid SX-70 image of *Newspaper Rock* in Arizona, illustrates vividly how the choice of substrate material influences how your image is initially rendered and subsequently perceived. It also is a reminder of how the substrate plays an important role in determining how long an image will last. *Petroglyphs and the Painted Desert, Arizona*, Douglas Holleley, 1978.

CHAPTER 10

PRINTING SUBSTRATES AND MATERIALS

THE materials you choose profoundly affect print quality. This is particularly the case with paper. Your choice can make a basic printer look good, or a good printer look bad. Spend time testing various materials, *making notes* as you proceed. Wherever possible select materials that are of archival quality (i.e. materials that are neutral to slightly alkaline). Papers can differ widely in quality, and some of the cheaper varieties are extremely acidic. High acid levels will cause the book to deteriorate quickly. If in doubt, spend a little more money. Compared to the time invested making your book, and the high cost of printing inks, the paper component of your budget is small. Do not be tempted by false economies.

In addition to printing your book on paper, you may wish to consider publishing it on CD ROM. There are many advantages to this procedure. The screen image can be vivid, imbuing your images with a quality that may well suit the nature of your work. A book published in this form can resemble an intimate, and interactive, movie. There are also significant cost advantages, especially if your book contains many color images. At the end of this chapter, *pp. 202–203*, there are instructions for publishing and distributing your work in this way.

PAPERS AND SUBSTRATES FOR INKJET PRINTING

What makes inkjet printing so interpretive is that ink and paper interact with each other at a fundamental level. If ink comes in contact with porous paper such as newsprint, it is quickly absorbed into the surrounding fibers. Although a fine droplet might have been emitted, it expands on the paper. As adjacent droplets are deposited, they bleed into each other. Consequently, the image looks unsharp. In contrast, if the ink is deposited on a more sympathetic surface, this phenomena is kept to a minimum. Each individual droplet dries quickly, maintaining its size and shape.

Additionally, when ink is absorbed into paper, it loses its intensity of color. The more absorbent the paper, the less the brightness and saturation of the printed image.

An example of cuneiform script. The writing is made by pressing wedge shaped tools into soft clay which is then allowed to harden, and in some cases is even fired. This particular tablet records an ancient commercial transaction.
Sumerian clay tablet, c.1700 B.C.
Courtesy of the Elmira College Archives, Gannett-Tripp Library, Elmira College, Elmira, N.Y.

This interaction suggests that in choosing and testing papers, you must do this in combination with the printer controls. As mentioned in the previous chapter, use the paper type settings, not as literal descriptions of the paper you are using, but as a way of applying either light or heavy amounts of ink. Try the same paper with a variety of settings before making a final decision.

Essentially, ink will print on (almost) anything, giving you a wide variety of choices over how your book will look and feel when finished. Consider color and texture as well as surface. Printing on crisp white coated paper communicates a completely different sensation to printing on a textured, off-white, or even colored, hand-made stock.

There are two main sources for inkjet printing papers.

PROPRIETARY INKJET PAPERS

Printer manufacturers as well as increasing number of paper manufacturers, produce a vast selection of paper stocks designed and manufactured specifically for inkjet printers. They include:

Matte, coated stocks of white paper

These papers have a coating, usually on one side, which maximizes sharpness and saturation. Double-sided coated papers are also available. You will recall in Chapter 2, *Printing Issues, pp. 27–29,* there was a caution against printing on both sides of the paper with an inkjet printer. If you are contemplating the use of a double-sided coated stock, test it before you decide. Despite the fact that these papers are usually thicker than normal, they still may wilt under the pressure of being printed on both sides, particularly if you are printing images with large areas of black. The real advantage is the fact that the verso is the same color and texture as the recto. Single-sided coated papers are often very yellow on the back.

Regrettably, coated paper is not as archivally-stable as a good-quality, uncoated stock. However, if your book demands the image quality that a coated paper provides, then you will have little choice. You can be consoled by the fact that the cover will protect the contents as much as is reasonably possible. Almost always any deterioration is a function of the interaction of light with these materials, and a book, with its protective cover, will provide the best possible environment for the preservation of the paper.

When selecting such papers, look for the designation "photo quality." A particularly good product is made by Epson.

Two examples of the use of vellum. This material, made of calf skin, is still obtainable, and can be used in an inkjet printer.
Top:
Missal. Vellum Leaf from Illuminated Medieval Manuscript, France, Beauvais, Late XIII Century.
Bottom:
Book of Hours. (Horae Beatae Mariae Virginis.) Vellum Leaf, France, Early XVI Century.

Photo quality high-gloss papers

High-gloss coated surfaces most resemble conventional photographs and usually produce the most saturated colors and the highest levels of sharpness. However, these papers, unless "tipped in," are generally unsuitable for bookmaking. Their surface often causes them to stick together when bound in a single volume. They are also very easily marked by fingerprints. Their plasticized finish, and sometimes brittle nature, can also make them difficult to bind.

Transparency materials

These materials are of great interest to the bookmaker. Although they share the drawbacks of glossy photo paper, being easily marked and difficult to bind, they nevertheless can provide unusual design solutions. The shiny surface can contrast well with matte paper pages. You can print text, allowing an image to show through, or you can print images on them that mask out either text or other images. A little of this effect goes a long way.

Above and Below:
Dianne Longley uses transparency materials to partially mask (and partially reveal) the image on the subsequent page. In so doing she literally constructs layers of meaning. Such a strategy also introduces the element of surprise and anticipation as the (visual) story is progressively unveiled. *Sensory Memorandum,* Illuminations Press, Adelaide, South Australia and the Visual Studies Workshop Press, Rochester, N.Y., 1998.

Sized cloth and canvas

Using these materials can give the book a very different "feel." One can use them to make the pages of a soft book, or you can join them together to form a scroll. They are also useful for making custom bookcloth.

Transfer material

Closely related is the use of transfer material, usually used to apply photographic images to t-shirts and other articles of clothing.

You can print an image and then place it on a variety of surfaces. These need not be cloth. It could be paper too thick to pass through your printer or any other similar surface. Like the sized cloth, it is also useful for making custom bookcloth.

There are also other transfer materials often used to place an image on a cup or mug. These materials can transfer an image to any hard, non-porous substrate such as metal, ceramic tiles or plexiglass. They permit interesting alternatives to conventional cover materials.

FINE ART PAPERS

Another source of papers for inkjet printing is an art supply store. The papers stocked by these stores are usually not designed for this purpose but can often be used with great effect.

Watercolor, drawing, and printmaking papers

Fine Art papers often come in a range of colors, especially varieties of white. They can range from a brilliant white to a soft, subtle cream and many of them provide a sympathetically textured surface on which to print. They offer an alternative to the harshness that can often accompany the use of a standard white stocks.

Not all such papers will print satisfactorily. Some of them have a highly textured surface which can cause problems with an inkjet printer. Those papers designated "hot press" have the smoothest (and hardest) surfaces and usually work best. Next in order of increasing texture is "cold press" paper. After this you can choose a variety of textures. Ask your paper supplier for advice when you choose and when in doubt buy a single sheet and do a test print. Of the stocks available *Arches, Rives* and *Fabriano* work well. These papers are 100% rag content and acid free.

This book uses transparency material as well as regular wallpaper. Notice how the text is visible correctly on the recto but reversed on the verso, forming a connecting visual element.
Roberley Bell, *Home,* Visual Studies Workshop Press, Rochester, N.Y., 1995.

Despite the fact that high cotton fiber content is usually a desirable feature (because of its archival stability), often the inks work better if there is some wood fiber present. Stocks with archival properties but having wood fiber are *Magnani Incisione* and *Stonehenge.*

All these papers are usually thicker than those designed by the inkjet paper manufacturers. Watercolor and other art papers are often 90 to 140 lbs. (185 to 300 gsm.) and up. This weight is often desirable from an aesthetic perspective, but it can cause printing problems. Most inkjet printers are designed to use paper up to about 37 lbs. (around 140 gsm.).

Manufacturers generally prefer that you did not use such papers. They can put strain on the printer, both on the paper drive train and also on the actual printing heads if there is insufficient clearance. Usually the thicker the paper the more difficulty you will experience. Addressing this problem will be discussed shortly.

Inkjet Fine Art Papers

Manufacturers are now beginning to appreciate the increasing use of inkjet printers to make fine prints and some of them are making papers specifically designed for this kind of printing. These papers are usually variations on their regular stocks but are specially sized and/or coated for optimum results. They are even more costly than the already expensive Fine Art papers but are well worth trying. Again, the best course of action is to make a series of tests.

Specialty Papers

Also in the art supply store you can often find unusual papers with interesting tactile and visual qualities. They are worth trying to see if they work with your printer and images. Experiment with Japanese rice papers, hand-made papers of various types, metallized papers and papers made out of unusual materials such as banana fibers. (The latter works very well indeed.) There is no way to tell which paper will work other than to test it. You will find that some papers work well while others are hopelessly porous. You will only know if you try.

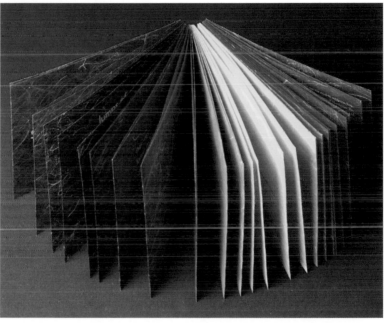

Consider also using colored paper in your book if it suits your content. This example contains two separate, but related, texts about travel in Australia. The title *Dream Time/Rainbow Travel* prompted the choice of multi-colored pages.
Bruce Chatwin, *Dream Time.*
Christian Ide, *Rainbow Travel.*
Alinea Presse, Berlin, 1993.

As problematical as papers that are too soft, are those that are too hard. These include certain kinds of metallized stocks and "papers" that are not paper at all but are instead some variety of mylar or plastic. Usually these materials will not allow the ink to dry and the result may well be a mess. If you test a few stocks you will quickly develop an appreciation of what is likely to work and what is not. Be prepared for surprises. Some good, some bad!

Usually all these papers are of very high quality (and priced accordingly) but there are others that you might not immediately consider, which are more prosaic but can have interesting properties if used with discretion and taste. Printing on brown paper bags and other industrial papers can be quite appropriate for certain applications. (I have even heard stories of people printing successfully on fine sandpaper!)

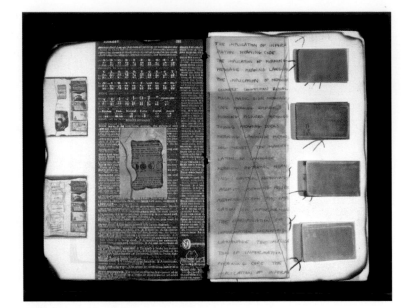

Do not limit yourself to simply choosing one paper with which to work. This example shows how a variety of stocks can be employed to give texture and vitality to a double-page spread.
Helen M. Brunner, *Primer: Ritual Elements (Book 1),* Writer's Center, Bethesden, Mo., 1982.

USING FINE ART AND SPECIALTY PAPERS

The main problem, apart from the quality of the printed image, is persuading thick paper to pass through your printer. Some printers accept such papers more easily than others. There are two variables. Firstly, the nature of the printer paper path and secondly, the direction of the grain of the paper.

If the path is relatively straight (usually found in machines where the paper feeds in the rear and exits in the front) then you will have an easier time than if the printer both loads and ejects the paper from the same side. Paper in such printers must describe a quite tight "U-turn" to be able to feed correctly. There are however, a few procedures you can adopt to maximize your chances of success.

The first of these is how you use the printer. Most printers have a setting which is recommended for printing envelopes. This setting allows for their extra thickness and thus provides a good base setting when working with heavier paper. There are usually two places of adjustment. The first of these is in the paper tray where the throat of the printer can be widened to accept thicker paper. Usually there is a lever with the icon of a page in one position, and the icon of an envelope in the other. Set the lever to the latter. The second is a lever on the print head itself. Again, there will most likely be two icons.

Opposite Page:
This book also uses a variety of substrates and materials. The bookmaker has used a combination of leather, gouache, inkjet printing, Polaroid transfers and Burgra art papers.
Peter Lyssiotis (In collaboration with Theo Strasser) *The Use of Ashes.* Self-published in an edition of 5, Melbourne, Vic., 1999.

Choosing the envelope setting will raise the head further away from the paper to provide extra clearance. (Check your manual. Epson, for example, uses a plus "+" sign rather than an envelope icon to give the print head more clearance.)

Always bear in mind that you are doing something that the manufacturer would not like to see and there is a chance you might void your warranty. If this is a critical issue for you, then stick to thinner stocks.

The second thing you can do to maximize your chances of success is to ensure that the grain of the paper is aligned correctly. Fine Art and specialty papers usually come in large sheets (approximately 22″x 30″). They will have to be cut or torn to fit in your printer.

To ascertain the direction of the grain, take one edge and bend it over to touch its opposite. See if it tends to stay in this position or whether it snaps back flat sharply. Do this again using the other two edges. The paper will bend more easily in one direction than the other. When it bends freely the grain is parallel to the bend. (See the diagrams at right.) The paper will go through the printer more easily if the grain is parallel to the rollers that carry it through the printer. If the grain is pointing towards the rollers it will resist bending as it tries (often unsuccessfully) to curve through the paper path. This can be enough to cause the printer to jam.

FINDING THE DIRECTION OF PAPER GRAIN

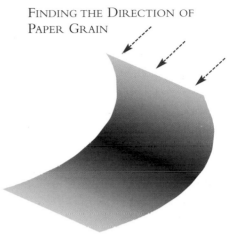

1. To find the direction of the grain, take one edge of the paper and bend it so it touches the opposite edge of the sheet. Do this in both directions.

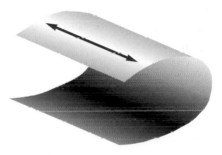

2. You will find that in one direction the paper bends freely and tends to stay in the bent position rather than spring back flat. When this occurs the grain is parallel to the bend (see arrow).

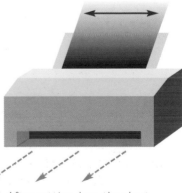

3. After cutting down the sheet, minimize jams and misfeeds in the printer by ensuring the grain of the paper is parallel to the rollers. (Red arrow.)

CHOOSING INK FOR THE INKJET PRINTER

One of the greatest expenses of inkjet printing is the cost of the inks. The printer manufacturers strongly recommend that you purchase their proprietary brand. In theory it should make no difference what brand of ink you use, but in practice the same printer can respond quite differently when different types are employed. There are no easy answers. It is simply a matter of trying a different brand of ink and seeing if you are happy with the results.

   There are three problems that can occur. The first of these is that the color calibration will alter, sometimes significantly. The only way you can see if this is happening with any accuracy is to create a test page to check a new brand of ink cartridge. The easiest way to do this is to open a new page layout document and create a series of picture or text boxes. Assign to these boxes the color sets of red, green, and blue, yellow, magenta, and cyan, and black. It is also helpful to create shades of these colors. (See the example below.)

   You should create this test sheet and use it when you first set up your printer with the manufacturer's inks in place. Should you decide to then try another (usually cheaper) brand, you have a basis on which to evaluate your choice. You will often find the colors vary significantly.

It is useful to make a test sheet like the one below to provide a standardized point of reference when testing new ink/paper combinations. To make one, create a number of text or picture boxes and fill them with the additive (Red, Green, and Blue) and subtractive (Cyan, Magenta, Yellow, and Black) primary colors as shown. By using the *Duplicate* command you can easily create a number of such boxes which will automatically overlap as in the example below. Shade each color at about 50% and 20% as well as leaving a box where the color is solid. It is also useful to have a neutral gray scale. Save this file and print a copy each time you use a new material.

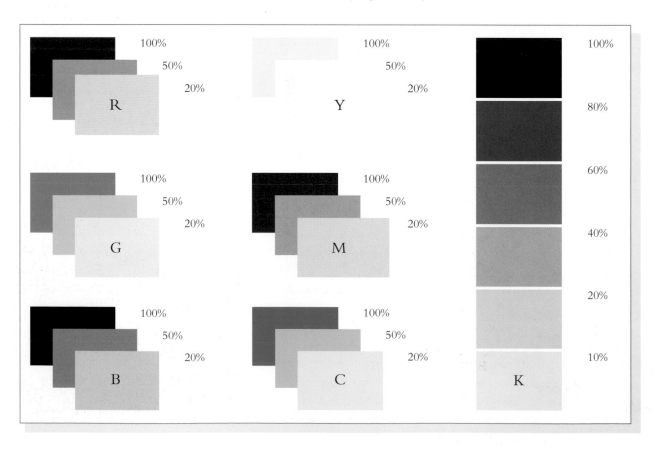

It is hard to advise on what you should do. The cost of ink is so high that any reader would be forgiven for attempting to reduce this bill. However, it is false economy to do this at the expense of something as critical as color balance.

The second problem that can occur is mechanical failure of the replacement cartridges. This is less of an issue now than it was in the past when often even ink-only cartridges simply failed to print after only a few pages. These days they are considerably more reliable. However, keep your receipts as most manufacturers offer some kind of warranty and will give you a refund if you are not happy. Be aware that some ink replacement cartridges also come with a new set of nozzles as well as the ink itself. These are more prone to problems than cartridges which provide only the ink to a fixed head in the printer.

Thirdly, and more difficult to test is the permanency of the ink. The ink in inkjet printers is different from regular inks. Conventional archival inks contain inert pigments suspended in a mild solvent medium. However, these inks will not work in an inkjet printer as the suspended particles cannot be ground finely enough to pass through the ultra thin nozzles of the inkjet print head. To get around this problem manufacturers use chemical dyes to color the ink. These dyes are intrinsically unstable in comparison.

This issue is being addressed at a variety of levels, including attempts to produce pigment particles small enough to pass through the print head nozzles, as well as making more permanent dyes. As things stand, the quality of dyes can vary from one manufacturer to another. Usually the original manufacturer's ink will provide you with the best result in this regard. As this aspect of printing becomes more of an issue, expect to see ink sets being produced which will claim to have enhanced durability. However, they are likely to be considerably more expensive than standard inks, and for the forseeable future, will have a more restricted color range, or gamut.

Finally on this issue, be always mindful of the fact that the *combination* of ink and paper is as much an issue as the ink or paper itself. (The same ink, printed on different substrates, can behave quite differently. Many of the cheaper coated papers are particularly prone to fading and/or color shifts.) There is no simple solution other than to always use the best materials you can afford, and maintain a rigorous testing regime.

Shinro Ohtake, *Atlanta, 1945–50*, Nexus Press, Atlanta, Ga., 1996.

Consider also utilizing the very materials of bookmaking as content. In this sculpture, one hundred feet of handmade paper is rolled into a delicate scroll. In so doing the artist makes reference to one of the earliest forms of bookbinding.
Sidewalk Scroll, John Diamond Nigh, 1998. Handmade paper, wooden base.

Papers and Substrates for Laser Printing

Laser printers do not permit the same amount of substrate choice as inkjet printers. The paper path is often quite convoluted, prohibiting the use of paper that is either too stiff or too thick. They are designed for high-volume, high-speed printing. This requires that the paper be cut perfectly square and be sufficiently flexible to negotiate the printer's mechanism. As such, deviating too much (in either direction) from a weight of 18 to 24 lbs. (80 to 120 gsm.) can cause paper jams, possibly damage your printer, and put your warranty at risk.

You will usually have to purchase papers specifically designed for such printers. Within the category of laser printer papers, there are many choices of quality, color and finish. When purchasing a stock, check that it is of archival quality. There is much paper available labeled Laser Paper that has very poor keeping qualities. Most manufacturers will state whether their stocks are archival or "acid free." It is essential to use paper of this quality as papers high in acid will deteriorate, becoming brittle and yellow in a surprisingly short period of time.

Most good quality office supply stores will offer a good range. Worth considering is paper recommended for color laser copiers. This is usually bright white, acid free and has a smooth hard finish. It is manufactured to maximize image sharpness and contrast.

However, these qualities, although useful for most purposes, may not always be appropriate to the nature and content of your book. If you want a softer effect, the use of art papers for laser printers is acceptable practice, as for inkjet printers. However, it will be unlikely you can use paper that is heavier than about 50 lbs. (170 gsm.) If you wish to use such papers you will have to perform a series of tests. Some printers have the ability to accept heavier papers, usually called "cover stock" and may have settings on the printer, or in the software, (or both) that permit their use with no damage to the machine. Read the instruction manual to see if this is possible with your machine.

You will also find that you can purchase laser paper with the grain going either parallel to the "long" side, or to the "short" side. The latter is sometimes described as going "across" the paper. As with inkjet printers, the best results are obtained if the grain of the paper is parallel to the rollers, so wherever possible, consider this factor when selecting pre-cut paper, or when (carefully and precisely) cutting down larger sheets of Fine Art paper.

Such cautions suggest that your choices will be narrower when using a laser printer. However, there are some other specialty stocks that make up for these limitations.

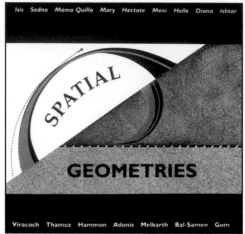

Wirth uses metallic inks in this complex die-cut book. Although such inks are (as yet) unavailable for most desktop printers, the product described on the next page under the heading *Specialty Products* can, with some careful work, duplicate this effect.
Karen Wirth, *Spatial Geometries*, Visual Studies Workshop Press, Rochester, N.Y., 1991.

Mylar and other plastic based papers

Some manufacturers make "papers" which are not papers at all but thin sheets of very stable, and often very archival, plastic. These products can be of great interest and they provide opportunities not available to inkjet printers.

Worthy of consideration are the stocks manufactured in Germany by Imperial. This company sells a product described as "metallic film." This plasticized stock closely resembles aluminum in appearance. Such stocks are not available for inkjet printers so be open to mixing and matching printing methods. Bear in mind that your book does not have to be printed exclusively on one system or another. You can print some pages on an inkjet printer, and others on a laser printer to take advantage of these different stocks.

Transparency Stocks

These are similar to those available to inkjet printers but have the advantage of being completely transparent. (They do not have a frosted coating to make the surface receptive to fluid based inks.) Again, consider their use even if the majority of the book is printed on an inkjet printer. Laser printers are particularly effective for printing text. The melted plastic toner produces a clean, rich, and very opaque black which works well on a transparent page, in contrast to the softness and tactility of the inkjet print on paper.

Above and below:
Although it is unlikely you will be able to use the simple gilding material described in the text to achieve results as precise and complex as this quite remarkable nineteenth century example, nevertheless be open to the emphasis and beauty provided by metallic effects.
Henry Noel Humphreys, *Sentiments and Similes of William Shakespeare. A classified selection of similes, definitions, descriptions, and other remarkable passages in the plays and poems of Shakespeare.* 3rd Edition. Longman, Green, Longman, Roberts and Green, London, c. 1870.

Specialty Products

One example is made by Letraset (Copy FX), a metal foil designed to adhere to the plastic toner, converting the black areas of the image or text to silver, gold or a variety of metallized colors. Investigate this and other similar products carefully. Many of them are packaged to emphasize a particular use. The product above encourages the purchaser to use it to enhance the text of invitations, certificates of achievement and other similar announcements. However, it can do quite extraordinary things to images. Be flexible, and experiment with alternative uses of such products.

PRINTING YOUR BOOK ELECTRONICALLY

There are ways to print your book other than using paper. One way of doing this is to print the work on CD ROM which offers the following advantages for the dissemination of your book.

- They are inexpensive. A blank CD costs very little money compared to the cost of producing a work on paper.
- They can reproduce color images with high quality.
- They are portable and inexpensive to transport via mail.
- They protect your investment. Unlike posting information on the Web where it can be accessed for free, the CD must be either purchased or specifically handed to the recipient.
- It is possible to print copies on demand.
- CD ROM's are, above all, an object. The data is in tangible form. The disk, its case and any accompanying material, can be purchased and catalogued like any book.

Peter E. Charuk, *Men's Work*. CD ROM, self-published, Sydney, New South Wales, 1995.

The easiest way to make a CD ROM is to purchase the program Adobe Acrobat Exchange/Distiller.[1] This program allows your book to appear on the screen as a PDF (Portable Document Format) file where it can be read by anybody who has Adobe Acrobat Reader (supplied free by Adobe and often "bundled" as part of the system software).

After installing Acrobat, a *Virtual Printer* will appear in the *Chooser* as if there was another printer connected to your computer. This form of printing works best with the Single-page set-up, and to a lesser extent with the Double-page spread. Because the document appears much as it looks in QuarkXPress with the guides turned off, it is quite unsuitable for the French-fold page set-up where you have pages on the screen that are not adjacent to each other. If you have set up your document in this fashion, you will have to re-format it.

Select the *PDF Writer* (the virtual printer) in the *Chooser* and go to *Page Setup*.

You will observe that the box asks for much of the same information as a conventional printer. In addition to allowing you to print to standard page sizes you can also select a *Custom* size. The main difference is the nature of the options that are available. Selecting the *Compression* option will produce a dialog box like the one on the opposite page.

This box enables you to compress the file so it occupies very little disk space. This is very useful if you decide to put your book (or a selection from it) on the web.

1. If you do not have Acrobat, you can use the PostScript driver to save the document as a file (See Chapter 9, *Printing with a PostScript Printer, p. 200.*) rather than a printed paper document. You can then take this file on a disk to be written or "distilled" in the universal PDF format at a bureau such as Kinko's. If you make your intentions known in advance, you will be given detailed written instructions on how to best prepare your files and what other material will need to accompany them. In the case of a QuarkXPress document, you will also need your image files and fonts.

Below: The Adobe Acrobat *Page Setup* dialog box.

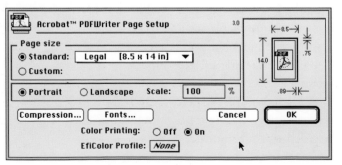

You may even find that your whole book will now fit on a floppy disk. The compression here has been set to the *Default* values. These work well for most documents. If you want better image quality, do not select any compression at all. However, if you do this your document will scroll very slowly. Compressing the images also adds a level of protection to your work as it reduces their file size and print quality making them less susceptible to unauthorized use.

The *Compatibility* option selected to 2.1 means the document can be read by older versions of Acrobat Reader.

The next dialog box is labeled *Fonts*. The Acrobat PDF writer will need to access all the fonts used in the book. Do this by selecting the option *Embed All Fonts*. Then select *Rebuild*.

The final step is to select *Print*. This box, by this stage, will look very familiar. You will see that all of the conventional options to print from QuarkXPress are present. You will observe that there are two additional options. These are *View PDF File* and *Short (DOS) File Names*.

Ensure both are selected. The *Short (DOS) File Names* is particularly important. PDF files are cross-platform. That is, they may be read by any computer, Macintosh or PC. By selecting this option the files you create can be recognized by the DOS system and will open without any problems in any computing environment.

The final step is to transfer this file to a suitable media. CD ROM's are particularly suitable as almost every recently purchased computer has such a drive. Additionally, they can be formatted to be recognized by both Macs and PC's. If you do not have access to a CD burner, you may find that the file has been compressed enough to fit on a floppy disk, or if not, a Zip disk. However, try wherever possible to write to CD for the reasons mentioned above. Then design a suitable cover to present your book effectively and attractively in this new form. In doing so consider your choice of materials carefully. You may try placing the CD in a binder more reminiscent of a conventional book rather than simply relying on the ubiquitous "jewel case."

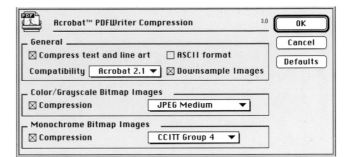

Above: The Adobe Acrobat *Compression* dialog box.

Below: The Adobe Acrobat *Fonts* dialog box.

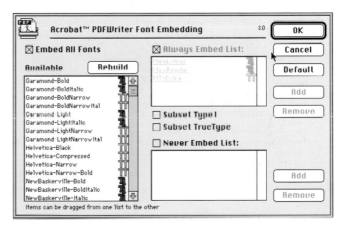

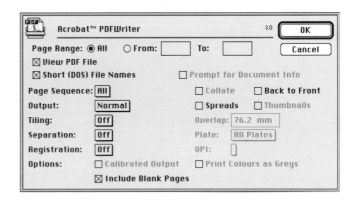

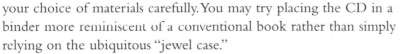

Above: The Adobe Acrobat *Print* dialog box.

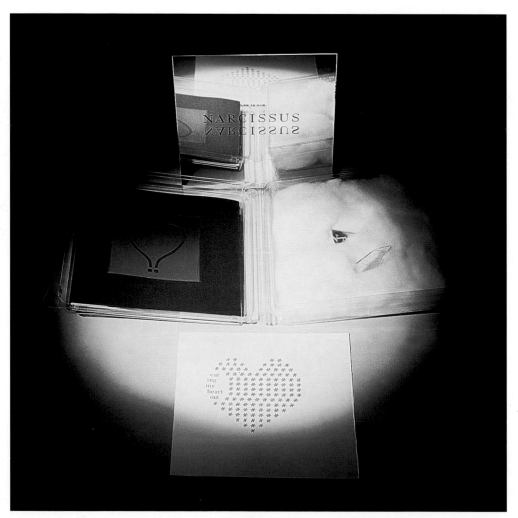

Binding can take many forms and use many different materials. It is more than simply making a cover for your book. Think of it instead as a coherent and sympathetic extension of your content. Seize the opportunity to add both complexity and clarity to your message. In this artist's book of typographical poems, Ruth Cowen's binding combines etchings, silkscreens, and an engraved mirror. *Real Estates of the Heart*. Graphic Investigation Workshop, Canberra School of Art, Canberra, 1991.

CHAPTER 11

BINDING THE BOOK

THE final stage in making a book is to bind it in a manner sympathetic to the contents. Despite the cliché that you cannot judge a book by its cover, the selection of an appropriate binding style and the careful choice of materials can suggest much about the content and intention of the author.

Although the binding of a book is the final stage in its presentation, do not be tempted to adopt a solution at the last minute to make it "look good." Do not be like those photographers who "mat" their prints, whether it suits their images or not, or those who automatically dry mount their prints on black cardboard (because it is thought that this will make the print "stand out"). The act of presentation is more complex than this. Good presentation is a mark of respect for the reader of your book. It is an act of generosity and giving. It should say to the reader that he or she is invited to view the work, and that his or her opinion is valued and respected.

Ideally you have been considering the cover of the book from the beginning. As you are now aware, bookmaking requires that all stages of the process be considered simultaneously, if for no other reason than one decision in the chain of production inevitably conditions the next. As early as the creation of your maquette, many factors that ultimately will affect the binding are in play. Decisions about page size, image and text sequence and how these pages are to be physically connected, already made very early in the process, will now be a factor in how the book is to be bound.

However, this is not to say that when arriving at this stage, all of the decisions have been made for you. There is still plenty of scope for creativity and choice that can either enhance or diminish your efforts so far. As the discussion of the maquette implied, it is important to remember that you are always making a statement, whether you like it or not. When you hand someone your book, you should be saying, "This is my work, I take it seriously and I have considered all of the aspects of its creation and presentation, and I would like you to take the time to read and appreciate it."

As advised elsewhere (and often) in this book, spend as much time as you can researching books for examples of techniques of the past. For example, the late nineteenth and early twentieth century era was a wonderful time for complex and exuberantly decorated book covers. It is not being suggested you simply emulate these techniques but rather, be *aware* of the richness of decoration from this period.
H. R. Millar, (Illustrator), *Headlong Hall / Nightmare Abbey*, Macmillan and Co., London and New York, 1896.

Do not allow it to imply you did not think through all the issues sufficiently. You may as well be saying, "Here is my book, take it or leave it. Really, I don't care what you think!"

This may seem like hyperbole. However, appreciate that your final touches are another's first impression. When you hand your book to the reader, the binding is the first thing that is seen and touched. Its appearance and tactile qualities create an impression which can either enhance the appreciation of the contents or can undermine them. Even simple things like color can transcend decoration. Think of the potent symbolism of Mao's "Little Red Book."

A leather hard-bound book creates a totally different impression from a book bound in bright, shiny vinyl. Depending on materials, a soft cover can convey anything from cheapness and easy availability to rarity and sophistication. This is because a good quality paper cover can sometimes communicate a sensation of gentleness and warmth impossible to achieve using cloth covered board, no matter how well crafted. No impression is necessarily "better" than any other. The material should be chosen on the basis of what is appropriate to what you are trying to convey. For example, if your book is about popular culture, then the use of a traditional leather binding may be incongruous.

The importance of touch at this stage cannot be underestimated. Unlike most works of art, the book is held in the hands. Its weight, texture and "feel" are potent transmitters of sensation. Because you are publishing the book yourself, you have the freedom to use any material you judge appropriate to enhance your message. If you are thinking creatively, you can adopt the advice given at the end of Chapter 1, and deliberately question conventional practice. You could conceivably create a cover with nails or thumbtacks emerging from the cover board resulting in a book so spiky, so unexpected, that a whole new dynamic emerges. But these effects only work when such an approach is appropriate to the contents. Effect for its own sake is a hollow experience. Cleverness without relevance will alienate rather than engage the reader. Conventions and assumptions are made to be questioned. But they must be questioned intelligently and sensitively.

Finally, it is important to appreciate that a cover performs the valuable function of protecting the contents of your book. The cover protects your images and text from the degrading effects of light and the paper from physical damage. You may also wish to consider making some kind of box to further protect your work.

Although made for expressive rather than informational purposes, this image shows something of the structure underneath the neat, clean finish of a well-bound book. Dismantling books is a good way to gain an understanding of bookbinding methods and techniques.
Bound to Come Unstuck, Douglas Holleley, direct scanned image, 1996.

BOOKBINDING TOOLS AND MATERIALS

Before proceeding you will need to purchase or obtain the following tools and materials. They are cheap and relatively easy to obtain with the exception of the bookbinding "nipping press" which is both heavy and expensive. Although it is helpful to have such a press, serviceable results may be obtained without one.

You will need the following tools:

1. A bone folder. This piece of equipment is essential for bookmaking. It is used to fold paper, burnish edges, and coax pasted paper and cloth into position.

2. Some good quality, unbleached linen thread. This is best obtained from a bookbinding supply store. Using the correct thread will ensure that your work will last.

3. Bookbinding needles, again best purchased from a bookbinding supplier.

4. A device for making holes in your paper. Traditionally this is an awl, a small tool with a sharpened point which bores holes in the paper. However, a small hand drill, either manual or electric, works as well, if not better.

5. A metal ruler for measuring and tearing paper and perhaps a heavy metal straight edge for cutting paper, cloth, and board.

6. A brush to apply your adhesive. A bookbinding supply house can supply you with a wide choice of brushes specifically designed for bookbinding work. A good substitute is a sash brush obtainable from a hardware store. These brushes have a circular ferrule and rounded bristles. They are usually around three quarters of an inch in diameter. A smaller brush for delicate work is also useful.

7. A sharp knife. You can purchase a bookbinding knife which can be kept sharpened. Equally good, and more easily purchased is a "Stanley" type knife, or a knife with scored "snap off" blades. All these choices ensure you are always working with a sharp edge. More errors and poor results are caused by using blunt knives than perhaps any other reason.

8. A cutting board.

Awl

Bone Folders

Knife

Paste Brush

9. A bookbinding press or a suitable substitute. Traditionally bookbinders use two kinds of press. To place initial pressure on the work and flatten the finished book, a nipping press made of cast iron with a heavy platen (or top pressure plate) is screwed down on the book. It gives the book a single initial "nip" (one brief exposure to a quite strong pressure). This flattens the book and ensures that all the (pasted or glued) surfaces are well bonded to each other. After this the book is then usually transferred to a drying press which puts gentle, continuous pressure on the book while it slowly dries.

However, such specialized pieces of equipment are quite expensive. An excellent temporary measure can be simply using a thick composition woodchip board, ideally a stock finished with a smooth surface, and a few common bricks. These simple substitutes can provide enough pressure to result in a serviceable job. The heavier and thicker the composition board, the better. Excellent results can be obtained by laminating several layers of board together until they are about two inches thick. You should have two, one to provide a firm base and the other to be placed on top of the book, its weight supplemented by paper or cloth covered bricks if necessary.

In addition to these tools you will also require the following materials:

1. A selection of papers for endpapers, covers, and lining papers for boxes. When selecting and cutting down paper, always consider the direction of the grain. In Chapter 10, *p. 211,* you will recall there was discussion of paper grain and how to ascertain its direction. It is correct practice when binding to ensure that the paper grain runs from the top (head) of the book to the bottom (tail). Paper folded with the grain will lie flat and crease without damage, but if folded against the grain, will likely crack, and not lie flat. Sometimes, especially if this is your first book, you may find the grain goes from left to right. If this is the case, ensure at minimum that all pages are the same. Pasting paper together so that the grain is "crossed" will cause warping. Most problems will occur where the endpapers connect with the contents. As most of the bindings in this chapter minimize the point of contact between the contents (known as the "text" or "book" *block)* and the endpapers, you are unlikely to have serious problems. Of all the bindings herein, the butterfly binding is most critical. The result will be certainly unsatisfactory if the grain is going the wrong way. It will be a complete "dog's breakfast" if you have the grain of the spine arranged at cross purposes with the pages.

It is also helpful to understand that paper will stretch when you wet it with the paste. Paper stretches most in the direction perpendicular to the grain. So if you have endpapers with the grain

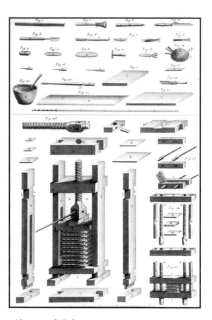

Above and Below:
These two pages are from the first book on bookbinding techniques to have large detailed plates which were helpful not only to those learning bookbinding, but also to those who planned to make standing—and other presses.
Réne Martin Dudin, *L'Art du relieur-doreur de livres,* L.F. de la Tour, Paris, 1772. *Courtesy of the Cary Graphic Arts Collection, Rochester Institute of Technology, Rochester, N.Y.*

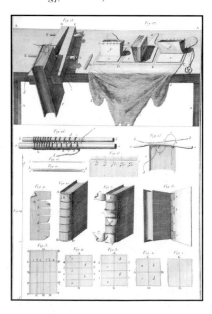

correctly oriented from head to tail, the paper will get wider as you paste it. Ideally you should compensate for this effect (simply wetting a sample of the paper you intend to use will give you an accurate idea of how much it will stretch). However, if this is your first book it is sufficient to be aware of this phenomenon and observe what happens as you proceed. Make notes and keep samples of the materials you use. Your skills will quickly improve with practice.

2. If you are making a hardcover book, you will need bookcloth to cover the cover boards. See *pp. 256–259.*

3. Cardboard, ideally acid free, to make your cover.

4. Clean scrap paper to protect the surface when you are pressing the book or pasting printed pages together.

5. Old newspapers which you will use when applying paste or glue to the various components of your book.

6. Glue and paste. Good quality polyvinyl acetate (PVA) glue (available from a bookbinding supplier) is only used for smaller, structural tasks. For large surfaces, wheat paste is preferred. To make about 12 ounces of wheat paste, measure two and a quarter cups of cold water and half a cup of regular pastry flour. (The ratio is 4.5:1.) Mix the two together in a saucepan and put on high heat. Stir constantly. The mixture will thicken as it heats, becoming smooth and translucent. You will know when it is done if you briefly stop stirring and allow the boiling liquid to bubble. If the bubbles are large and thick, resembling lava rather than water, it is ready. Pour the mixture into a well-washed jar and allow it to cool to room temperature. It will keep for about two to three weeks in the refrigerator. After this it will become moldy. Anti-mold agents (thymol) can be added, but are not essential.

This mixture is inexpensive, non-toxic and easy to prepare, taking no more than five minutes to make. However, it does require some planning. It is best made when you start to print your book as it will be on hand when you are finished and ready to bind. Equally satisfactory is "instant" paste, a powder (usually methyl cellulose) that you simply mix with water and can use immediately (available from a bookbinding supplier). If however, you have left it all to the last minute and have a deadline to meet, you can get by using PVA glue diluted with water (about 70 parts PVA to 30 parts water). The water slows the drying time and increases "spreadability." However, this mixture is unforgiving of error. You will also find a good quality glue stick (such as the Uhu brand) extremely useful.

Below:
You may also wish to purchase headband material to give your book a more "finished" look. Originally it was woven by hand, incorporating the same material used to sew the signatures together. Now you can purchase this material in pre-fabricated form from a bookbinding supply house and simply attach it to the edge of the contents of the book with PVA glue. Headbanding lends an elegant air to your binding and protects the spine when you remove the book from the bookshelf.

THE COMPONENTS OF A BOOK

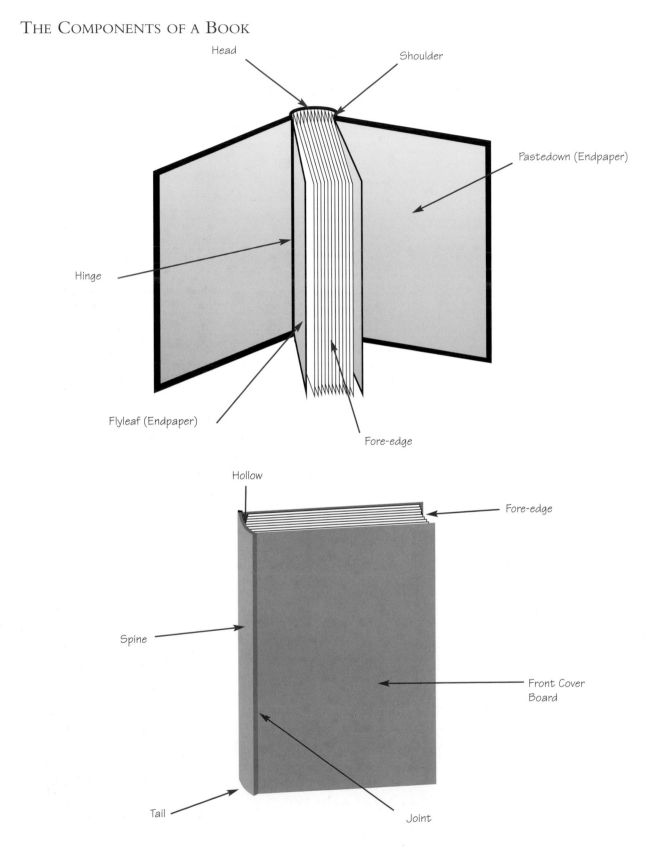

JOINING THE PAGES TOGETHER

CHOOSING A BINDING STYLE

This choice, to a large extent, has been made by your subject matter and the page set-up you have decided to adopt. If you have read Chapter 4, you will understand that to choose a page set-up is also a decision about how the book will look when it is finished. However, some choice still exists at this stage. The following table lists some of the binding options available with the page set-ups described earlier.

BINDING STYLE		COVER STYLE	SUITS THE FOLLOWING PAGE SET-UPS	
Coil or Spiral Binding	p. 226	Soft or Hard	Single Page The French-fold	p. 59 p. 69
Stab Binding	p. 227	Soft or Hard	Single Page The French-fold	p. 59 p. 69
Edge-to-Edge Binding	p. 229	Soft or Hard	Double-Page Spread (Straight)	p. 64
Concertina Binding	p. 231	Soft or Hard	Double-Page Spread (tab) The French-fold	p. 66 p. 69
Butterfly Binding	p. 232	Soft	The French-fold	p. 69
Saddle/Pamphlet Stitch	p. 233	Soft or Hard	Saddle Stitching	p. 71
The Box	p. 248	Usually Hard	All of the Above	

To a degree, the binding style is independent of the decision whether to cover the book with a hard or soft cover. The binding styles, for the most part, describe various ways of attaching the pages, either to each other, or gathering them so that they are attached at the spine. Once this has been done then you can decide whether or not you wish to employ a soft or hard cover to enclose the contents.

First consider the various means of assembling the inside of the book. Later we will look at various ways of attaching either a hard or soft cover to the bound contents.

All the following methods are simple. Traditional bookbinders may feel some of the techniques have been greatly simplified and some of the niceties have been glossed over. Certainly anyone interested in this highly specialized and beautiful craft is encouraged to read further and attempt more sophisticated bindings. However, the following binding processes work and will produce sturdy and beautiful objects.

COIL OR SPIRAL BINDING

This is the simplest and quickest of all methods and is most appropriate for the single page and French-fold set-up. You need only take your book to a printer or a stationery supply store where it can be punched and bound, often while you wait. Books bound this way open easily and lie flat.

Metal coils and spirals are superior to those made of plastic. They are stronger and allow more choice of coil pattern. Some of these are wonderful structures in their own right. However, you may find that if you desire a more sophisticated pattern you will have to do some research to track down a printer/binder with a suitable machine. Be cautious when you request such binding because the terminology can be confusing. "Spiral" binding is often not a spiral at all, but instead a series of plastic "combs." These are not as functional, or good looking, as a coil. If you decide to use one of these methods, invest in a test. Create a blank maquette with the paper you intend to use and have it bound to be sure the color, size (diameter) and binding pattern are suitable and serviceable.

Above and Below:
King uses a coil binding system to construct a book with two spines. This permits the reader to explore the contents of the book in a variety of ways. The coil is also particularly suitable for binding different types of paper together. In this book transparent pages alternate with opaque paper. Susan E. King, *Treading the Maze, An Artist's Book of Daze.* Published by *Montage 93: International Festival of the Image,* Rochester, N.Y., 1993.

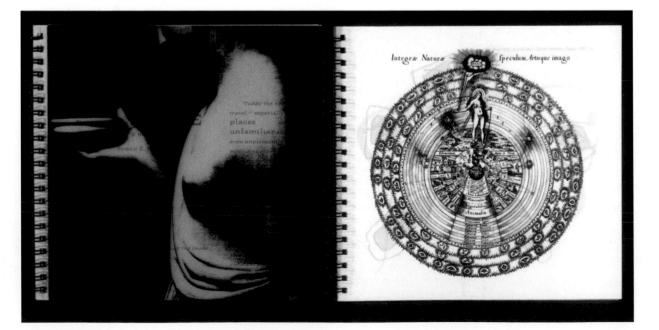

STAB BINDING

This method is also suitable for binding books that use either the single page set-up or the French-fold. In both cases we are presented with a series of sequential pages that need to be joined into a single unit. If you have printed your book using the French-fold page set-up then this stitching will not only hold the pages in position but also join the two rear edges of the folded page together at the spine.

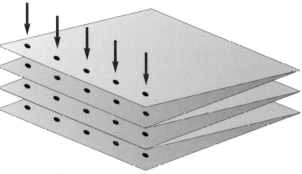

Stab binding is simple, strong and easy to do. The disadvantage of this method is that the book does not easily lie flat when open. The nature of the stitching tends to favor the book being closed, and the gutter of the book is quite deep. However, it produces a book that will never fall apart and looks extremely elegant. This binding also allows you to decide at a later date whether you wish to enclose it with a hard or soft cover. It is also a good way of cheaply and quickly binding any collection of papers together to make them easy to read and store.

Take your stack of papers to be bound and align them by bending them slightly and knocking them on a flat firm surface. Do this to the top and sides of the book so that the stack of paper is perfectly square. Then place the stack of papers on a flat surface protected by a layer or two of cardboard. This is necessary as we will be perforating the papers with either an awl or a drill. The holes should be made as shown in the figure at right.

The holes are 0.125″ from the left-hand side of the paper. The top and bottom holes are 0.5″ from the top and bottom of the sheet. In this case the remaining distance was divided in half then each segment divided in thirds so that holes are *about* an inch apart. The example to the right shows a book 11″ high by 8.5″ wide. The distance between the top and bottom holes was 10 inches so a hole was drilled every 1.25″ resulting in a total of seven holes. The distance between the holes is not crucial. Anything from 0.75″ to 1.5″ is fine. The main aim is to get the intervals even. Thus if your book was 8.5″ high then you might divide the 7.5″ by 7 to get a spacing of a little over an inch to distribute them evenly.

Lay out the holes on a spare sheet of blank paper the same size as the pages of the book. In this way you can draw the 0.125″ line directly on this paper and then mark where each hole will go. When you have finished, place this paper on top of the stack, weight it down securely, and make your holes.

Above:
This exploded view shows three folded sheets lined up to be stab-stitched at the spine to form a French-fold book. The stitching not only holds the pages together but also hides the rear of the printed sheet from view.

Below:
To prepare the folded sheets for stitching, draw a guide line on a scrap sheet of paper, one eighth of an inch from the edge. Create the holes with an awl or drill being sure to space the holes evenly, about an inch apart from each other.

The next step is to stitch the leaves of the book together with bookbinding thread. Cut a length of thread three times as long as the edge you are binding. Thread your needle and start at the second hole from the top of the book. The initial point of entry is from the rear of the book. When you have finished threading you will end up at the same spot and can tie off the thread at the rear of the book.

The following diagram(s) will make this clear. Start threading from the back of the book, beginning at the second hole from the head. Keep threading until you come to the hole nearest the tail.

1.

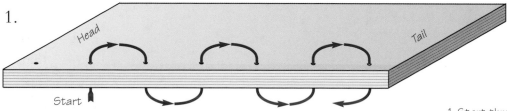

Then return in the opposite direction. The thread will form a series of loops as it travels back to the starting point. When you get to the hole just before the one you started with, push the thread (down) through this hole, then jump over the first point of entry and come up though the hole nearest the head. You then come back to the second hole where you began. Push the thread down through so that the two ends are coming out the same hole.

1. Start threading, from the back of the book, through the second hole from the head. Keep threading until you come to the hole nearest the tail.

2.

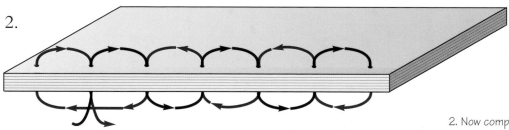

At this stage your book will be secure enough to remove it from the weight or clamp which held it together. Place it face down on your workbench. The two threads will be coming out of the second hole from the head. Ensure there is a free end on either side of the thread that joins the the first and third hole at the back of the book. Now gradually work the loops placing tension on the thread so that the book pulls into shape. Do not place too much tension on the thread as it will distort the book. Keep the thread just tight enough to hold the book square and tight. Tie off the two ends with a square (reef) knot, over the top of the thread that is between the first and third hole and trim the threads about 0.125″ from the knot. The book now will be very secure and you can read it as if it were finished. Shortly we will discuss how you can enclose it with either a hard or soft cover.

2. Now complete the stitch by returning to the head of the book using the same holes you first stitched through, bypassing the original thread in the opposite direction. When you come to the hole you started with, jump over it and pass the thread up through the last hole at the head of the book. You will now be able to pass the needle and thread down the same hole where you began.

Carefully tighten the loops and tie the two ends of the thread with a square knot after ensuring each of the ends of the thread are on either side of the loop between the first and third holes at the back of the book.

Edge-to-edge Binding (To Suit the Symmetrical Double-Page Spread Set-up)

This straightforward binding method forms the book by using a glue stick to join the folded double-page spreads together at the edges of the sheet. This is a simple but effective method of joining your pages together. It forms a precursor to the concertina binding discussed next.

Firstly, fold your pages in half so that the printed side is on the inside. Use the point of your folder to score the folds and then use the broad side to burnish the folds so the pages lie as flat as possible.

This diagram shows how double-page spreads are first folded and then joined at the edge. A thin (about half an inch) strip of glue is applied to the rear of the edge of a sheet with a glue stick. The next double-page spread is then attached. It is helpful to make a jig so they aligned correctly. (See overleaf.)

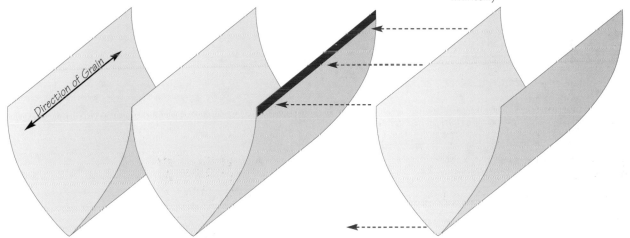

Direction of Grain

A thin line of paste or "glue stick," about 0.5″ wide, is then applied to the rear of the right hand edge of the first sheet. The second folded double-page spread is then placed exactly over the first so that the two sheets are attached at the edges. The second diagram below shows how you can use a piece of scrap paper to define the area to receive the adhesive. Make sure each time you paste or "glue-stick" a page, you use a fresh piece of paper both on top to define this edge, and underneath to keep your pages and work space clean. You will generate a lot of (sticky) waste paper while binding. Have a cardboard box nearby to place the waste.

The most difficult aspect of this method of binding is to get the pages exactly aligned so that when the book is finished, and all of the pages joined together, it is perfectly square. The most common error is to attach the pages together so they form an uneven shape.

To apply the glue, mask off a strip about half an inch wide with a piece of scrap paper. Best results are obtained by using a glue stick, preferably one that is acid free.

Scrap Paper

.5″

Apply glue to protruding strip

The best way to ensure that this does not happen is to make a jig. You can use the blocks of composition board you have made for weighting your work, and place each folded double page spread firmly up against the edge of the block. If you use two blocks to create a right angle you can align the pages both up and down and side to side thus ensuring your finished book will align perfectly.

When you have completed the task of joining all your pages together the book can either be read conventionally, one double page at a time, or it can unfold to show all of the pages simultaneously. You will find however, that it does not lie perfectly flat. If this is a problem consider refining the system by adding a "tab" to function as a hinge to join the pages to each other.

To make a simple jig, glue two pieces of wood together at right angles, as shown in this diagram. You will use it frequently when binding your book(s). It will work for most binding styles and is a quick and easy way to ensure the pages align properly.

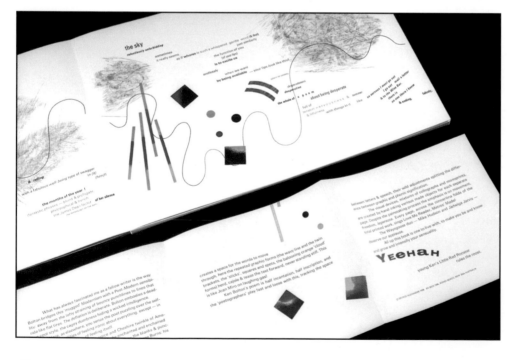

Above:
This book shows the advantage of using a tab to hinge the pages together rather than simply edge-gluing them back to back. A hinge allows the pages lie flat when the book is extended. Ken Bolton (Author), *The Terrific Days of Summer.* Designed, letterpress printed and published by the Wayzgoose Press, Katoomba, New South Wales, 1998.

CONCERTINA BINDING

Concertina binding is a variation on the edge-to-edge method. However, because we have a folded, flexible tab on the edge of each double-page spread, the finished book will have the advantage that if you choose to display the book spread out open, it will lie flat.

This method is slightly more difficult to work with at the design stage because you are working with an asymmetrical page layout view of your document. However, the finished result is well worth the extra trouble. The tabs that join the pages together give the document a sense of planning and purpose. Additionally the document is stronger as well as being more flexible.

When printed your double-page spread will have a small tab on the right or left hand side of the sheet. This sheet will then have to be folded so that the printed contents are within the fold, and the tab is then folded in the opposite direction. Use the point of your bone folder to score the folds and then use the broad side to burnish the folds so they are as flat as possible.

As with edge binding, place the folded sheets on top of each other. This time, however, (Uhu) glue the tab of one double-page spread to the rear of the following spread. To maintain squareness, again use blocks of wood as a jig to hold them square.

NOTE: You can also use this method to bind a French-fold (with tab) page layout. If you do the tabs will fall in the gutter, and the edges of the page will show a fold rather than a join. This can look neater from a binding perspective but you sacrifice the design freedom of working with an uninterrupted double-page spread with no gutter other than a fold down the center.

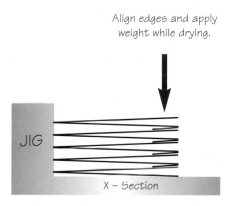

Align edges and apply weight while drying.

Above:
A cross-section of double-page spreads (with tabs) placed in position on the jig. It is almost impossible to get correct alignment without such a device.

Below:
This exploded view of the double-page layout shows how the tab functions as a hinge.

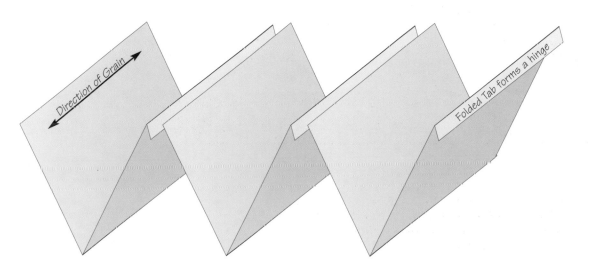

Direction of Grain

Folded Tab forms a hinge

BUTTERFLY BINDING

This method suits only the French-fold page set-up. Use it as an alternative to either stab stitching the folded pages or joining them with a tab. This style produces a soft cover. It is an elegant and quite decorative method. When the spine of the book is a different paper stock and color, it forms a dramatic contrast to the contents. The hand-worked feel and soft cover suits small, intimate books of a personal nature.

It is important to use strong, thin paper for the spine. Because of the amount of paper that goes into making the spine it is easy to end up with a book where the binding is twice as thick as the pages, producing a lop-sided and clumsy result. The key concept is delicacy. Using complementary materials creates a soft, handcrafted sensation of intimacy and softness. There is one caution. It is quite difficult to align the pages when gluing them to the corrugated spine. Despite this, the simplicity and self-evident elegance of the finished product makes it worthy of serious consideration.

The first diagram shows the nature of the paper spine. You make it by folding paper into a corrugated shape. Use a piece of paper the height of your book and fold it in half on the vertical axis. Then fold each half in half again. Keep doing this until the height of the ridges is about 0.5″. You might have to experiment until you have found the correct width of the paper, which when folded, gives you ridges of 0.5″ and produces a sufficient number of them to accommodate all of the pages of your book. There is no quick and easy way to do this and trial and error is the best course of action, no matter how imprecise a suggestion this might seem. You can save material by doing your trials with a narrow strip of paper instead of one the height of the book. Be sure the grain is parallel to your folds.

The French-fold pages are then attached with a glue stick, to either side of the ridges formed by the folded paper. The cover, usually of slightly thicker stock is glued to the first and last upward facing ridge. (See the diagram at right.)

Despite its apparent simplicity this is a binding method that greatly depends on skill of implementation. It is advisable to make a mock up of this method before trying it on your finished work. The thickness of the spine material, and the precision with which you attach the pages to the spine, will mean the difference between success and failure.

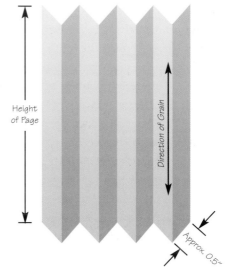

Height of Page

Direction of Grain

Approx. 0.5″

Above and Below:
The spine is formed of corrugated paper. The pages are attached by gluing them on either side of the corrugations as seen below. Although using simple materials and techniques, this is a binding system that requires considerable skill in execution. The pages must be set exactly square, and the paper gauge of the spine must be exactly correct (ideally a little thinner than the pages).

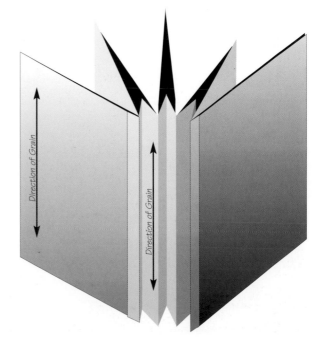

Direction of Grain

Direction of Grain

SADDLE, OR PAMPHLET STITCHING

This is the simplest of all the binding methods, but requires some skill in setting up. It relies on each of the pages to be correctly positioned on the double-page, double-sided printed sheet so the page sequence is logical and linear when the book is assembled. Depending on the thickness of the paper, saddle stitched books are usually a maximum of 64 pages, and more often between 16 and 32 pages. A single, saddle-stitched section is called a signature.

Saddle stitching joins folded pages together in the manner of a standard staple-bound book. However, using thread produces a softer, more handcrafted effect and there is no problem with staples rusting and damaging the paper. This is called pamphlet stitching.

After printing your pages, fold them in half, burnish the fold with your folder and assemble the book. We will assume you have a book of 12 pages comprised of three sheets with four pages on each sheet. You will also need a cover.

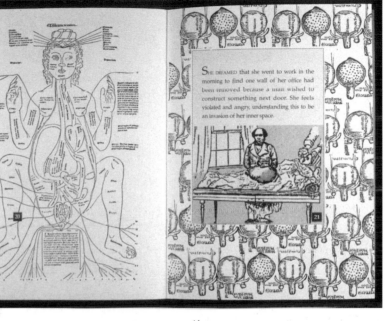

Above:
Joan Lyons, *The Gynecologist,* Visual Studies Workshop Press, Rochester, N.Y., 1989.

Below.
Carol Flax, *Some (M)other Stories; A Parent(hetic)al Tale,* Southeast Museum of Photography, Daytona Beach, Fla., 1995.

This cover can be either printed or, if a suitable decorative stock has been obtained, left plain so a title label may be pasted on to identify the book. Customarily the cover is a thicker stock than the pages inside.

Place the sheets together in correct order. Open the book to the center double-page spread and make three holes in the gutter/fold between the two pages with an awl or strong needle.

Push your threaded needle through the middle hole from the outside of the cover. Then go to the top hole and go back though to the outside of the book. Skip over the middle hole and go back through to the inside through the bottom hole. Then proceed to the middle hole, go though to the outside, and the thread will finish where it began. Tie off the thread with a square (reef) knot, making sure that there is an end on either side of the vertical thread that will extend from the top hole to the bottom hole. Trim the ends 0.2″ from the knot. Either sew on the cover at the same time or cover the book with a paper cover wrapper, much as you would a school exercise book.

1. Fold and assemble the pages in correct order.

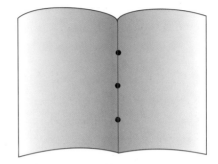

2. Using an awl or strong needle, punch three holes through the spine.

3. Start threading from the outside, entering through the centre hole. Follow the arrows. You will end up exiting (with the thread going in the opposite direction) through the hole where you began. Ensure that each of the two thread-ends are on either side of the loop that extends from the top hole to the bottom hole on the outside of the book. Tie the thread with a square knot.

Left:
Because the pages must be printed on both sides of a single sheet of paper, saddle stitching is best suited for offset publications, or as is the case here, color laser printed books. These printing methods minimize show through problems as in both cases the ink (or toner) does not penetrate the paper to the extent that occurs with inkjet printing.
Rachel Siegel, *Haircut,* Strong Hair Press at the Visual Studies Workshop, Rochester, N.Y., 2000.

COVERING THE BOOK BLOCK

When the contents are bound together, ready for covering, they are termed a book or text "block." There are two main strategies for covering the block. You can use a soft cover or a hard cover. The construction will vary slightly depending on how you have joined the pages together.

You may also choose to enclose your book in a box. This will suit any of the page binding methods.

Lyssiotis combines many techniques in this elaborately presented set of books. Each of the individual volumes are saddle stitched, and the entire set is housed in a matching box.
Nick Doslov (text) and Peter Lyssiotis, *The Products of Wealth*. Published by Peter Lyssiotis, Melbourne, Vic., 1997.

Soft Cover Binding

Soft Cover Glued to Book Block

This is a simple but elegant way to cover a stab-stitched book. Cut a piece of cover stock, with the grain running north to south, or if you prefer, head to tail. (See Chapter 10, *p. 211*, for instructions on ascertaining the direction of the grain.) Trim it so that the front and rear cover are the size of the page, leaving an allowance for the spine which is defined by the thickness of the contents. Score the paper to define the folds for the spine.

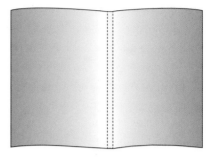

Prepare the cover by cutting it to size, allowing for the spine. Score and fold it as shown above.

The cover is attached to the block with undiluted PVA glue. With a small, stiff brush, apply the PVA along the edge of the spine. Work the glue into the paper to reinforce the book block. Next, apply the glue to the front and rear pages for a depth of 0.25″. In doing this you will be brushing over the stitching which is 0.125″ in from the edge of the spine.

Firmly but carefully, push the spine into the cover so it forms a snug fit. Place the finished book flat and weight it gently while it dries (about an hour) with a book from your bookshelf that is about two inches thick. Do not apply so much weight that the book thread shows through the paper cover when the book is finished.

Apply PVA glue to the spine and endpapers of the book block as shown in red. About 0.25″ is a sufficient bead. Lower the block into the cover as above, and weight lightly for at least an hour. If you have used a stab stitch, be careful not to over-weight the book. Too much pressure can cause the stitches to distort the cover.

Left:
Soft (paper) binding allows you to print both images and text on the cover using your desktop printer. Be careful, however, to select a stock that will resist scuffing and water damage. For best results it is preferable to have the cover printed by a color laser printer at a bureau or printshop as this form of printing is more robust, water resistant, and light fast. An inexpensive compromise is to print a color master-cover at home and then have this color-photocopied rather than printed from disk. Douglas Holleley, *Adaminaby,* Rockcorry, Rochester, N.Y., 1998.

FOLDED WRAP-AROUND SOFT COVER

The following procedure is suitable for a number of binding methods. It can be used in place of the glued method just described for the stab-stitch. It is also useful for the double-page spread either with, or without, tab.

The simplest way to understand this method is to remember how you may have covered exercise books at school. However, don't just think of the cover as protection. Be sensitive and choose a paper stock appropriate to your book. Try to imbue the book with a feeling of warmth and tactility, inviting the reader to open and read.

You will require a sheet of suitable paper twice as high and twice as wide as the opened book. Using such a large sheet will ensure that the cover completely encloses the first and last page of the book, providing structural integrity and conveying a sense of purpose. Some planning is necessary if you intend to use this method as you will have to have included in your binding an extra sheet of paper front and back to be enclosed by the paper cover.

On the next page is a guide to setting up your folds and cuts. Folds are shown by dotted lines and cuts by solid lines. Lay your open book down on a suitable sheet of cover stock and lay out the cover as shown. Cut the sheet according to the diagram being sure to provide the tabs to protect the spine of the book.

First fold in the flaps top and bottom to the horizontal center of the page. Then fold in the flaps that are formed on the left and right hand side of the book. Burnish each fold with the folder to ensure a snug fit and a flat cover. The spine tabs on the head and tail in the middle of the cover, are "turned in" within the cover to provide reinforcement at the head and tail of the spine.

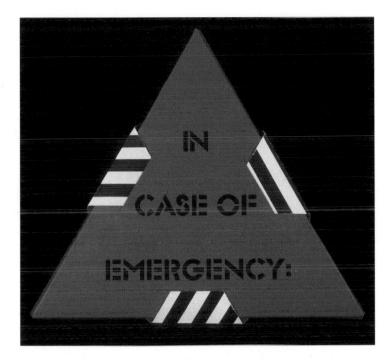

Wrap-around soft (paper) covers are ideal for experimenting with unusual shapes.
Scott McCarney, *In Case of Emergency*, Nexus Press, Atlanta, Ga., 1984.

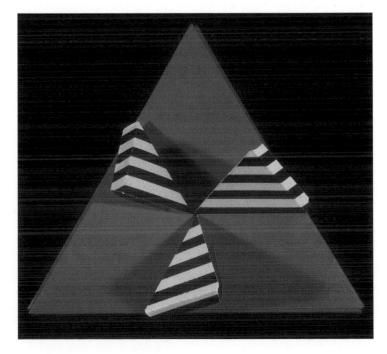

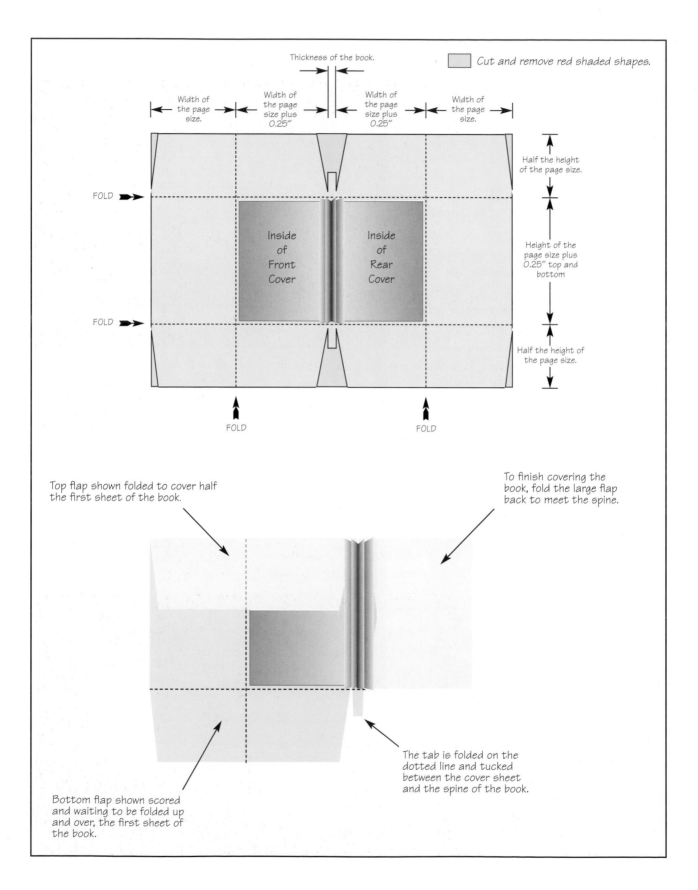

Thickness of the book.

Cut and remove red shaded shapes.

Width of the page size.

Width of the page size plus 0.25"

Width of the page size plus 0.25"

Width of the page size.

Half the height of the page size.

Height of the page size plus 0.25" top and bottom

Half the height of the page size.

FOLD

FOLD

Inside of Front Cover

Inside of Rear Cover

FOLD

FOLD

Top flap shown folded to cover half the first sheet of the book.

To finish covering the book, fold the large flap back to meet the spine.

The tab is folded on the dotted line and tucked between the cover sheet and the spine of the book.

Bottom flap shown scored and waiting to be folded up and over, the first sheet of the book.

THE HARD COVER

A hard cover can be applied to most of the binding systems described in this chapter. The method shown overleaf is particularly suitable for the stab-stitch method and a saddle-stitched book. You may also use this method to enclose either of the two concertina style bindings. However, if you do, you will not be able to view the books open and extended. This may not be a problem if you have chosen these binding methods because of their uninterrupted (without gutter) double-page spread views. If this is the case you will be happy reading the book page by page.

However, if you really want to view the book extended, then there is a compromise solution. You can make a hard cover board for both the front and rear of the concertina, but omit the spine which normally would connect these together. This method will be discussed in more detail later.

The basic principle in hard cover binding is to create a cover (and usually a spine). This cover is then attached to the inside of the book by using the endpapers as hinges.

To make such a cover you will need cardboard, bookcloth, and suitable paper for the endpapers. Because the endpapers serve the function of actually joining the contents of the book to the cover, the endpaper stock will have to be sufficiently strong enough to perform this task. Choose paper that is at least 90 lbs. or 200 gsm. weight, and is (ideally) of all rag composition so it will be strong and flexible. It is also important that the grain of the paper is aligned so that it runs from north to south so the crease will not become brittle, and so the book will lie flat when opened.

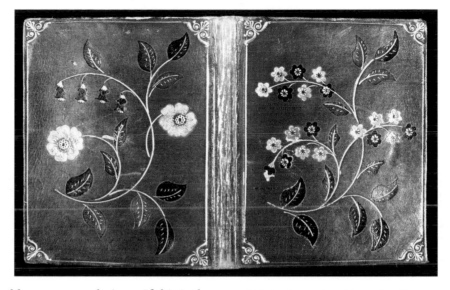

This book was found in a pile of discarded rubbish in London by Dr. Peter Stanbury, a gifted and sensitive collector, indeed savior, of often idiosyncratic cultural artifacts and other ephemera. The tooled leather cover is most likely that of a commercially made autograph book. Inside miniature drawings (presumably made by Ms. Wyatt) have been lovingly mounted. The book radiates a delicate, even fey sensibility. A true artist's book.
The scrapbook of Martha Wyatt. Inscribed May 3, 1830. *From the collection of Dr. Peter Stanbury.*

The first task is to attach endpapers to the text or book block. Using the criteria described above, select a stock that is sympathetic to the nature and tone of your book and cut two pieces of endpaper the height of your book and twice as wide.

The diagram to the right shows the relationship of the end papers to the bound book itself. The endpapers form a hinge connecting the book itself to the cover. Sheet (a) both front and rear, is attached to the book itself with a thin strip of glue, 0.25″ wide. This glue also reinforces the stitching in the same way as in a (glued) soft cover. When the actual cover has been constructed then sheet(s) (b) front and rear are pasted to the inside of the cover. In this way the cover and contents become one unit. As you can see from this diagram, the fold of the endpaper endures a lot of stress. Not only is it asked to flex each time the book is opened and closed, it also must hold the book block securely within the covers.

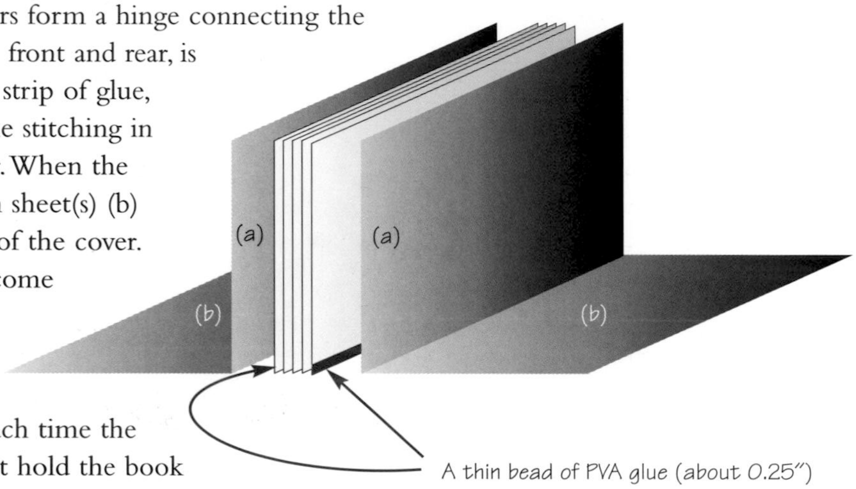

For this reason it is sometimes advisable, if the book is particularly large, to reinforce the connection between the endpapers and the bound volume. A simple way of doing this is to PVA a reinforcing strip of sized, cheesecloth-like material called "super" to the spine of the bound book and the endpapers. This reinforces the hinge of the endpaper and helps to stop the contents pulling away from the cover.

After you have glued the "super" to both the spine and the endpapers, apply more glue to the outside of the "super" so that it penetrates the fibers forming a strong, but flexible hinge.

The contents of the book are now ready for the hard cover. After allowing the glue to dry you may, if required, trim the top and the bottom of the book with a guillotine. (Depending on the thickness of your book you may have to take it to a printer to have it trimmed in a power guillotine.) If the book is comprised of single sheets you may even trim the outside edge to ensure that the contents and endpapers are both square and line up exactly. However, if your book consists of French-folded sheets, remember that the outside edge is a fold. If you trim it you will separate the front of each individual page from its obverse. This will result in every second double-page spread showing the rear of the folded pages which you had intended to be hidden.

(a)   (a)

(b)   (b)

A thin bead of PVA glue (about 0.25″) on either side of the pages attaches endpapers to the bound contents of the book.

You can reinforce the hinge by gluing (PVA) a piece of "super" to the spine and endpapers.

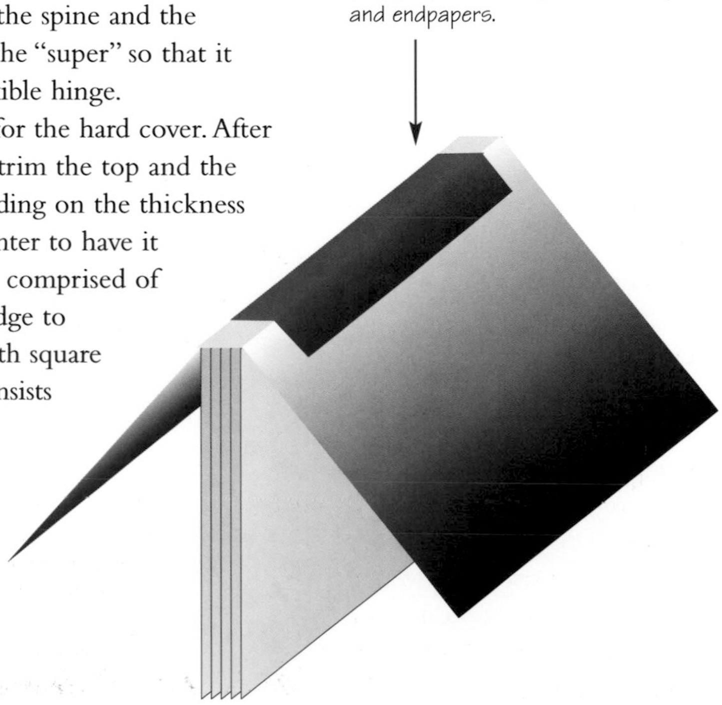

To make the hard cover, cut two pieces of cardboard to form the core of the cover. This board will then be covered with bookcloth. Between the front and back cover there must be a space the thickness of the book for the spine. These two boards should have the following characteristics.

- The grain of the board must run from north to south.
- The size of the boards must be slightly larger than the bound contents to form a protective lip. The amount of this overlap is 0.125″ on the top, the outside edge and the bottom. At the spine the board will be flush with the contents. Thus if you are binding a standard vertical US Letter size book you will cut two pieces of board each 8.625″ wide and 11.25″ high.

Place these down on the bookcloth on a cutting board as shown in the diagram below. Measure a one inch overlap around the cover boards. Mark out the corners (as indicated in red) so that the line at 45° to the board is the thickness of the cover boards plus a sixteenth of an inch away from the corner(s) of the boards. (Do not cut them just yet.)

The distance between the boards, (a), will require calculation for your particular book. The basic formula for determining this value is as follows. You must allow:

1. The thickness of each of your cover boards (cover boards are usually about an eighth of an inch, but measure them to be sure) plus...
2. The thickness of your bound pages, plus...
3. About a sixteenth of an inch. (This is to allow your spine to have a slight curve when the book is finished.)

You can have the spine finish square by leaving no allowance for curvature, or you can add a little more, depending on how much you desire. About a sixteenth of an inch, however, usually works quite well. It is also good practice to line the inside of the spine with paper, but you can omit this step.

An elaborately decorated leather binding by Mike Hudson. Ross Burnet, *A Bookseller's Diary*, Wayzgoose Press, Katoomba, New South Wales, 1993.

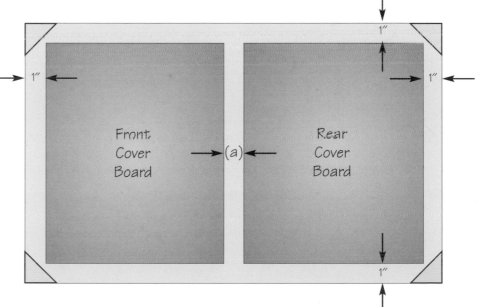

To the right is a cross section of the book showing the two cover boards and the book block. The the gap (a) in the diagram above is the height of (x) plus one sixteenth of an inch.

Constructing the Hard Cover

NOTE: In the series of diagrams on the opposite page remember you are looking at the book from the inside. The bookcloth is face down and the boards are pasted to the rear of the cloth. This is why the front cover board is on the left and vice versa.

1. Calculate the distance you must leave to allow for the spine. Measure out your bookcloth as in the diagram on the previous page drawing guidelines in pencil on the rear of the bookcloth to indicate where the cover boards must go.

2. Cut the bookcloth one inch around the border of the boards. DO NOT cut the corners off the bookcloth yet.

3. Place some scrap paper under your bookcloth and apply the wheat paste (or watered down PVA glue) to the bookcloth. It is good practice to also apply paste to the board which can be very "thirsty." Immediately dispose of the scrap paper to keep your work clean.

4. Place each cover board in position. Burnish these boards down with your folder to ensure they are firmly attached to the cloth.

5. Cut the corners of the bookcloth at 45°, leaving around 0.125″ between the cut corner and the corner of the cover board. The correct amount is the thickness of the board plus a sixteenth of an inch.

6. Begin wrapping the bookcloth over the cover boards. Start at the top first. Pull the pasted cloth up towards you and then round it over the top of the cover board and burnish it down flat with your bone folder. Repeat this step on the bottom. Use your folder to burnish the cloth in the spine, making sure that where it attaches to itself (the "turn in") is well joined. You will find that the cloth, when wet, stretches quite easily and can be worked into shape.

7. Now work on the the flaps at either side. You will notice at each of the the corners where you have turned over the cloth, that a little triangle of doubled over bookcloth is formed. You must pinch this down with your folder so the triangle is firmly adhered to the back of the bookcloth. This will ensure that the bookcloth completely covers the cardboard.

8. Now, fold each of the flaps on the sides. Use your folder to burnish them to the board so that they adhere firmly.

9. If you have a nipping press, nip the cover. If not, place your heavy boards on it and press it firmly. Allow it to dry for about 15 minutes. Now you are ready to attach the inside of the book to the cover.

Apply paste to both the bookcloth and the boards and then lay the boards in position on the cloth. Trim the cloth corners so they are a little more than the thickness of the board (usually 0.125″) away from the corners of the board.

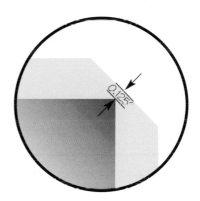

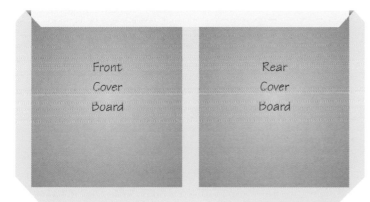

Begin folding the bookcloth over the boards, starting from the top. Burnish the cloth onto the board. Next fold the bottom flap. A small triangle of double thickness bookcloth will be formed at the corners when the flap is folded. Push it down with your bone folder. (See below.)

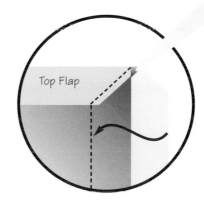

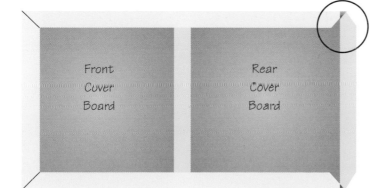

Now fold either side. Ensure the corner of the board is fully covered with cloth by pushing down the small triangle before folding over the remaining flaps. (See the magnified view of the corner above.)

ATTACHING THE CONTENTS (BOOK BLOCK) TO THE COVER

As mentioned before, the endpapers form a hinged joint between the cover and the contents. You will have to carefully paste each of the end papers and then attach them in turn to the inside front, and inside rear, of the cover.

To apply paste to the endpapers place a sheet of clean scrap paper, larger than your page size, inside the book block under the endpaper and spread the paste quickly and evenly. Work from the center of the sheet to the edges. Do this to the endpaper that will be at the front of the book only. Wait a minute or so and apply a second coat.

Now, take the cloth-covered cover and place it face down on a clean surface. Carefully place the pasted endpaper down on the left hand side of the open cover so that the bound edge of the block aligns with the edge of the cardboard nearest the spine. It should show 0.125″ of cloth covered board on all the outside edges of the book, but it may show less on the fore-edge if the endpapers stretched when moistened by the paste.

Next, place a scrap of paper under the rear endpaper of the bound contents and apply paste as you did before. Remove the scrap sheet carefully.

Now carefully lift the rear cover and close it so that the book is square and the rear endpaper meets the inside rear cover so it aligns with the edge of the cardboard as you did with the front. You only get one chance to do this. The best approach is to lift the rear cover, bend the spine, and try to put the cover on the contents of the book as squarely and as definitely as possible. You have to make this motion with confidence. Be definite in your actions and trust yourself. Nip the book or place it under a *very* heavy weight for a few moments. Allow it to dry, at least overnight, under moderate weight.

To give the book extra "finish" you may wish to attach a headband to the bound contents before placing them in the cover. When the book is bound it will look like the diagram to the right.

Apply paste twice to front endpaper. Brush from the center to the edges. The endpaper will then be pasted to the inside of the front cover.

Scrap sheet inserted under end sheet to protect fly leaf and contents.

Align spine of book block with the edge of the cardboard.

Rear Endpaper.

Inside Rear Cover. The cardboard will be visible.

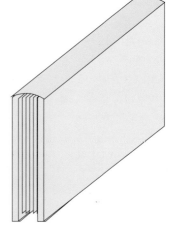

HARD COVER FOR CONCERTINA STYLE BOOKS

As mentioned earlier you can also employ the previous method to cover a concertina book. However, if you do it will be impossible to extend the book into a flat, single line of connected pages. You will have to be content to enjoy only the simplicity of page set-up and layout and the fact that the book will exhibit a folded, rather than stitched, gutter.

There are however, two cover styles that allow you to have the advantages of a book that can be viewed in two ways and still have a hard cover. The first is to use the binding method detailed above, but do not attach the book to the front cover. Alternatively you can make a separate hard cover for the front and the rear of the bound contents, and completely omit the spine.

The diagram, top right, shows how the finished book will look with the first of these two methods. You have to print your concertina in such a way that the first fold (page) is the title page for your book. Thus when the cover is opened, the concertina is sitting on the right hand side of the inside of the cover and is ready to read. The left-hand side of the cover is not attached in any way to the contents. It merely protects the pages from handling and light by folding over the contents of the book when it is closed. The book is attached to the cover by pasting the rear fold (blank page) to the inside rear cover.

Because the inside of the cover is visible, it will be necessary to conceal the cardboard and spine by pasting a decorative sheet over it. As such the following modifications have to be made to the basic hard cover.

Lay your cloth and cardboard out as shown at right. You will observe it uses most of the principles described in the previous covering method. However, there are two major changes. Firstly, the spine is now reinforced by attaching a strip of the same cardboard you are using for the covers. Secondly, the width of the spine is calculated differently. The spine is the thickness of the book block. Be sure the grain of the spine and endboards is aligned north to south.

View of a partially expanded concertina attached to the rear of a hard cover binding.

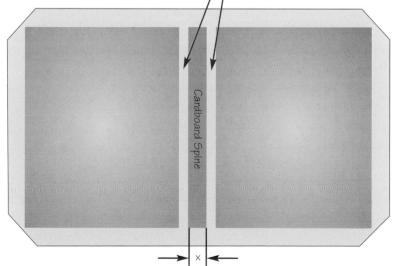

Allow three sixteenths of an inch (0.1875", say 0.2") to form the hinge between the spine and the cover boards.

Cardboard Spine

The reinforced spine (x) is as wide as the pages of the book are deep. (See overleaf.)

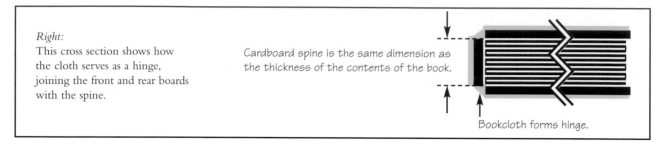

Right:
This cross section shows how the cloth serves as a hinge, joining the front and rear boards with the spine.

Cardboard spine is the same dimension as the thickness of the contents of the book.

Bookcloth forms hinge.

As before, leave one inch of cloth surrounding the boards, and trim the corners after the boards have been pasted in position. Fold the bookcloth over the cardboard being sure to pinch down the small triangles of bookcloth when you cover the corners.

Your cover will now look like the diagram at right. As you can see the cardboard and the folded-over bookcloth are visible. To finish the cover it is necessary now to line the inside with a suitable paper. This may be either the same paper you have used to print your book or you may choose a stock that complements the contents. Cut this paper so that it is 0.25″ shorter than the height of the bound cover. The width will need to be cut the same length as the actual inside dimensions but it will be set 0.125″ from the fore-edge when you paste it down. This is so because this paper will shorten as it is worked into the hinges formed between the spine board and the two end boards. The gap of 0.25″ on either side of the spine will reduce the width of this paper so that it finishes 0.125″ from both the left and right-hand edges to match the border at the top and bottom.

Start by placing the pasted paper on the left-hand side of the book 0.125″ in from the edge and centered top and bottom. Burnish this down with your folder as you work the paper onto the cover from left to right. Take special care at the hinge. Work the paper into this gap with your folder so that it adheres to the bookcloth and the edges of the cardboard.

Finally, keep burnishing the paper and allow it to finish on the right-hand side of the book 0.125″ from the right-hand edge. The cover should be "nipped" or pressed, and then allowed to dry, under weight, at least overnight. When finished the inside of the cover should look like the diagram at right.

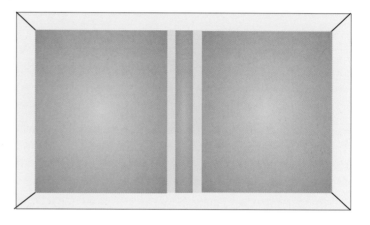

Above:
Inside of the cover showing the cover boards and spine in position with the bookcloth wrapped around the edges.

Below:
View with the lining paper pasted down. Ensure the lining paper is well adhered to the bookcloth and boards by running your bone folder along the groove.

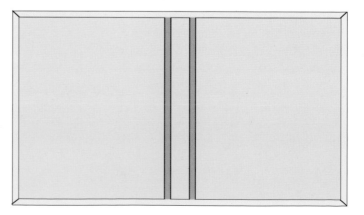

Now simply paste the last page of your concertina bound contents onto the right hand side of the cover.

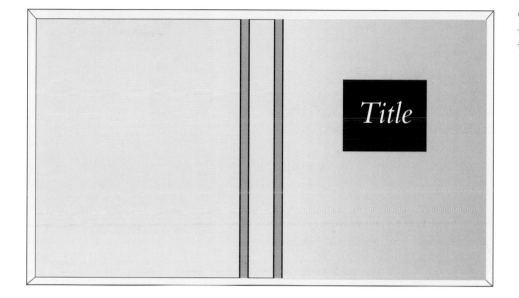

View of the finished book with the concertina attached to the inside rear cover.

The second way to attach a hard cover to a concertina binding requires you to make two separate covers for the front and rear of the concertina. There is no spine. To make this cover, cut two pieces of cardboard as you would for the cover method above. Each of these boards is the height of the page plus 0.25″ and the width of the page plus 0.25″.

Cover each board individually. Finally, paste the front and rear sheets so they are centered on the boards.

Below:
The simplest way to hard cover a concertina book is to make two, single-page size cloth covered boards, one for the front and one for the back. You then paste them to the first and last sheets of the concertina as shown below.

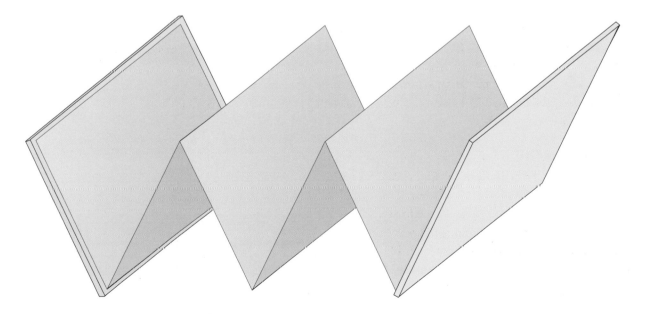

Making and Covering a Clamshell Box

An alternative to conventional binding is to make a box to hold the contents of your book. If you do this you may decide not to bind the pages of your book together. You can place the loose pages in the box, in order, to form a kind of hybrid portfolio/book made up of either single or folded sheets. This can be an excellent compromise form of presentation. You can maintain the coherence and intimacy of the book, but you can also remove the pages and hang the work for exhibition. Such a box can also house a fully bound and covered book, adding another level of protection to the work.

The box structure which most suits the book is the clamshell. This has a lid and base connected to each other in much the same way as a spine connects the front and rear boards of a conventional book. It is moderately difficult to construct. However, if you allow time to read the instructions carefully, and proceed slowly and patiently, you will succeed. To begin you will need to determine the dimensions of the box.

Start first by determining the size of the base. To allow 0.125″ (¹/₈″) clearance around the book block, add 0.25″ (¹/₄″) to the overall dimensions. Thus if the book is 8.5″x 11″, the base will be 8.75″x 11.25″.

The lid of a clamshell box is more difficult to calculate because it must not only overlap the base on three edges to enable the sides of the lid to clear the sides of the base, but it must also finish directly over the base at the spine. (See diagram lower right.) The amount of overlap required whenever two sides meet in this way is 0.1875″ (³/₁₆″). This means when calculating the lid, you must add 0.1875″ to the dimensions of the base for the head, tail and fore-edge, but nothing where the lid meets the spine.

Thus for a base measuring 11.25″x 8.75″ you will need a lid of length, 11.625″ (11¹/₄″ + ³/₁₆″ + ³/₁₆″ = 11⁵/₈″) and width, 8.9375″ (8³/₄″ + ³/₁₆″ = 8¹⁵/₁₆″).

The depth of the box will depend entirely on how thick your book is when finished. For the purposes of this example we are going to assume it is ¹/₂″ thick. Thus the height of the base sides will be 0.5″, plus the thickness of the cardboard. Assuming the cardboard you are using is about 0.125″ thick, the base sides will be 0.625″ (⁵/₈″) high.

The sides of the lid need to be deeper so that when the box is closed the lid is flush with the bottom of the base. Thus the sides of the lid will be 0.75″ (³/₄″) deep. The spine joining the lid and the base will be 0.5″.

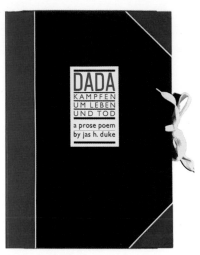

Above and Below:
Here a modified clamshell box encloses a concertina bound book. Note how the binder has created a "pocket" on the inside cover to house the introductory essay which was printed on a separate sheet.
Jas H. Duke, *Dada Kampfen um Leben und Tod,* Wayzgoose Press, Katoomba, 1996. Binding by Mike Hudson.

Below:
Cross-section of a clamshell box looking from the head. Here you can see the relationship between the the lid and base, and how the sides and spine align when the box is assembled.

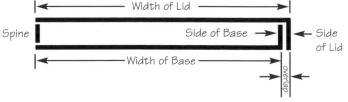

Mark out your board as shown below. This may look a little intimidating at first but it is logical and will make sense as you proceed. Note that the dimensions of the two longer sides are greater than the lid or base of the box itself. This is because they will overlap the shorter sides at the corners to form a neat, square joint. The amount of overlap is determined by the thickness of the board at each end. Assuming the board is 0.125″ thick, the longer sides will each be 0.25″ greater than the lid or base.

The spine width is the same as the inside height of the finished box. In this case this is 0.5″. Also, as the spine forms a "bridge" between the base and lid, its length is measured so it is half way between these two elements. In this case this amount is 11.6875″ (11 $^{11}/_{16}$″).

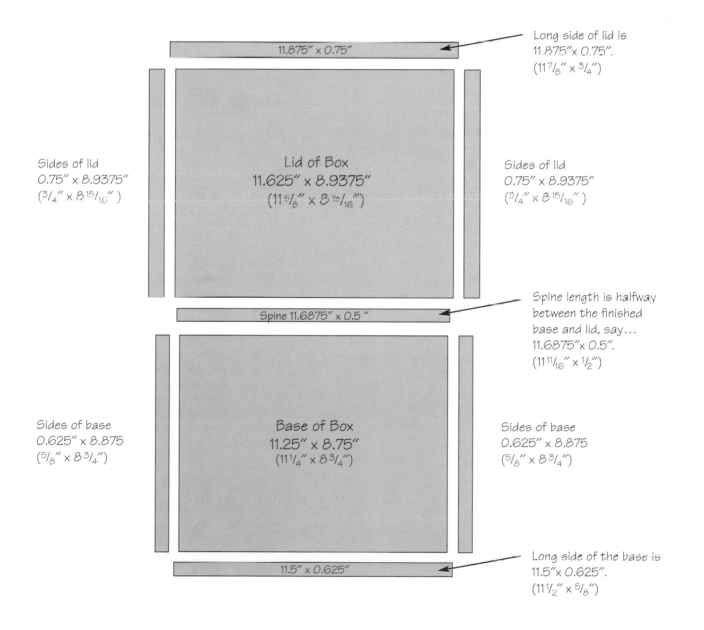

11.875″ x 0.75″

Long side of lid is
11.875″x 0.75″.
(11 $^{7}/_{8}$″ x $^{3}/_{4}$″)

Sides of lid
0.75″ x 8.9375″
($^{3}/_{4}$″ x 8 $^{15}/_{16}$″)

Lid of Box
11.625″ x 8.9375″
(11 $^{5}/_{8}$″ x 8 $^{15}/_{16}$″)

Sides of lid
0.75″ x 8.9375″
($^{3}/_{4}$″ x 8 $^{15}/_{16}$″)

Spine 11.6875″ x 0.5 ″

Spine length is halfway
between the finished
base and lid, say…
11.6875″x 0.5″.
(11 $^{11}/_{16}$″ x $^{1}/_{2}$″)

Sides of base
0.625″ x 8.875
($^{5}/_{8}$″ x 8 $^{3}/_{4}$″)

Base of Box
11.25″ x 8.75″
(11 $^{1}/_{4}$″ x 8 $^{3}/_{4}$″)

Sides of base
0.625″ x 8.875
($^{5}/_{8}$″ x 8 $^{3}/_{4}$″)

11.5″ x 0.625″

Long side of the base is
11.5″x 0.625″.
(11 $^{1}/_{2}$″ x $^{5}/_{8}$″)

To begin construction, attach the side pieces to the base and the lid. This is going to be achieved by simply butt joining them together with PVA glue. You will be surprised how strong this is when the glue dries. However this gluing, as effective as it is, is not what gives the box its full strength. When we finish this stage, the entire assembly, inside and out, is going to be covered with book cloth. When this layer is applied the box will assume extra strength from this cloth "skin." The construction is analogous to monocoque construction in modern automobiles where the cocoon of the bodywork, not the strength of a chassis, gives the car its structural integrity.

Construct the lid first. Place the largest board on a piece of newsprint. Apply a thin bead of glue to one of the shorter side boards and attach it to the base as shown at right.

Attach the other two sides in turn. You will see that one of the three sides is longer than the lid by the thickness of two pieces of cardboard. Glue this piece to the adjacent sides as well as the base.

Now proceed to the base of the box and repeat this operation. Do not attach the spine at this stage. When you have finished you will have the lid and base of the box each with three sides attached. (See the diagram at the foot of this page.) Brace the box with bricks or heavy old books while the glue dries.

Because the box gains strength by being covered in bookcloth, it is good practice to begin to cover the board within an hour so of construction. In this way the cardboard butt joints, and the bookcloth, dry at similar rates. If you do this the whole structure will gain extra strength. However, if this is your first attempt, you will have more success if you wait for the butt joints to dry overnight. This way you will be covering a structure that is completely dry and rigid. This makes the task considerably easier. Additionally, after the joints have dried, you can sand them with abrasive paper to remove any excess glue or other inconsistencies.

Below:
This view of the base shows the far side already glued in position. Observe the thin bead of glue on the lower inside edge of the side piece to the right of the base. Attach this piece to the base of the box. You will also need to glue it to the adjoining side piece as shown in the diagram. Do the same for the third, and final side of the base. Repeat for the lid.

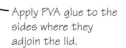

Apply PVA glue to the sides where they adjoin the lid.

Lid of the box

Thin bead of PVA glue is applied to the sides which are then attached to the lid.

Below:
When the base and lid of the box are assembled they will look like the diagram below. Allow them to dry before covering them with bookcloth. You may find it necessary to brace the cardboard as it dries with old, unwanted books, or bricks covered with paper or cloth. Ensure all the corners are joined and the box is square. The spine, at this stage, is not connected to either the lid or the base.

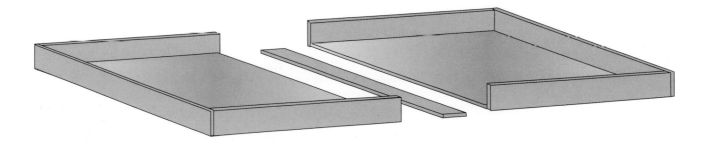

You will next need to mark out the bookcloth. The accompanying diagram will help you to do this. We will cover the entire structure with cloth, inside and out. The corners will require some care so as to completely hide the cardboard. Again, the principle of leaving a small amount of extra (triangular) material for this purpose, will also apply here. (See the hard-cover binding section *p. 243.*) Box corners however, are slightly more complex than the book corners as they are three-dimensional rather than flat.

Lay the bookcloth face down on a clean surface. Place the assembled top, spine and bottom of the box on the bookcloth as shown at right. The distance between the spine and the lid, and the spine and the base, is 0.2″ (just under a quarter of an inch).

You can see that the bookcloth extends well past the lid and the base of the box. You have to leave sufficient material to cover the sides outside and in and then have enough left over to paste it to the (inside) bottom of the base and lid. For a box 1″ deep you will need about 2.5″ to 3″ of overlap. The amount of overlap is determined by:

- measuring the outside height of the box,
- adding 0.125″ for the thickness of the board,
- adding the inside height of the box, and finally,
- adding about an inch of overlap to paste on the inside of the lid and the base.

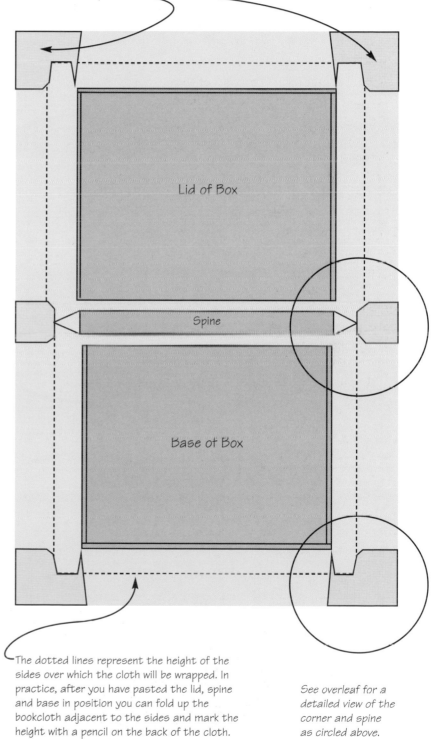

Cut on the red lines and remove all the red shaded areas to form the flaps that will enclose the cardboard structure. As before, the spine will be the trickiest part of the job as there is not a lot of material to work with. Be patient!

Lid of Box

Spine

Base of Box

The dotted lines represent the height of the sides over which the cloth will be wrapped. In practice, after you have pasted the lid, spine and base in position you can fold up the bookcloth adjacent to the sides and mark the height with a pencil on the back of the cloth.

See overleaf for a detailed view of the corner and spine as circled above.

A simple formula is to allow two and a half to three times the height of the box. The amount of overlap inside the base and lid of the box will be hidden by a liner and is therefore not critical.

Essentially you will be wrapping the box with cloth, reinforcing and at the same time completely covering the corners, giving the box strength and structural integrity.

Now cut the corners and area around the spine as shown in the following diagrams.

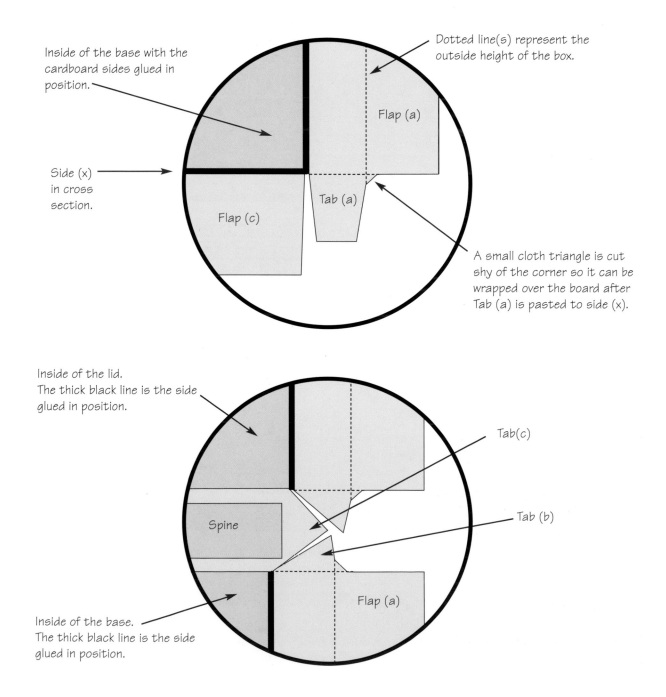

Inside of the base with the cardboard sides glued in position.

Dotted line(s) represent the outside height of the box.

Flap (a)

Side (x) in cross section.

Tab (a)

Flap (c)

A small cloth triangle is cut shy of the corner so it can be wrapped over the board after Tab (a) is pasted to side (x).

Inside of the lid.
The thick black line is the side glued in position.

Tab(c)

Tab (b)

Spine

Flap (a)

Inside of the base.
The thick black line is the side glued in position.

Covering the Box, Step by Step

The biggest aid to success is having a large, unimpeded space to work and plenty of scrap paper. Take the time to properly clear your work table. Also it is advisable to have a good supply of paper towels and a clean, damp rag to wipe any excess paste from the bookcloth if you get some in the wrong place.

1. Lay the lid, spine and base in position on the cloth and mark their position in pencil. Paste the entire cloth. Attach the base, lid and spine on the cloth after first also applying paste to the cardboard. Burnish to adhere the cardboard to the cloth.

2. To cover the sides, start with the base. Pull Flap (a) and attach it to the outside only of the side. Burnish it to the board with your bone folder. Leave the flap that will eventually cover the inside hanging loosely inside the box at this stage.

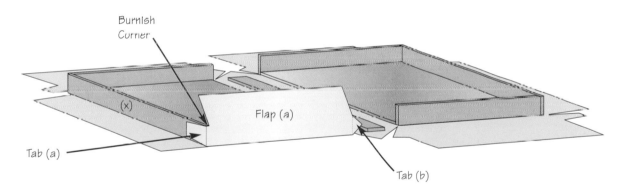

3. Wrap Tab (a) around the adjacent side (x) to cover the vertical corner of the board.

4. The little triangle of cloth that remains can now be wrapped over the top of the corner and burnished into position.

5. Next wrap Tab (b) around the exposed edge of the side nearest the spine, again burnishing the small triangle into position, ensuring the cardboard is completely covered. You will find that there is not a lot of material at this end as it is being shared with the spine. Use your bone folder to stretch and pull the tab into position.

6. The remaining material of Flap (a) that was hanging loosely inside the box should now be burnished firmly to the inside of the side of the box and to the inside of the base. Work the cloth carefully into the inside corner joints.

7. Repeat for the opposite side of the base.

8. Now wrap Flap (c) over the third side to cover all three sides of the box.

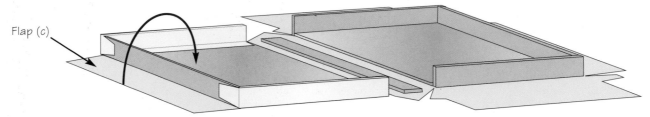

Flap (c)

9. Repeat this series of operations on the lid of the box.

10. The spine will have only a small triangle on either end to wrap over its edges. You will have to use your folder to stretch the cloth over the spine. The box is now completely covered on the outside.

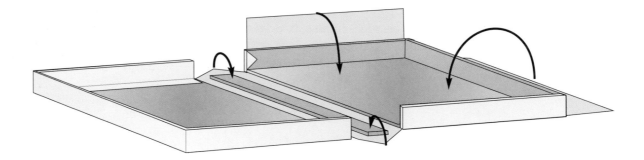

11. Finally, cut a piece of cloth or lining paper so that it is 0.25″ in from all the sides. (You will find if you use cloth rather than paper, it will be easier to work with, and will be more forgiving of any measurement errors.) Paste and attach it to the inside of the box. Work the cloth into the hinges with your folder and burnish it down thoroughly. Place a protective sheet of clean paper over the box and weight it while it dries. This can take several days.

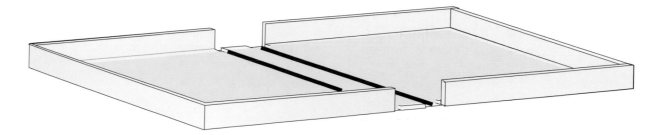

MAKING A SIMPLE PRESENTATION BOX

This box is easy to make and may be used either to hold loose pages or to provide a decorative and/or protective cover for a bound book. The best material to use is heavy drawing paper such as Rives, Arches or Stonehenge. The diagram below shows the dimensions, cuts and folds for a box that holds a book 8.5″ x 11″ and is about half an inch thick. It is useful to simply make this box using the dimensions as given. If you do you will understand the principle and can then change the dimensions to suit other sized books. You can use the test box to store printing paper, or extra prints.

The solid lines are cuts. Score and fold all the dotted lines in the same direction. All the spaces between the scored lines are 0.75″. Using the photograph at right as a reference, fold the flaps (b) so they form the sides of the box and meet in the middle over the base (d). Fold the two flaps (c) so they form a double flap or "pocket" over flap (e). To close the box insert flap (a) into the double flap.

This solution is inexpensive and elegant and should be attempted.

Above:
The simple paper box can be used to either store individual sheets, or protect a previously bound book. An inviting impression can be created by using the same materials for the box that you used for the cover of the book.
Douglas Holleley, *Past and Future Tense,* Rockcorry, Rochester, N.Y., 1998.

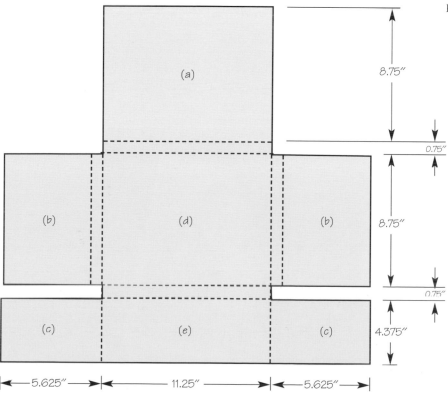

ADDENDUM: MORE ON BOOKBINDING MATERIALS

There are a host of materials available for covering your book. Some of the more common choices will be described below. Additionally, there are many other unconventional materials which will perform this task admirably and give your book a distinctive quality.

Almost any cloth can be used to bind a book. A trip to a craft or sewing supply store will present you with a range of possibilities. You can find lamé, ginghams and a variety of other materials any of which may be the ideal cloth to suit the nature of your contents. Be aware that some curtain materials come with a sized backing that facilitates pasting the cloth to the cardboard covers. Such (unpatterned) materials also allow you to print your own cover artwork on them.

There are a few principles to keep in mind when selecting a cloth.

Firstly, it should not be too thick. Bulky materials seldom look good when wrapped around the cover boards. The edges of the cover should be sharp and well-delineated, not thick and clumsy looking. Additionally, the corners may be very difficult to cover. Problems are also created when it comes time to affix the lining paper. The result can look "lumpy" and awkward, rather than slim and precise.

Secondly, try to select a material that can be wiped clean if you accidentally get paste on it while working. It is easy to get some where you do not want it to be. This will not be a problem if the material you select is suitably sized as you can wipe it clean with a damp cloth.

When you bind a book yourself you can adopt solutions and use materials that are particular to your expressive and communicative concerns. Despite the fact there are "proper" methods and materials designed specifically for bookbinding, keep an open mind and experiment with a variety of materials and binding solutions. In this case a simple hessian material has been hand painted and a pocket created inside the front cover to hold loose photographs. Author unknown. *Day book/journal.* Germany, 1919. *From the collection of Dr. Peter Stanbury.*

If you are new to the craft, it is advised that you stick with purpose designed book cover materials. With the exception of some leather stocks, which can be thick and difficult to work with, most are optimized for thickness and ease of use, and will thus provide the greatest opportunity for a successful job.

Bookcloth

This is the classic material for covering books. As the name suggests, this is cloth developed specifically for this task. There are many levels of quality available. It is well worth spending extra on a good quality stock as the covering material you select is the first thing that will be noticed (and judged) when you hand your book to a prospective reader. Usually the better cloths have excellent wearing and tactile qualities and are easy to work with. An example of a good cloth to use when you are first starting is:

Crash canvas

This cloth is a neutral color and works well with a variety of books. It has the virtue of being extremely easy to work with and is very forgiving. Any paste you may accidentally splash while working can be easily wiped off, and even should you miss a spot, its neutral appearance and textured surface will make most marks invisible. It also has the virtue of being very flexible and will conform to almost any shape. It is also very good for hinges as it is strong and retains its flexibility over a long period of time.

The main disadvantage is that it is quite light in color and can get dirty with continual handling. If you use it, you should spray the finished book with a silicon based, upholstery protective spray.

Buckram

This is probably the most common material employed to create a book cover. As a rule buckram is relatively inexpensive, although good quality stocks attract a premium price. It is similar to bookcloth but the mercerized surface is more robust, sometimes seeming a little "plastic" in comparison with better quality bookcloths. It is usually used for binding library books which are handled often, and need the extra protection this material offers.

The cover of this beautifully printed and presented book is made of papier maché coated with shellac. This method of construction was also used to make daguerreotype cases in the nineteenth century. The principle of creating a mold and then casting a cover is worth consideration, either using traditional materials as above, or adapting new materials such as fiberglass resin or plastic.
Henry Noel Humphreys, *Sentiments and Similes of William Shakespeare.*
A classified selection of similes, definitions, descriptions, and other remarkable passages in the plays and poems of Shakespeare. 3rd Edition, Longman, Green, Longman, Roberts and Green, London, no date, c. 1870.
Courtesy of the Cary Graphic Arts Collection, Rochester Institute of Technology, Rochester, N.Y.

Leather

Leather is the material of choice for traditional bookbinding. The main disadvantage is that it is expensive and relatively difficult to work with. Difficulty arises because it is often quite thick and/or uneven in thickness. Thus it usually requires paring down with a sharp knife if it is to be wrapped around an edge or a corner. However, it is a beautiful and very permanent material, and will imbue your book with a sensation of solidity and authority. If you wish to try it, consult a text on advanced bookbinding for detailed instructions on how to reduce the thickness of the material where required.

Also available, and somewhat cheaper, and easier to use, is composition leather. This material is composed of recycled, shredded natural leather, formed into sheets of standard thickness and color. This material works very well and can be used in the same way as any conventional bookcloth.

In this collection of essays on private press printing, the bookbinder Mike Hudson makes reference to the letterpress process by incorporating what appears to be a splash of molten lead on the cover.
Jagwiga Jarvis and Mike Hudson, *Collected Private Impressions,* Wayzgoose Press, Katoomba, New South Wales, 1995–96.

Heavy papers

Heavy paper cover stocks are available which are strong and have good folding and hinging characteristics. These materials can be either plain or come with printed designs. They are often used as endpapers. Elegant effects can be created by employing complementary or contrasting papers in combination, as both cover stock and endpapers.

Custom printed covers (cloth and paper)

As mentioned in Chapter 10, *p. 207,* there are heavyweight paper and cloth/canvas stocks which can allow the creation of highly individualized covers. These can be printed using an inkjet printer or by using any conventional printmaking process such as silk screen, linoleum cuts or woodblocks. Even simple rubber stamps can be used for this purpose.

Synthetic materials

In addition to natural materials such as cloth, paper and leather, there is a wide variety of synthetic materials created expressly for bookbinding. These include plain and patterned vinyl materials which replicate the look of leather.

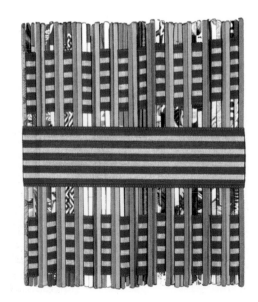

However, synthetics are often used to fabricate bookbinding materials which do not replicate existing materials but have their own, often idiosyncratic, characteristics. Gold and silver "cloths" are but one example. As these materials are designed specifically for bookmaking, they are straightforward to use and allow easy cleanup.

Wood, metal and other unusual materials

Finally, be open to the consideration of unusual and unconventional materials such as wood, metal, glass, plexiglass, sheet plastic and anything else that can be worked with tools and joined together to form a cover. Often such materials will necessitate the creation of unconventional binding solutions employing piano hinges, conventional door hinges or various combinations of rings and/or coils to hold the book together. Such bindings run the risk of being cumbersome and gimmicky. However, when used sensitively, they can greatly enhance the appreciation of your work.

Simply to describe materials in words quickly gives you an insight into the kinds of impressions that can be generated by the cover alone. Consider the differing qualities of wood.

There is old, silver, weathered timber, polychrome stained plywood, lacquered wood, sliced driftwood, carefully carved and burnished wood, hand-painted wood, scorched wood, etc.

Notice how each description generates a different sensation in your mind. The moral of the story is simple. Try it and see.

Above, below and below opposite:
This unusual binding by Keith Smith of Rochester, N.Y., incorporates a variety of materials, including variously printed and decorated papers as well as colored ribbons. Smith is a master binder and the reader is encouraged to refer to his many texts on the subject. The book is an album of photographs made by Philip Zimmermann of his son, Nicholas. Privately published in an edition of 1, 1984.

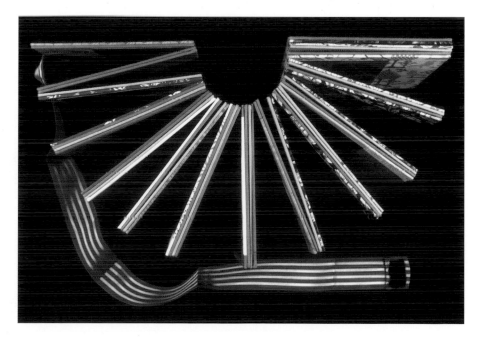

In this chapter we pay homage to one of the first and arguably
finest, self-publishers in the history of bookmaking, William Blake.
Poems by Mr. Gray. A New Edition, London. Printed for J. Murray,
1790. *Courtesy of the Cary Graphic Arts Collection, Rochester Institute
of Technology, Rochester, N.Y.*

CHAPTER 12

COMPUTERS, COPYRIGHT AND THE LAW

NOTE: This chapter represents the author's observations and views only. It is not a definitive legal document. Readers must obtain qualified legal advice to be sure their activities will not result in prosecution.

BECAUSE digital technology is a relatively new and rapidly evolving field, the law is constantly changing in response to unforseen circumstances and practices. As such the material contained within this chapter should not be regarded as a definitive statement of the legality, or otherwise, of certain practices. The purpose of the chapter is to illustrate many of the dilemmas that present themselves and suggest protocols and methods which are centered on basic values of respect for property, both tangible and intellectual, and informed by basic common sense and good manners.

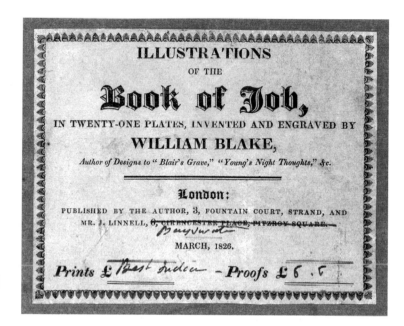

One of the issues with which legislators and the legal profession are struggling to come to grips is the ease with which digital data can be transmitted, copied and stored. The ability of the computer to render any information in a discrete code and subsequently process, amalgamate, modify, transform and re-present this information makes it the ideal medium for a Postmodern world. These attributes, however, make it easy for the individual to access the intellectual property of others to the point where the boundary between fair usage and plagiarism becomes blurred and difficult to differentiate.

This can occur at a number of levels and in a variety of media. The rights of visual artists, once protected by the skill required to practice their craft, are now easily appropriated by anyone with image processing software. On a more prosaic level, the ability to cut and paste text removes the drudgery of copying quotations and makes it possible for an individual to create an essay entirely from a pastiche of the words and thoughts of others.

Looking at the positive side, such possibilities suggest that knowledge may grow and become more complex as new ways of

To compare the process of copyright observance to the trials of the Biblical Job is perhaps unfair. It should not be seen as a trial to respect the property of others. When observing these conventions and laws, remember that they are there also to protect your work when it is finally printed, published and distributed. Without these protective mechanisms it could be you that is plagiarized by others. Imagine how you would feel if this occurred. The black and white illustrations in this chapter are all from William Blake's book, *Illustrations of the Book of Job.* Published by the Author and Mr. J. Linnell, London, 1826. This proof copy, printed by Blake himself, is held by the Elmira College Archives, Gannett-Tripp Library, Elmira College, Elmira, N.Y.

integrating data facilitate new connections and reveal unexpected and interesting juxtapositions. The downside is that such practices can erode the concept of originality and scholarship, turning the individual into another kind of box, much like the computer itself, able only to function as an editor of an endless loop of second hand thoughts.

Ultimately, it is the individual who must take responsibility for the way he or she uses the computer. As with most things in life, if it feels wrong then it most likely is. This guiding principle will prevent most problems from occurring. However, there are some practices which seem harmless because they are relatively commonplace. Protestations of "everybody does it" will be of little use if the individual finds him or her self in a position where a software company or another individual decide to exercise their rights to protect their property.

Many of these problems arise because activities that were once relatively self-limiting in the analog world of objects, things, and complex mechanical processes have actually changed both in character and ease of production in the digital domain.

The Problematical Nature of Computers

The Ability to Make an Identical Copy

Until the advent of digital technology, to make a copy was to create an object that differed from the original item. However, it is now possible to make an unlimited number of identical copies of anything that appears on the computer screen. The code that represents an image, document or piece of software can be copied an infinite number of times and in each case the copy is exactly the same as the original.

There are many implications for practice as a result. Perhaps the most seductive notion, and the one that is most likely to cause an individual to commit an offense, is the notion that there is no actual theft of an object, only a copy has been made. However, whether the original string of code represented a computer program or utility, an image or a written document, each (digital) copy has the same qualities as the original. This is a significant change from analog practice.

This book is an excellent, and very early, example of self-publishing. Blake drew on the Bible for his inspiration (and copyright free text) and then illustrated the work with his own engravings and calligraphy. Although the images and text are each kept in their own space (or box), Blake has integrated the two mediums of words and images by using the text as a framing and decorative device, in addition to being a communicator of the sense and meaning of the story. William Blake, *Illustrations of the Book of Job,* op. cit., *Plate 2.*

For example, one can theoretically make an infinite number of prints from a single photographic negative. In practice, however, variations are inevitable as the negative is translated into print. Changes in paper stock, temperature variations of the developer, deterioration of the chemicals and a host of other variables all combine to make it extremely difficult to make an edition where each print exhibits identical properties. Additionally the negative itself, with repeated use, can become scratched or otherwise altered. The problem is exacerbated if the negative is duplicated, either from the negative itself, or through the fabrication of a copy negative made from a print. As each generation is created so is there an accompanying drop in the quality of the image.

In comparison, digital code, no matter how many times it is copied, remains the same, irrespective of whether it is recorded on magnetic tape, floppy disk or CD. Unlike the vagaries of photographic paper or other analog forms of media, the carrier of the code exerts no influence on the content of the digital document. Whether one uses a cheap floppy disk or a gold plated CD ROM, the media has no effect on the contents, other than its mechanical reliability in the disk drive of the machine. The code remains the same.

There are a number of implications for the individual, all of which conspire to lessen the apparent seriousness of the activity.

It is no longer necessary to possess the "original." One does not have to physically steal an object when a copy will function just as well.

As discussed above, each copy of a digital file is an exact clone of its "parent." Thus, a copy of a digital file has the same qualities, and value, as the original. A common rationalization is that "nothing has been taken, but simply a copy has been made." However, such a defense is inappropriate with respect to digital files where the copy and the original are indistinguishable from each other.

William Blake, *Illustrations of the Book of Job,* op. cit., *Plate 3.*

The cost of making a copy is low.

All that is required to infringe copyright in the digital domain is a personal computer. The pirated file can be stored on an inexpensive floppy disk. As such the act of infringing copyright of digital files carries with it little economic investment. This lack of a financial barrier minimizes the apparent seriousness of the infringement. The offense seems minimal if not trivial. Can a fifty cent floppy disk suddenly become worth hundreds, even thousands, of dollars?

The ease of making a copy.

Because a digital file can be easily copied, usually by simply dragging its icon from one location to another, the ease of this process contributes to perceiving this act as relatively harmless in nature.

THE HOMOGENIZATION OF PHYSICAL AND INTELLECTUAL PROPERTY.

William Blake, *Illustrations of the Book of Job,* op. cit., *Plate 5.*

Computers are capable of re-presenting and representing data from all media in a uniform manner. Through the process of digitization, where conventional analog forms of knowledge are converted into mathematical equivalents, it is possible to reduce the particular qualities of otherwise quite disparate media into a single uniform format. The sound of a musical instrument, the combined sounds of a symphony orchestra, a painting, a photograph, a book of poetry or scientific theories, can all be rendered in the same digital language.

There is no discrimination in terms of qualitative worth. This process subtly suggests that all information is of equal value or equal non-value. Great works and small, masterpieces and doodles, the efforts of both the master and the apprentice, all are reduced to the same format, and may be transmitted and stored in the same way.

This has the ability to engender a position of moral confusion. Data becomes data becomes Dada (read nonsense). When everything can be seen to be the same, then all things come to assume equal value.

It is thus very easy to adopt and maintain the perception that all knowledge stored and transmitted on electronic delivery systems is a kind of intellectual smorgasbord, free for the taking. There is nothing intrinsic to the process that makes it self-evident that one set of code is free and another must be paid for. Often the only differentiation that exists is a claim made by the originator, manufacturer or distributor that the information is protected by copyright.

Some freeware, software that is distributed for little or no charge, works as well, if not better, than commercial software with a high price tag. Such anomalies do little to encourage compliance with manufacturers' efforts to protect their products. To the average individual there is no justification for this apparently arbitrary distinction.

Of course things are not this simple. The average individual has only minimal comprehension of the complexity of software or other sophisticated files, and knows only that they can be easily duplicated on floppy discs or other media. The same goes for all files, big, small, simple or complex. Unlike the analog world which deals with objects and things, the digital world has no tangible existence in three dimensional form. The digital world has no sense of reality, nor does it discriminate between expensive and inexpensive, exotic or familiar. Unlike previous publishing and artistic practice, digital code cannot distinguish itself through its appearance and quality.

William Blake, *Illustrations of the Book of Job,* op. cit., *Plate 9.*

THE LACK OF A HIERARCHICAL STRUCTURE OF SKILL ACQUISITION

Within the computer domain itself, once the basic skills have been learned then one quite quickly gets to the point where doing something sophisticated requires only a little more skill than doing something simple. When one learns to scan an image, or download something from the web, then the skill is learned. What you then choose to scan or sample is simple repetition. Compare this to past practice when if you wanted to forge a painting, or a dollar bill, you had to acquire almost as much skill as the person that made the original object. It took years of practice to acquire the skills to be able to be a forger. Now with a scanner and a printer anyone can make a facsimile of almost anything. Do not be a thief or a forger.

All these characteristics combine to create pitfalls and traps, making it easy to break laws and conventions. These can have serious and unfortunate consequences. The single most common trap is that of infringing copyright. This most frequently occurs at two levels, software copyright and creative copyright.

SOFTWARE COPYRIGHT

Because of the ability to make an exact clone of digital code, it is very tempting to simply copy a piece of software. This is particularly the case when the software is expensive. Not only is this illegal, it is also extremely disrespectful to the creative people who devised and refined this software. It is enough to say that copying software is illegal and the penalties can be severe. A software company may decide to pursue the matter in court. If you are enrolled as a student, it can result in you being suspended or expelled from the school.

The days where computing information and knowledge were not seen as property, but as challenges, are gone. We are no longer in the halcyon days of the 1960s, where inside the MIT lab at Cambridge, young men (sic) lived and breathed computers, creating a culture of "hacking" and experimentation. These hackers approached computing from the idealistic perspective that knowledge (especially computer software knowledge) should be free, that results and software solutions should be shared, and that authority was to be distrusted.[1]

These ideals were perhaps once appropriate and at that time and place, helped create elegant solutions. The environment of total commitment and fierce competition produced much good work. However, in the very different corporate climate of the new millennium, such attitudes look less like free-spirited individualism and

William Blake, *Illustrations of the Book of Job,* op. cit., *Plate 12.*

1. Steven Levy, *Hackers, Heroes of the Computer Revolution,* Anchor Press/ Doubleday, Garden City, N.Y., 1984. See Chapter 2, *The Hacker Ethic.*

more and more like anarchistic intellectual theft. Certainly, they will be perceived as the latter by a software company protecting its property. It is also much easier to get caught than you might think. Be aware that if you are connected to an ethernet network, then the network manager can, at any time, from the comfort of his or her office, search the entire contents of your computer and identify suspicious software.

TEXT COPYRIGHT

The laws concerning the copyright of text have been little changed by the digital revolution. The use of small quotations and properly attributed ideas was, is, and will likely continue to be permitted.

What has changed, however, is the ready availability of vast amounts of information on the Internet which can be quickly and easily copied and pasted into an essay or text. This activity can seem less like plagiarism because of the sheer volume of information on the net, and the quite often idiosyncratic way it is presented and "published." This can contribute to a perpetuation of the hacker "creed" that all information should be free and distributed without restraint.

However, quite simply it is wrong, and illegal, to use the work of others without attributing the source. It is worse to do so using large "slabs" of text which pose as your own individual thoughts. If nothing else, your book will not be your book at all. Instead, it will be a pastiche of the work of others.

William Blake, *Illustrations of the Book of Job,* op. cit., *Plate 14.*

Where legitimate difficulties occur is when and if you find some prose, or a poem, that you would like to use with your images. Many fine artist books of the past have used this very approach. If this is the case, you will have to ascertain whether the material you wish to use is still protected by copyright, or is so old that the copyright has expired. It is for this reason that so many books use texts from the past, often as far back as Biblical times. Do not assume however, that because a text is old, that it is free of encumbrances.

Check with the publisher of the book where you found the text, and if in doubt, seek legal advice. Dover Publications are a very good source for copyright free material and usually make it very clear which material you may use, and which is protected.

IMAGE COPYRIGHT

For the bookmaker and the digital visual artist, this is perhaps the most contentious area of all. The problem is particularly exacerbated by a prevailing visual aesthetic which encourages and promotes photo assemblages and collages. This aesthetic is a direct function of the computers ability to cut and paste with seamless precision. Mitchell[2] makes the point that in the past, collages remained a fringe activity in photography because they were "usually technically difficult, time consuming and easily detectable." This, however, is no longer the case. As mentioned earlier, the traditional notion of skill hierarchy has been largely eroded by the computer. Now even a novice can, with some success, graft a number of visual sources together to create a photo-collage.

2. W. J. Mitchell, *The Reconfigured Eye,* MIT Press, Cambridge, Mass., 1994.

The problem is further exacerbated by Post Modern trends in art where existing images are re-contextualized for reasons of irony, social comment, or visual incongruity. Barbara Kruger's work is an excellent example. However, artists like Kruger go to considerable trouble to obtain the necessary clearances or find copyright free material. To simply emulate this method, with no consideration of the source of your material, will inevitably lead to trouble.

William Blake, *Illustrations of the Book of Job,* op. cit., *Plate 15.*

Again, this problem is compounded by the fact that the Internet is full of images waiting to be downloaded. Their access is so immediate and so simple that the temptation can be very strong to simply help yourself. If the image you select is copyright-free, then there is no problem. If it is copyrighted, and the copyright holder exercises his or her rights, then the ease with which you were able to access it, is no defense.

In addition to the 'net, it is also possible to scan images from books. Some scanners even come with a de-screening option to remove the halftone screen from the (pirated) image. This is an abomination. If you must scan a preexisting image, you can only use copyright-free material or material for which you have received permission to use.

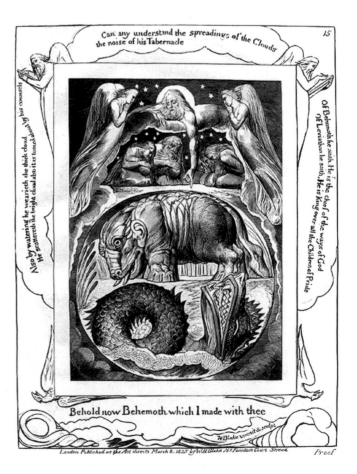

MORAL RIGHTS

Be also aware that artists possess moral rights to their work. If you substantially change the context of even a copyright-free image, to the point where its original intention has been grossly distorted, you may encounter problems. These problems can include your work being dismissed as naive or gauche, corrupt or offensive and depending on the level of debate, can become a legal matter.

    This is not an area where absolute values prevail. Sometimes it is important in art practice to subvert convention. For example, much of the power of Joel Peter Witkin's photographs comes from his references to the visual structure of classical religious painting. Within these structures he unexpectedly depicts strange, often grotesque events to present new, and often disturbing, visions. However, artists of Witkin's calibre do this with intelligence and understanding, and accept responsibility for their actions. Such a stance is courageous and justifiable. To do the same thing without this understanding and sense of responsibility, is at best insensitive, and at worst offensive. It is a serious ethical and legal issue, especially if you are oblivious to your actions.

William Blake, *Illustrations of the Book of Job,* op. cit., *Plate 16.*

WHAT MATERIAL CAN YOU USE?

Creative material is protected by copyright. When this copyright expires it is said to be in the public domain. The general rule of thumb is that if an image was published before 1922 it is in the public domain and you are free to use it (subject to the provisos discussed above). However, it is wise to assume that all images are protected and accordingly you should seek permission from the copyright holder. Even images produced prior to 1922, and held in public collections, have restrictions on their use. The institution that holds these works will itself have to grant permission if you wish to use one of the images from its collection.[3]

3. An excellent layman's guide to the complexities of copyright can be found in the book by Adele Droblas Greenberg and Seth Greenberg, *Digital Images: A Practical Guide.* Osborne McGraw-Hill, Berkeley, 1995.
  Detailed copyright information and forms can also be obtained from the Library of Congress who administer copyright law in the United States.

Copyright Office, Library of Congress
101 Independence Ave, S.E.
Washington, DC, 20559–6000.
URL: *www.loc.gov/copyright*

PROTECTING YOUR WORK

The discussion until now has been centered on respecting the rights of others. However, as a creative author, you have rights as well. Prior to 1978, to protect your work you had to place a copyright notice on your book and register it with the United States Copyright Office. However, the law now protects creative work the moment it is placed in tangible form. This protection extends to 50 years after your death.

It is no longer necessary to register your work with the Copyright Office to gain this protection. This will only be required if you wish to sue for copyright infringement. However, it is wise to place a notice in your book claiming copyright. This notice must include the following information…

- The word "Copyright" or the symbol "©."

- The year of first publication.

- Your name, or that of the copyright holder.

For more information contact,
The Copyright Office
Library of Congress
101 Independence Ave, S.E.
Washington, DC, 20559–6000.
URL: *www.loc.gov/copyright*

William Blake, *Illustrations of the Book of Job,* op. cit., *Plate 20.*

CONCLUSION

The purpose of this discussion has been to warn the reader of the many traps and pitfalls that can occur when constructing a book using digital technology. Making a book requires that you use many smaller programs (utilities) and other copyrighted material such as fonts, in addition to the larger and more obvious programs such as Photoshop and QuarkXPress. As such the possibility of (even unwittingly) committing a software copyright infringement is greater than normal. When this is coupled with the use of both text and images (the use of which is governed by certain laws and conventions of usage in themselves) then it should be apparent that considerable caution must be exercised at each step. Most of these problems will evaporate if the book is comprised entirely of your own work. It is anticipated that this will be the case for the majority of readers. However, as the discussion of image usage suggested, even basic concepts such as authorship and originality have been severely questioned, if not re-defined, because of the unique characteristics of digital technology and the ready availability of pre-digitized material on the Internet. When in doubt, try wherever possible, to substitute an image of dubious title with either a known copyright-free image, or better still one of your own making.

This, the last of Blake's Job images, has been digitally modified by the author. In so doing the joyful tonality of Blake's final illustration has been significantly altered, to be replaced by a somber, even bleak vision. The reader is asked to consider this modification in the light of the previous discussion. Is this a fair interpretation, or does it change, if not distort, Blake's intention too much?
William Blake, *Illustrations of the Book of Job*, op. cit., *Plate 21.*

GENERAL GOOD PRACTICE

The following simple rules will
help guide your practice. Some of
these rules apply to legal practice,
others to more general principles
of computer etiquette, especially in
a communal situation, such as a
public library, college or university.
In such places resources are shared,
and can often be scarce. As such, it
is important to exercise some
consideration for others when
using the equipment to ensure a
harmonious and mutually
respectful working environment.

These are best addressed by a
simple list of do's and don'ts.

DO…

•   credit your sources, both text
    and images, in an academically
    responsible manner.

•   acknowledge any assistance you
    may have received above and
    beyond normal help.

•   save your work often.

•   if you find there are no computers vacant, but there is one where
    work is in progress but the operator is not able to be found,
    perform a "Save as" operation and rename the open file (adding
    the date is good) before starting work. In this way you keep the
    "missing person's" original file and also the progress made to the
    point where you commenced working on the machine.

•   when saving your work, create a folder with your name on it and
    be sure to save your files to this destination. Don't accidentally, or
    unthinkingly, save them to folders on the hard drive (especially
    program folders such as QuarkXPress or Photoshop).

Above and Opposite:
In keeping with this homage to one of
the first and arguably finest, self-publishers in the history of bookmaking,
here are two (further) pages from
Blake's book, *Poems by Mr. Gray. A New
Edition,* London. Printed for J. Murray,
1790.

Do Not...

- do to other's work what you would not like done to yours.

- copy software or other files for which you have not paid and for which you are not the registered owner.

- use large (or small) quantities of unattributed text.

- use other people's images.

- as a general rule, scan from a commercially printed book. The quality will in all likelihood be awful and it is also most likely protected by copyright.

- walk out leaving your work open and un-saved. Leaving the computer with open windows and work in progress while you disappear for "a few minutes," is extremely inconsiderate.

- use imaging computers to email or net-surf, if the demand for computer access is high.

- leave folders or files on the computer, especially if they are large. Put them on your portable storage disk and trash the originals.

- look at other people's files or folders. Respect privacy.

- go into the system folder without seeking the advice of the technical support staff.

- use a computer attached to a scanner, printer or any other specialized device if there are other computers vacant, and you do not require access to the specialized equipment.

William Blake, (Illustrations) *Poems by Mr. Gray. Illustrations by William Blake. A New Edition,* London. Printed for J. Murray, 1790.

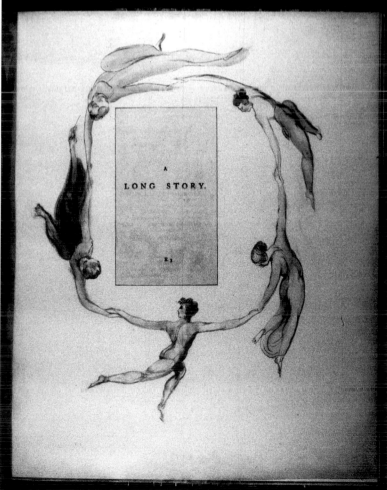

The biggest book of all is, of course, the world. Like any book, it is full of messages and signs, admonitions and exhortations, promises and threats. You have only to open your eyes and read.

This image is from Nathan Lyons' thoughtfully sequenced book, *Riding First Class on the Titanic,* Addison Gallery of American Art, Andover, Mass., 1999.

BIBLIOGRAPHY

ARTIST'S BOOK HISTORY AND THEORY

Artist's Books Yearbook 1996/97. Stanmore, UK: Magpie Press, 1996.

Crimp, Douglas. "The Museum's Old/The Library's New Subject." In *The Contest of Meaning.* Edited by Richard Bolton. Cambridge, Mass.: MIT Press, 1993.

Drucker, Johanna. *The Century of Artists' Books.* New York: Granary Books, 1995.

Dugan, Thomas. *Photography Between Covers.* Rochester, N.Y.: Light Impressions, 1979.

Eaton, Timothy A. *Books as Art.* Boca Raton, Fla.: Boca Raton Museum of Art, (n.d.).

Jennett, Sean. *The Making of Books.* New York: F. A. Praeger Inc., 1951.

Lauf, Cornelia and Clive Phillpot. *Artist/Author, Contemporary Artist's Books.* New York: DAP/Distributed Art Publishers Inc. and the American Federation of Arts, 1998.

Levy, Steven. *Hackers: Heroes of the Computer Revolution.* Garden City, N.Y.: Anchor Press/Doubleday, 1984.

Lyons, Joan, ed. *Artists' Books. A Critical Anthology and Sourcebook.* Rochester, N.Y.: Gibbs M. Smith, Inc., Peregrine Smith Books in association with Visual Studies Workshop Press, 1985.

Mitchell, W. J. *The Reconfigured Eye.* Cambridge, Mass.: MIT Press, 1994.

Rothenberg, Jerome and Steven Clay, eds. *A Book of the Book: Some Works and Projections about the Book and Writing.* New York: Granary Books, 2000.

Smith, Keith. *200 BOOKS, An Annotated Bibliography.* Rochester, N.Y.: keith smith BOOKS, 2000.

Smith, Keith. *Structure of the Visual Book.* 3d ed. Rochester, N.Y.: keith smith BOOKS, 1995.

Smith, Keith. *Text in the Book Format.* 2d ed. Rochester, N.Y.: keith smith BOOKS, 1997.

Thomas, Lew. *Louisiana Artist's Pages.* New Orleans: Contemporary Arts Centre, 1989.

Wye, Deborah. *Committed to Print.* New York: Museum of Modern Art, 1988.

BOOKBINDING

Cockerell, Douglas. *Bookbinding and the Care of Books.* London: Pitman, 1901.

Johnson, Arthur W. *Manual of Bookbinding.* New York: Charles Scribner's and Sons, 1978.

La Plantz, Shereen. *Cover to Cover, Creative Techniques for Making Beautiful Books, Journals and Albums.* Asheville, N.C.: Lark Books, 1995.

Lewis, A. W. *Basic Bookbinding.* New York: Dover, 1957.

Smith, Keith. *Bookbinding for Book Artists: Sewn & Pasted Cloth or Leather Requiring No Special Tools or Equipment.* Rochester, N.Y.: keith smith BOOKS, 1998.

Smith, Keith. *Non-Adhesive Binding. Vol. 1. Books without Paste or Glue.* Rev. and enl. Rochester, N.Y.: keith smith BOOKS, 1999.

Smith, Keith. *Non-Adhesive Binding. Vol. 2. 1- 2- & 3-Section Sewings.* Rochester, N.Y.: keith smith BOOKS, 1995.

Smith, Keith. *Non-Adhesive Binding. Vol. 3. Exposed Spine Sewings.* Rochester, N.Y.: keith smith BOOKS, 1995.

DESIGN AND TYPOGRAPHY

Carson, David. *2nd Sight.* Text by Lewis Blackwell. London: Laurence King Publishing, 1998.

Carson, David. *The End of Print, The Graphic Design of David Carson.* Text by Lewis Blackwell. London: Laurence King Publishing, 1995.

Carter, Rob, Ben Day and Philip Meggs. *Typographic Design: Form and Communication.* New York: Van Nostrand Reinhold Co., 1985.

Higgins, Dick. *Pattern Poetry.* Albany, N.Y.: SUNY Press, 1987.

Lawson, Alexander S. with Dwight Agner. *Printing Types, An Introduction.* Rev. and enl. Boston: Beacon Press, 1990.

Livingston, Alan and Isabella Livingston. *Encyclopædia of Graphic Design and Designers.* London and New York: Thames and Hudson, 1992.

Massin, Robert. *Letter and Image.* New York: Van Nostrand Reinhold, 1970.

Solt, Mary Ellen. *Concrete Poetry: A World View.* Bloomington, Ill.: Indiana University Press, 1971.

Williams, Emmett. *An Anthology of Concrete Poetry.* New York and Villefranch: Something Else Press, 1967.

PHOTOGRAPHY AND DIGITAL IMAGING

Davis, Phil. *Photography.* Dubuque, Iowa: Wm. C. Brown Publishers, 1990.

Day, Rob. *Designer Photoshop.* New York: Random House, 1993.

Eastman Kodak Co. *Conservation of Photographs.* Rochester, N.Y.: 1990.

Greenberg, Adele Droblas and Seth Greenberg. *Digital Images: A Practical Guide.* Berkeley: Osborne McGraw-Hill, 1995.

Szarkowski, John. *Looking at Photographs.* New York: Museum of Modern Art, 1973.

White, Minor. *Mirrors, Messages, Manifestations.* New York: An Aperture Monograph, 1969.

PRINTING

Bunnell, Peter C. *Non Silver Printing Processes: Four Selections 1886–1927.* Facsimile Edition. New York: Arno Press, 1973.

Burkholder, Dan. *Making Digital Negatives for Contact Printing.* San Antonio, Tex.: Bladed Iris Press, 1995.

Coe, Brian. *Colour Photography, The First Hundred Years 1840–1940.* London: Ash and Grant, 1978.

Cost, Frank. *Pocket Guide to Digital Printing.* Albany, N.Y.: Delmar Publishers, 1997.

Crawford, William. *The Keepers of Light: A History and Working Guide to Early Photographic Processes.* Dobbs Ferry, N.Y.: Morgan and Morgan, 1979.

Berry, W. Turner and H. Edmund Poole. *Annals of Printing.* London: Blandford Press, 1966.

PERIODICALS

AbraCadaBra. Alliance for Contemporary Book Arts, PO Box 24415, Los Angeles, Calif., 90024.

Emigre. 4476 D Street, Sacramento, Calif., 95819.

JAB. Journal of Artist's Books, 535 Means Street, Atlanta, Ga., 30318.

Koob Stra. The Centre for Book Arts, 626 Broadway, New York, N.Y., 10012.

Umbrella. PO Box 3640, Santa Monica, Calif., 90408.

URL's

www.loc.gov/copyright: This site provides extensive and useful information on all aspects of copyright law.

www.inkjetmall.com: This site contains much practical advice as well as providing access to materials.

BOOKS, ARTIST'S BOOKS, AND PORTFOLIOS BY THE AUTHOR

Holleley, Douglas. *A Passing Show.* Sydney: Macquarie University, 1973.

——. *Far Fetched.* Rochester, N.Y.: Visual Studies Workshop, 1976.

——. *The Ray-Gun Catalog.* Webster, N.Y.: Published at the Xerox Facility, 1976.

——. *Visions of Australia.* Sydney: Angus and Robertson, 1980.

——. *Points of Entry.* Canberra: Limited edition portfolio, 1983.

——. *Voyelles / Twenty Four Years.* Photographs by D. Holleley with text by Arthur Rimbaud and Dylan Thomas. Hand set by Thierry Bouchard. Canberra: Graphic Investigation Workshop, Canberra School of Art, 1988.

——. *Through the Eye of the Needle.* Woodford, New South Wales: Rockcorry, 1990.

——. *Travels in Time.* Photographs by D. Holleley with text by Dr. Peter Stanbury. Limited Edition catalogue hand-printed by Wayzgoose Press. Woodford, New South Wales: Rockcorry, 1991.

——. *Paper, Scissors and Stone.* Text and direct scanned images. Woodford, New South Wales: Rockcorry, 1995.

——. *Love Song.* Text and direct scanned images. Woodford, New South Wales: Rockcorry, 1995.

——. *Momento Mori.* Portfolio of direct scanned images with essay. Woodford, New South Wales: Rockcorry, 1996.

——. *Paper Planes.* Text and photograms. Woodford, New South Wales: Rockcorry, 1996.

——. *Soft Landing in a Hard Place.* Direct scanned images and essay. Woodford, New South Wales: Rockcorry, 1996.

——. *Luna Park; the Image of a Funfair.* Ph.D. thesis. Sydney: University of Sydney, 1997.

——. *Adaminaby.* Story and illustrations. Rochester, N.Y.: Rockcorry at the Visual Studies Workshop, 1998.

——. *The Frock.* Story and digital images. Ithaca, N.Y.: Rockcorry, 1998.

——. *Past and Future Tense.* Stories and digital photographs. Ithaca, N.Y.: Rockcorry, 1998.

——. *Re-reading the Book; a Photographic Analysis of Albrecht Dürer's Hierin sind begriffen vier Bucher von menschlicher Proportion.* Limited edition portfolio with essay and digital photographs. Rochester, N.Y.: 2000.

Glossary

Additive color: Colors made by mixing together the light of the three additive color primaries, red, green and blue, *p. 185.*

Ampersand: Shorthand character (&) representing the word "and."

Ascender: See *p. 42.*

ASCII: Abbreviation for American Standard Code of Information Interchange. A standard of using numbers to represent the characters and commands on the keyboard.

Backup: In printing, the relationship of shapes between one side of the paper and the other, *p. 28.* In computing, making a copy of a document and storing it safely.

Baseline: See *p. 41.*

Bezier curve: A means of drawing curved lines in object-based programs (such as Adobe Illustrator) using mathematically defined curves constrained by anchor and control points assigned to the line.

Binary code: A number system using combinations of only two digits, zero and one.

Bit: The building block of the digital binary code. A simple yes/no or on/off represented by a zero (0) or a one (1).

Bitmap image: An image made up of colored or toned pixels, rather than mathematically drawn objects. All scanned photographs and images are bitmap images. Also known as Raster images, *p. 121.*

Bleed: Images printed to the edge of the page. Having no border.

Block: The pages of a book after being sewn or glued together.

Body size: Measurement of type size (in points) based on the height of the body of metal type, *p. 43.*

Body type: Text material, usually under 12 points.

Bold type: Type with thicker strokes, *p. 44.*

Byte: A byte is comprised of 8 bits and usually corresponds to one character such as a letter or number, on the screen, *p. 131.*

Calibration: The adjustment of the separate components of a system to an agreed upon standard. In digital terms, a monitor, printer and program can be calibrated to produce consistent results, *pp. 183–185.*

Cap height: Height of capitals from the baseline to the capline, *p. 41.*

Capitals or Upper Case: The larger letters of the alphabet.

Capline: The imaginary line that runs along the tops of the capital letters, *p. 41.*

Caps: An abbreviation for capital letters.

Caption: Supporting material, usually an explanation or description accompanying photographs or illustrations, *p. 8.*

Central Processing Unit: CPU. The part of the computer with the logic board, chip and hard drive, where operations are performed.

Character: Any component of a font including alphabets, punctuation or numerals.

Chase: The frame in which movable type is fixed on the bed of the press prior to printing, *p. 79.*

Clamshell: A box hinged so that the lid is connected to the base, *pp. 248–254.*

Codex: A book bound with a spine along one edge. Compare to the Concertina.

Colophon: Inscription placed either at the front or the back of the book which contains details about its production. This might include appropriate credits for design, details of the typeface used, and how it was set, and other items of note and/or interest, *p.35.*

Color Table: Similar to separation table. A set of algorithms or preferences which are used to calculate the transition from RGB to CMYK formats. These algorithms also usually take into account the color rendition of different output devices..

Color temperature: A measure of the degree to which a light source represents the appearance of white according to the proportion of the spectrum it emits. It is measured in units of degrees Kelvin (°K). For example the color temperature of daylight is 5,200°K. The color temperature of a household incandescent light is about 3,200°K.

Comprehensive Layout or "Comp": An accurate representation of a layout, showing positioning and size of images and typography. Same as (Final) Maquette.

Compression: Making a file smaller so it will occupy less disk space. Compression either averages pixel values or instead "maps" the position of identically valued pixels so they are stored as a unit rather than as pixel by pixel data.

Concertina: Pages joined to each other, either in the gutter or the outside edge so that there is no single spine, *p. 231.*

Condensed type: See *p. 44.*

Cursor: The shape that moves about the screen when you move the mouse. It can be a pointer (arrowhead), an I-beam or can be other shapes depending on the function you are performing in a program.

Descender: See *p. 42*.

Desktop: The metaphor for the screen display, especially when you are in the Finder. However, all screen displays are often said to appear on the desktop.

Dialog box: A box that appears on the screen in which you usually have to either enter information or make a decision.

Dingbats: Various decorative signs, symbols and bullets used for emphasis.

Dog's breakfast: An Australian slang expression (probably British in origin) used to describe a chaotic mess.

DPI: Dots per inch. This is usually a measure of the resolution of an output device such as a film or paper printer. Often (somewhat incorrectly) used interchangeably with PPI or pixels per inch.

Dry transfer: Type characters attached to paper backing sheets. These characters could then be burnished onto the finished artwork in preparation for plate making.

EPS: Encapsulated PostScript, a standard file format for high resolution PostScript illustrations.

Exquisite corpse: A form of random organization of either images or words. In the case of images, different parts of the body, such as the head, torso and legs, are allowed to be combined in various configurations to create new hybrid images, *p. 7*. Poets have also used this technique to allow poems to be created by the chance juxtaposition of independent phrases, *p. 20*.

File: A single cluster of information representing one document. This can be an image, or a self contained written text. It is indicated by an icon and file name.

Finder: The basic program that controls the computer. The finder is displayed as the Desktop where the Hard Disk (containing the System Software) and Trash are displayed.

Folder: A group of files in the same location indicated by an icon that looks like a conventional office folder. See *p. 91* for the importance of using folders when printing from QuarkXPress.

Fonts: In traditional (letterpress) printing, the term fonts described a complete set of characters, including alphabets, numerals and punctuation for one size of typeface. In digital printing it is used to describe a typeface, irrespective of size, *p. 41*.

Fusing: Method of fixing powdered, colored toner to paper by either heat or chemical reaction. This method is used by laser printers.

Gamma Adjustment: The alteration of the middle values of an image so that the contrast is altered by either the compressing or expanding of shadow or highlight areas, *p. 147*.

Gamut: The range of colors able to be rendered by a particular output device.

GCR: Gray Component Replacement. This control, used when printing replaces gray tones of an image, comprised of a mixture of colors, by a graded replacement of these values with pure black ink.

Grayscale: An image comprised of 256 shades of gray, ranging from pure black to paper base white.

Grid/layout: Schematic representation of the position of images and type in a layout, *pp. 30–32.*

Gutter: The space between two pages of a double page spread where they meet at the binding. Can also refer to the space between columns on the same page.

Hairline: The thinnest strokes within a typeface.

Halftone: A rendition of a continuous tone image such as a photograph into a series of larger or smaller black or white dots (or a clustering of same size dots) to create the illusion of a continuous tone image.

Hard disk: A plate, or series of plates covered with magnetic material, which is where the System Software, Programs and Files are stored.

Histogram: The visual representation of gray values on a scale of 256 levels, ranging from 0 (black) to 255 (white), *p. 137.*

Hue: Pure colors of the spectrum with no white or black component.

I-beam: The shape the cursor adopts when working with text.

Imagesetter: High resolution device for printing screen and line negatives from disk in preparation for offset printing.

Imposition: The arrangement of pages in a signature so when printed all are in correct order, *pp. 71–73.*

Index color: A system for displaying color where there are 256 or less colors available.

Interpolation: The sampling of adjacent pixels and calculating new pixels to place between them when an image is enlarged digitally. A similar process is involved when the image is reduced in size, *pp. 163–4.*

Italics: Type based more closely on written script.

Item: A QuarkXPress term used to describe any drawn element on the page. Typically items are text boxes, picture boxes, lines (rules) and text paths.

JPEG: Joint Photographic Experts Group. An image file format that reduces the file size by generalizing similarly colored pixels into a single value. It always results in some loss of quality.

Justified: A column with vertical left and right-hand edges, *p. 48.*

Kerning: Optical adjustment of the space between two letters, *p. 51.*

Kilobyte: 1024 bytes. Abbreviated K.

Laser: A concentrated light source.

Laser printer: A printer that uses powdered plastic toner to image on paper. Laser printers usually employ PostScript software to "draw" the image on the page.

Leading: The adjustment of the space between lines of type. Once performed by inserting lead strips, *p. 52.*

Letterspacing: The interval between individual characters.

Letterpress: Printing from raised characters, usually made of lead, but sometimes wood. The lines of type are placed on the "bed" of a printing press. The type is inked, either manually or mechanically, paper placed over the type, and then pressed in contact with the type with a roller.

Line Art: Images, usually drawn as black lines on white paper, which have no intermediate gray values. The values are either black, or white.

Line breaks: The point where one line finishes in a non-justified column. Harmonious patterns formed by the line breaks are indicative of thoughtful and skilled typesetting.

Linotype: The Linotype machine was a keyboard device which aligned molds of the various letters into a line which were then be filled with molten lead to form "lines of type."

Lossless: A compression algorithm where data is not lost.

Lossy: A compression algorithm where data is lost.

Lower case: The smaller letters of the alphabet, usually possessing ascenders and descenders. The opposite of upper case or Capital letters.

LPI: Lines per inch. Units of measurement of the resolution of a half tone screen, *pp. 127–128.*

Maquette: An accurate representation of a layout, showing positioning and size of images and typography, *pp. 21–24.*

Margin: The un-printed area surrounding a block of type.

Master Page: (QuarkXPress and other page layout programs.) A page on which guides, and other items can be placed which will appear automatically on each new page created within the same document.

Meanline: The line that runs along the top of the body of lowercase letters. It corresponds to the top line of the x-height of the characters.

Megabyte: A measure of computer memory equal to a kilobyte squared, i.e. 1024^2 (1,048,576 bytes) Abbreviated MB.

Menu: A list of commands, usually a "pull down" list but they can also "pop-up." Options not available will be displayed grayed-out.

Modern Style: Typeface. The serifs are straight lines, and the strokes vary greatly in weight from bold, thick strokes to fine hairlines, *p. 40.*

Monotype: A brand name of typeface. Sometimes (incorrectly) used to describe individual characters of cast metal type.

Noise: Texture added to a digital image to produce the illusion of photographic grain.

Offset Lithography: A plate is made, usually from a photographic negative. The ink adheres to the areas of the plate that are to be printed black. This ink is then transferred to a rubber roller, which then transfers this impression to the paper.

Old Style Figures: Numbers compatible with lower case letters. 1, 2 and 0 align with the x-height; 6 and 8 have ascenders; and 3,4,5,7, and 9, have descenders, *p. 44.*

Old Style: A category of Roman typefaces that originated in France in the sixteenth century. They are characterized by a lack of contrast between the thick and thin strokes of the letters, *p. 39.*

Orphan: An indented line of a new paragraph that begins at the bottom of a column, *p. 55.*

Phototypesetting: Type imaged from a master photographic negative containing all the characters of the alphabet on a single sheet of film. The master negative can be enlarged to produce type of any size.

PICT: Acronym for "picture." A standard file format for graphics files. Best used with multi-media programs rather than page layout programs.

Pixel: Short for picture element. The smallest element of a raster, or bitmap image.

PostScript: A programming language developed by Adobe that describes where and how text and graphics appear on the page.

PPI: Pixels per inch. The measure of resolution of a raster (pixel based) image file.

RAM: Random Access Memory. The "short term memory" of a computer which performs rapid calculations rather than commit them to writing on the hard drive of the computer.

Ranging Figures: Numbers that are the same height as the capital letters and sit on the baseline, *p. 44.*

Raster image: An image made up of colored or toned pixels, rather than mathematically drawn objects. All scanned photographs and images are raster images. (See bitmap.)

Recto: The right-hand page of a book. All odd numbered pages (which always occur on the right-hand side of the spread) are the recto. The obverse of these pages (even numbered) are called the Verso which are always on the left, *p. 59.*

Resample: See Interpolation

Resolution: The measure of how many units of information per fixed distance are employed to describe the subject of an image. In digital terms this is measured in pixels per inch. In photographic terms resolving power is usually expressed in lines per inch, in other words, how closely can adjacent parallel lines be drawn before the film fails to distinguish the gaps between them. See *pp. 126–133*.

RGB Color: See additive color.

Rip: Raster Image Processing. A program that translates page description (usually PostScript) files into a data stream that is subsequently rendered by the printer.

Rivers: Spaces between words, produced when text is justified. Sometimes these spaces connect vertically, from line to line through the block of text, forming distracting white lines which look like white rivers running through the text block, *p. 55*.

Rule: A line drawn on the printed page.

Sans serif: Literally "without serifs." A typeface stripped of all decorative embellishment, *p. 40*.

Saturation: The relative purity of a color. Literally free of white, thus full and rich.

Scratch disk: The hard drive allocated to a computer program to temporarily store data while calculations are performed.

Separation table: Similar to color table. A set of algorithms or preferences which are used to calculate the transition from RGB to CMYK formats. These algorithms also usually take into account the color rendition of different output devices.

Serif: The terminal stroke at the top and bottom of the main strokes of letters in a Roman style typeface, *pp. 45–46*.

Show-through: The impression of a printed image or block of text that appears on the rear of the sheet, *p. 27*.

Slug: A line of metal type created by a Linotype machine, *p. 38*.

Small Caps: Capital letters, usually the size of the x-height of the lower case letters. In QuarkXPress they are instead calculated as a percentage of the full sized upper case letters, usually about 80%, *p. 44*.

Smart quotes: Quote marks that change orientation depending whether they occur at the beginning or end of a quotation, e.g., "•••." These are quite different from inch marks •˝ with which they are often confused.

Storage: Any type of media you can store files on, eg. hard disks, floppy disks, "Zip" disks, CD Roms.

Stress: The degree to which the thicker parts of the stroke are angled.

Stroke: Any of the linear, as opposed to curved, elements within a letterform, *p. 42*.

Subtractive color: Colors made by mixing together pigment. The three subtractive color primaries are yellow, magenta and cyan, *p. 186.*

Super: An open weave cloth used in bookbinding to reinforce the hinge formed when endpapers are attached to the Block.

System Software: The essential operating software of the computer. Found in the System Folder on the Hard Disk.

Text type: See body type.

TIFF: Tagged Image File Format. A protocol for coding raster images so they can be transferred from one program to another.

Tile/Tiling: Printing an oversized image across several sheets of smaller paper, *p. 196.*

Transitional: Typefaces designed in the mid-eighteenth century. The contrast between the thick and thin strokes is exaggerated and the stress is vertical, *p. 39.*

Trapping: Adjacent colors in artwork are made to overlap so that if they go out of register when printed, the (usually white) paper will not show through.

Typo: Short for typographical error. A mistake in typesetting.

Typography: The art of setting type on a page. See Chapter 3, *Typography, pp. 37–57.*

Unsharp mask: A filter which increases the apparent sharpness of an image. Named after an analog photographic process where an "soft" transparency can be sandwiched with a high contrast contact positive to increase the apparent sharpness of the subsequent print, *pp. 161–162.*

Vector image: An image made up of mathematically defined objects which instruct the computer to "draw" a shape rather than define it pixel by pixel as does a raster or bitmapped, image.

Verso: The left-hand page of a book. These pages are even numbered (2, 4, 6, etc.) The opposite of the Recto, *p. 59.*

Virtual Memory: A process which imitates the function of RAM by writing and accessing calculations to the hard disk of the computer.

Weight: The visual lightness or heaviness of a typeface as determined by the ratio of the stroke thickness to the height of the character.

Widows: Very short lines (usually one or two words) that appear at the end of a paragraph, column or page, *p. 55.*

Window: A rectangular frame on the desktop that has a title bar or scroll choice.

X-height: This is the size of the lower case letter "x." The distance between the baseline and the meanline, *p. 41.*

INDEX
Italics indicate illustrations.

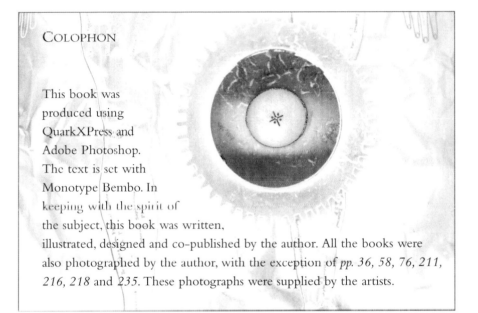

COLOPHON

This book was
produced using
QuarkXPress and
Adobe Photoshop.
The text is set with
Monotype Bembo. In
keeping with the spirit of
the subject, this book was written,
illustrated, designed and co-published by the author. All the books were
also photographed by the author, with the exception of *pp. 36, 58, 76, 211, 216, 218* and *235*. These photographs were supplied by the artists.

NOTES